S. Hrg. 113–407

ONLINE ADVERTISING AND HIDDEN HAZARDS TO CONSUMER SECURITY AND DATA PRIVACY

HEARING

BEFORE THE

PERMANENT SUBCOMMITTEE ON INVESTIGATIONS

OF THE

COMMITTEE ON HOMELAND SECURITY AND GOVERNMENTAL AFFAIRS UNITED STATES SENATE

ONE HUNDRED THIRTEENTH CONGRESS

SECOND SESSION

MAY 15, 2014

Available via the World Wide Web: http://www.fdsys.gov

Printed for the use of the
Committee on Homeland Security and Governmental Affairs

U.S. GOVERNMENT PRINTING OFFICE

89–686 PDF   WASHINGTON : 2014

For sale by the Superintendent of Documents, U.S. Government Printing Office
Internet: bookstore.gpo.gov   Phone: toll free (866) 512–1800; DC area (202) 512–1800
Fax: (202) 512–2104   Mail: Stop IDCC, Washington, DC 20402–0001

(II)

CONTENTS

WITNESSES

Thursday, May 15, 2014

Alphabetical List of Witnesses

APPENDIX

EXHIBIT LIST

Page

ONLINE ADVERTISING AND HIDDEN HAZARDS TO CONSUMER SECURITY AND DATA PRIVACY

THURSDAY, MAY 15, 2014

U.S. SENATE,
PERMANENT SUBCOMMITTEE ON INVESTIGATIONS,
OF THE COMMITTEE ON HOMELAND SECURITY
AND GOVERNMENTAL AFFAIRS,
Washington, DC.

The Subcommittee met, pursuant to notice, at 9:32 a.m., in room SD–342, Dirksen Senate Office Building, Hon. Carl Levin, Chairman of the Subcommittee, presiding.

Present: Senators Levin, McCaskill, McCain, Johnson, and Portman.

Staff present: Daniel J. Goshorn, Counsel; Mary D. Robertson, Chief Clerk; Henry J. Kerner, Staff Director and Chief Counsel to the Minority; Jack Thorlin, Counsel to the Minority; Brad M. Patout, Senior Advisor to the Minority; Scott Wittmann, Research Assistant to the Minority; Samira Ahmed, Law Clerk; Rebecca Pskowski, Law Clerk; Kyle Brosnan, Law Clerk to the Minority; Nick Choate (Sen. McCaskill); Brooke Erickson and Mike Howell (Sen. Johnson); and Derek Lyons (Sen. Portman).

OPENING STATEMENT OF SENATOR LEVIN

Senator LEVIN. Good morning, everybody. For almost a year, the Permanent Subcommittee on Investigations has been investigating hidden hazards to consumers' data privacy and security that results from online advertising. Our Subcommittee operates in a very bipartisan way, and our practices and our rules provide that the Ranking Minority Member may initiate an inquiry, and our tradition is for both sides of the aisle to work on investigations together, and our staffs work very closely together.

This investigation was initiated and led by Senator McCain, so I would like to call on him to give his opening statement first, after which I will add a few additional remarks. But first I would like to commend Senator McCain for his leadership and his staff for their very hard work in addressing the facts and issues that are the subject of today's hearing. Senator McCain.

OPENING STATEMENT OF SENATOR McCAIN

Senator MCCAIN. Thank you, Mr. Chairman. I appreciate you and your staff's cooperation in conducting this important bipartisan investigation, which has been the hallmark of our relationship together for many years. I believe that consumer privacy and safety in the online advertising industry is a serious issue and warrants this Subcommittee's examination.

With the emergence of the Internet and e-commerce, more and more commonplace activities are taking place on the Internet, which has led to major advances in convenience, consumer choice, and economic growth. These advances have also presented novel questions concerning whether consumer security and privacy can be maintained in the new technology-based world. We will examine these issues today specifically in the context of online advertising, where vast data is collected and cyber criminals exploit vulnerabilities in the system and use malware to harm consumers.

As we discuss this complex subject, it is important to keep in mind the following simple idea that I think everyone will agree on: Consumers who venture into the online world should not have to know more than cyber criminals about technology and the Internet in order to stay safe. Instead, sophisticated online advertising companies like Google and Yahoo!, whose representatives are here with us today, have a responsibility to help protect consumers from the potentially harmful effects of the advertisements they deliver. Deciding who should bear responsibility when an advertisement harms a consumer can be a technical and difficult question. But it cannot continue to be the case that the consumer alone pays the price when he visits a mainstream website, does not even click on anything, but still has his computer infected with malware delivered through an advertisement.

At the same time, online advertising has become an instrumental part of how companies reach consumers. In 2013, online advertising revenue reached a record high of $42.8 billion, surpassing for the first time revenue from broadcast television advertising, which was almost $3 billion less. With the continuing boom in mobile devices, online advertising will become even more lucrative in years to come.

With this hearing, we will outline the hazards consumers face through online advertisements, how cyber criminals have defeated the security efforts of the online advertising industry, and what improvements could be made to ensure that consumers are protected online and the Internet remains a safe, flourishing engine for economic growth.

Make no mistake. The hazards to consumers from malware in online advertising are something even a tech-savvy consumer cannot avoid. It is not a matter of simply avoiding shady websites or not clicking on advertisements that look suspicious. For example, in February of this year, an engineer at a security firm discovered that advertisements on YouTube served by Google's ad network delivered malware to visitors' computers. In that case, the user did not need to click on any ads; just going to YouTube and watching a video was enough to infect the user's computer with a virus. That virus was designed to break into consumers' online bank accounts and transfer funds to cyber criminals. A similar attack on Yahoo! in December 2013 also did not require a user to click an advertisement to have his computer compromised.

A consumer whose bank account was compromised by the YouTube ad attack has little recourse under the law as it currently stands. Of course, if an affected consumer managed to track down the cyber criminal who placed the virus, he—or relevant law enforcement agencies—could take legal action against that wrongdoer. But cyber criminals today are normally part of sophisticated professional criminal enterprises, often overseas. Tracking them down is exceedingly difficult—even for professional security specialists. A consumer has essentially no chance whatsoever of recovering funds from cyber criminals.

How can it be that cyber criminals can sneak malware into advertisements under the noses of the most technologically advanced companies in the world? Cyber criminals employ clever tricks to evade the current security procedures used by the online advertising industry. One of these key security procedures is scanning, essentially having a tester visit a website to see if a virus downloads to the test computer. Just as normal online advertisers can target their advertisements to run only in specific locations, cyber criminals can also target by location to avoid scanning. For example, if a cyber criminal knows that the facilities responsible for scanning ads are clustered around certain cities, they can target the malicious advertisement to run in other areas so that the scanners will not see it.

Cyber criminals have used even simpler techniques to bypass security. When law enforcement raided the hideout of a Russian cyber criminal network, they found calendars marked extensively with U.S. Federal holidays and 3-day weekends. These cyber criminals were not planning Fourth of July picnics, of course; they were planning to initiate malware attacks at times when the security staffing at the ad networks and websites would be at their lowest ebb. Just this past holiday season, on Friday, December 27, 2013—2 days after Christmas and 4 days before New Year's Eve—cyber criminals hacked into Yahoo!'s ad network and began delivering malware-infected advertisements to consumers' computers. The malware seized control of the user's computer and used it to generate "bitcoins," a digital currency that requires a large amount of computer power to create. Independent security firms estimate that around 27,000 computers were infected through this one malware-laden advertisement.

The result of these cyber criminal tactics has been countless attacks against consumers online. One major vulnerability in online advertising is that the advertisements themselves are not under the direct control of online advertising companies like Yahoo! and Google. These companies choose not to directly control the advertisements themselves because sending out all of those image or video files would be more expensive. Instead, online advertising companies have the advertiser himself deliver the ad directly to the consumer. While it is cheaper for the companies in the online advertising industry to operate in this way, it can lead to greater hazards for consumers. Malicious advertisers can use their control over advertisements to switch out legitimate ads and put in malware instead. The tech companies who run the online advertising industry frequently do not know when such a switch occurs until after the ad is served. Because those companies do not control the advertisement, their quality control processes are frequently purely reactive, often finding problems after they arise instead of before.

As the online advertising industry grows more and more complicated, a single online advertisement for an individual consumer routinely goes through five or six companies before ultimately reaching the consumer's computer. That fact makes it easier for the various companies in the chain to disclaim responsibility when things go awry.

One instance where that issue was apparent was the attack on Major League Baseball's website in June 2012. In that case, the malicious ad appeared to be for luxury watches and was displayed as a banner at the top of the MLB Web page. The ad was shown to 300,000 consumers before being taken down. In the aftermath of that attack, it was still unclear what entity was responsible for delivery of the malware. One security analyst noted at the time that ''the lack of transparency and multiple indirect relationships'' in online advertising made assigning responsibility for the attack virtually impossible.

One way to get an idea of how complicated the online advertising world and online data collection can be is to take a look at what happens when a consumer actually visits a website where advertisements are served by third-party ad companies.

When a user visits a website, that website instantaneously contacts an online advertising company to provide an advertisement. That ad company in turn contacts other Internet companies who help collect and analyze data on the user for purposes of targeting advertisements to him. Each company can, in turn, contact other companies that profit from identifying users and analyzing those users' online activities. Ultimately, hundreds of third parties can be contacted resulting from a consumer visiting just a single website.

Using special software called ''Disconnect,'' the Subcommittee was able to detect how many third-party sites were contacted when a user visits particular websites. These contacts are represented in a chart. In this first example—we will go to a video.[1] We see what happens when a user visits the website of an ordinary business that does not depend heavily on advertising revenues. In this case, our example is TDBank, a company whose website provides online banking services for its existing customers and, more importantly, not to generate income from people visiting the site. For that reason, it does not need to derive a large amount of revenue from online traffic and advertisements.

You can see there—it is very difficult to see, but what it—a few third parties were contacted. By contrast, when a consumer visits a website that depends much more heavily on revenue from advertising—based on the number of people who visit their website—the number of third parties can be enormously higher. For example, this video shows what happens when a consumer visits TMZ.com, a celebrity gossip website.[2]

And just to make that point even more clear, here are TDBank and TMZ side by side.[3]

Finally, another problem in the current online advertising industry is the lack of meaningful standards for security. The two primary regulators of online advertising are the Federal Trade Com-

---

[1] See Exhibit No. 3, which appears in the Appendix on page 164.
[2] See Exhibit No. 4, which appears in the Appendix on page 165.
[3] See Exhibit No. 5, which appears in the Appendix on page 166.

5

5

mission and self-regulatory groups like the Digital Advertising Alliance and Network Advertising Initiative. The self-regulatory groups have not been active in generating effective guidance or clear standards for online advertising security.

On the government side, the FTC has brought a number of enforcement actions against companies involved in online advertising for ''deceptive'' practices pursuant to their authority under Section 5 of the FTC Act. These cases all involve some specific misrepresentation made by a company rather than a failure to adhere to any general standards.

I will just summarize by saying that on the question of consumer privacy, there are some guidelines on how much data can be generated on Internet users and how that data can be used, but these approaches—including verbose privacy notices, ''do not track'' efforts, and ''notice and choice'' procedures—have only been partially effective.

A new approach to preventing abuses of consumer data and privacy may be necessary. A few years ago, Senator Kerry and I introduced ''The Commercial Privacy Bill of Rights.'' While updates will be necessary, it provides a framework for how to think about these issues moving forward—one that includes basic rights and expectations consumers should have when it comes to the collection, use, and dissemination of their personal, private information online, and specifically in prohibited practices; a clarified role for the FTC in enforcement; and a safe harbor for those companies that choose to take effective steps to further consumer security and privacy. That legislation also envisions a role for industry, self-regulators, and stakeholders to engage with the FTC to come up with best practices and effective solutions.

Consumers deserve to be equipped with the information necessary to understand the risks and to make informed decisions in connection with their online activities. Today one thing is clear. As things currently stand, the consumer is the one party involved in online advertising who is simultaneously both least capable of taking effective security precautions and forced to bear the vast majority of the cost when security fails. For the future, such a model is not tenable. There can be no doubt that online advertising has played an indispensable role in making innovation profitable on the Internet. But the value that online advertising adds to the Internet should not come at the expense of the consumer.

I want to thank the Chairman for working with me on this important hearing and the witnesses for appearing before the Subcommittee. I thank you, Mr. Chairman.

Senator LEVIN. Thank you so much, Senator McCain.

Today's hearing is about the third parties that operate behind the scenes as consumers use the Internet. In particular, the Subcommittee's report outlines the enormous complexity of the online advertising ecosystem. Simply displaying ads that consumers see as they browse the Internet can trigger interactions with a chain of other companies, and each link in that chain is a potential weak point that can be used to invade privacy or host malware that can inflict damage. And we have seen a very dramatic example of this risk in the visuals that Senator McCain presented to us, as well as in the example outlined in the report.[1] Those weak links can be exploited although consumers have done nothing other than visit a mainstream website.

The Subcommittee's report and Senator McCain's opening statement also highlight the hundreds of third parties that may have access to a consumer's browser information with every Web page that they visit. According to a recent White House report, more than 500 million photos are uploaded by consumers to the Internet each day, along with more than 200 hours of video every minute. However, the volume of information that people create about themselves pales in comparison to the amount of digital information continually created about them. According to some estimates, nearly a zettabyte, or 1 trillion gigabytes, are transferred on the Internet annually. That is a billion trillion bytes of data.

Against that backdrop, today's hearing will explore what we should be doing to protect people against the emerging threats to their security and their privacy as consumers. The report finds that the industry's self-regulatory efforts are not doing enough to protect consumer privacy and safety. Furthermore, we need to give the Federal Trade Commission the tools that it needs to protect consumers who are using the Internet.

Finally, as consumers use the Internet, profiles are being created based on what they read, what movies they watch, what music they listen to, on and on and on. Consumers need more effective choices as to what information generated by their activities on the Internet is shared and sold to others.

I want to thank all of today's witnesses for their cooperation with the investigation. And I do not know, Senator Johnson, do you have an opening statement?

Senator JOHNSON. No. Thank you.

Senator LEVIN. I will now call our first panel of witnesses for this morning's hearing: Alex Stamos, Chief Information Security Officer of Yahoo! Inc., Sunnyvale, California; George Salem, the Senior Product Manager of Google Inc., Mountain View, California; and Craig Spiezle, the Executive Director, Founder, and President of Online Trust Alliance, Washington, DC. We appreciate all of you being with us this morning, and we look forward to your testimony.

Pursuant to our Rule 6, all witnesses who testify before this Subcommittee are required to be sworn, so I would ask each of you to please stand and raise your right hand. Do you swear that the testimony that you will give to this Subcommittee will be the truth, the whole truth, and nothing but the truth, so help you, God?

Mr. STAMOS. I do.

Mr. SALEM. I do.

Mr. SPIEZLE. I do.

Senator LEVIN. We will be using a timing system. About a minute before the red light comes on, you are going to see lights change from green to yellow, giving you an opportunity to conclude your remarks. Your written testimony will be printed in the record in its entirety. We would appreciate your limiting your oral testimony to no more than 10 minutes. And, Mr. Stamos, we will have

[1] See Exhibit Nos. 3-5, which appear in the Appendix on pages 164-166.

you go first, followed by Mr. Salem, and then Mr. Spiezle. And then after we have heard all of the testimony, we will turn to questions.

Mr. Stamos, please proceed. Again, our thanks.

STATEMENT OF ALEX STAMOS,[1] VICE PRESIDENT OF INFORMATION SECURITY AND CHIEF INFORMATION SECURITY OFFICER, YAHOO! INC., SUNNYVALE, CALIFORNIA

Mr. STAMOS. Good morning.

Senator LEVIN. Good morning.

Mr. STAMOS. Chairman Levin, Ranking Member McCain, and distinguished Members of the Subcommittee, thank you for convening this hearing and for inviting me to testify today about security issues relating to online advertising. I appreciate the opportunity to share my thoughts and to discuss the user-first approach to security we take at Yahoo!. I respectfully request that my full written testimony be submitted for the record, Mr. Chairman.

Senator LEVIN. It will be.

Mr. STAMOS. Thank you, sir.

My name is Alex Stamos. I am Yahoo!'s Vice President of Information Security and Chief Information Security Officer. I joined Yahoo! in March. Prior to that I served as Chief Technology Officer of Artemis Internet, and I was a co-founder of iSEC Partners. I have spent my career building and improving secure, trustworthy systems, and I am very proud to be working on security at Yahoo!.

Yahoo! is a global technology company that provides personalized products and services, including search, advertising, content, and communications, in more than 45 languages in 60 countries. As a pioneer of the World Wide Web, we enjoy some of the longest lasting customer relationships on the Web. It is because we never take these relationships for granted that 800 million users each month trust Yahoo! to provide them with Internet services across mobile and the Web.

There are a few key areas I would like to emphasize today.

First, our users matter to us. Building and maintaining user trust through secure products is a critical focus, and by default, all of our products need to be secure for all of our users around the globe.

Second, achieving security online is not an end state. It is a constantly evolving challenge that we tackle head on.

Third, malware is an important issue that is a top priority for Yahoo!. While preventing the distribution of malware through advertising is one part of the equation, it is important to address the entire malware ecosystem and to fight it at each phase of its lifecycle.

Fourth, Yahoo! fights for user security on many fronts. We partner with other companies to detect and prevent the spread of malware via advertising and pioneered the SafeFrame standard to assure user privacy in ad serving. We have led the industry in combating spam in phishing. We continuously improve our product security with the help of the wider research and security communities. And we are the largest media publisher to enable encryption for our users across the world.

---

[1] The prepared statement of Mr. Stamos appears in the Appendix on page 55.

I would like to thank the Subcommittee for your focus on malware and the threat it poses to consumers. Internet advertising security and the fight against malware is a top priority for Yahoo!. We have built a highly sophisticated ad quality pipeline to weed out advertising that does not meet our content, privacy, or security standards.

This January, we became aware of malware distributed on Yahoo! sites. We immediately took action to remove the malware, investigated how malicious creative copy bypassed our controls, and fixed the vulnerabilities we found. The malware impacted users on Microsoft Windows with out-of-date versions of Oracle Java, a browser plug-in with a history of security issues, and was mostly targeted at European IP addresses. Users on Macs, mobile devices, and users with up-to-date versions of Java were not affected.

As I mentioned earlier, the malware ecosystem is expansive and complex. A large part of the malware problem is all the vulnerabilities that allow an attacker to take control of user devices through popular Web browsers such as Internet Explorer, plug-ins like Java, office software, and operating systems. Malware is also spread by tricking users into installing software they believe to be harmless but is, in fact, malicious.

We successfully block the vast majority of malicious and deceptive advertisements with which bad actors attack our network, and we always strive to defeat those who would compromise our customers' security. This means we regularly improve our systems, including continuously diversifying the set of technologies and testing systems to better emulate different user behaviors. Every ad running on Yahoo!'s sites and on our ad network is inspected using this system, both when they are created and regularly afterwards.

Yahoo! also strives to keep deceptive advertisements from ever reaching users. For example, our systems prohibit advertisements that look like operating system messages because these ads often tout false offers or try to trick users into downloading and installing malicious or unnecessary software. Preventing deceptive advertising once required extensive human intervention, which meant slower response times and inconsistent enforcement. Although no system is perfect, we now use sophisticated machine learning and image recognition algorithms to catch deceptive advertisements. This lets us train our systems about the characteristics of deceptive creatives, advertisers, and landing sites so that we can detect and respond to them immediately.

We are also the driving force behind the SafeFrame standard. The SafeFrame mechanism allows ads to properly display on a Web page without exposing a user's private information to the advertiser or network. Thanks to growing adoption, SafeFrame enhances user privacy and security not only in the thriving marketplace of thousands of publishers on Yahoo! but around the Internet.

We also actively work with other companies to create a higher level of trust, transparency, quality, and safety in interactive advertising. We are members of the Interactive Advertising Bureau's Ads Integrity Task Force, and we have proudly joined TrustIn-Ads.org.

We also participate in groups dedicated to preventing the spread of malware and disrupting the economic lifecycle of cyber criminals, including the Global Forum for Incident Response and Security Teams, the Anti-Phishing Working Group, the Underground Economy Forum, the Operations Security Trust Forum, and the Bay Area Council CSO Forum.

While preventing the placement of malicious advertisements is essential, it is only one part of a larger battle. We fight the monetization phase of the malware life cycle by improving ways to validate the authenticity of email and by reducing the financial incentives to spread malware. Spam is one of the most effective ways malicious actors make money, and Yahoo! is leading the fight to eradicate that source of income. For example, one way spammers act is through "email spoofing." The original Internet mail standards did not require that a sender use an accurate "From:" line in an email. Spammers exploit this to send billions of messages a day that pretend to be from a friend, family member, or business associate. These emails are much more likely to bypass spam filters, as they appear to be from trusted correspondents.

Spoofed e-mails can also be used to trick users into giving up user names and passwords, a technique that is generally known as "phishing." Here is how Yahoo! is helping the Internet industry tackle these issues.

Yahoo! was the original author of DomainKeys Identified Mail, or DKIM, a mechanism that lets mail recipients cryptographically verify the real origin of email. Yahoo! freely contributed the intellectual property behind DKIM to the world, and now the standard protects billions of emails between thousands of domains.

Building upon the success of DKIM, Yahoo! led a coalition of Internet companies, financial institutions, and anti-spam groups in creating the Domain-based Message Authentication, Reporting, and Conformance, or DMARC, standard. DMARC provides domains a way to tell the rest of the Internet what security mechanisms to expect on email they receive and what actions the sender would like to be taken on spoofed messages.

This April, Yahoo! became the first major email provider to publish a strict DMARC reject policy. In essence, we asked the rest of the Internet to drop messages that inaccurately claim to be from yahoo.com users. Since Yahoo! made this change, another major provider has also enabled DMARC to reject. We hope that every major email provider will follow our lead and implement this commonsense protection against spoofed email.

DMARC has reduced the spam purported to come from yahoo.com accounts by over 90 percent. If used broadly, it would target spammers' financial incentives with crippling effectiveness.

Yahoo! also incentivizes sharing to ensure our products are trustworthy and our users' data is secure. To this end, Yahoo! operates one of the most progressive bug bounty programs on the Internet. Our bug bounty program encourages security researchers to report possible flaws in our systems to us via a secure Web portal.

In this portal we engage researchers and discuss their findings. If their bug turns out to be real, we swiftly fix it and we reward the reporter with up to $15,000. In an age where security bugs are often auctioned off and then used maliciously, we believe it is critical that we and other companies create an ecosystem where both burgeoning and established security experts are rewarded for reporting, and not exploiting, vulnerabilities.

Yahoo! invests heavily to ensure the security of our users and their data across all of our products. In January, we made encrypted browsing the default for Yahoo! Mail. And as of March, domestic and international traffic moving between Yahoo!'s data centers has been fully encrypted. Our ongoing goal is to enable a secure encrypted experience for all of our users, no matter what device they use or from what country they use Yahoo!.

In conclusion, I want to restate that security online is not and never will be an end state. It is a constantly evolving, global challenge that our industry is tackling head on. Threats that stem from the ad pipeline, or elsewhere, are not unique to any one online company or ad network. And while criminals pose real threats, we are strongly dedicated to staying ahead of them.

Yahoo! fights for user security on multiple fronts. We partner with multiple companies to detect and prevent the spread of malware via advertising. We pioneered the SafeFrame standard to assure user privacy in ad serving. We have led the industry in combating spam in phishing. We continuously improve our product security with the help of the wider research and security communities. And, finally, we are the largest media publisher to enable encryption for our users across the world.

Yahoo! will continue to innovate in how we protect our users. We will continue to fight cyber criminals who target us and our users. And we will continue to view user trust and security as our top priorities.

Thank you very much for the opportunity to testify. I look forward to answering any questions you may have. Thank you, sir.

Senator LEVIN. Thank you very much, Mr. Stamos.

Mr. Salem.

STATEMENT OF GEORGE F. SALEM,[1] SENIOR PRODUCT MANAGER, GOOGLE INC., MOUNTAIN VIEW, CALIFORNIA

Mr. SALEM. Chairman Levin, Ranking Member McCain, and Members of the Subcommittee, thank you for the opportunity to testify on Google's efforts to combat malware on the Web. My name is George Salem, and I am a senior product manager. I lead the engineering team that fights the delivery of malware through advertising, a practice known as ''malvertising.''

Ensuring our users' safety and security is one of Google's main priorities. We have a team of over 400 full-time security experts working around the clock to keep our users safe. One of the biggest threats consumers face on the Web is malicious software, known as ''malware,'' that can control computers or software programs. Malware allows malicious actors to make money off of innocent victims in various ways. It may even lead to identity theft, which has now topped the list of consumer complaints reported to the FTC for 14 years in a row.

Advertising has had a tremendous role in the evolution of the Web, bringing more products, tools, and information to consumers,

---

[1] The prepared statement of Mr. Salem appears in the Appendix on page 59.

often free of charge. It has allowed the Web economy to flourish. In the last quarter, Internet ad revenues surged to a landmark $20.1 billion, and the ad-supported Internet ecosystem employs a total of 5.1 million Americans.

Even though only a tiny portion of ads carry malware, malvertising undermines users' faith in this ecosystem. Bad ads are bad for everyone, including Google and our users. Our incentive is to keep our online performance safe for everyone, or customers will not continue to use our products. This is why we believe in providing the strongest protections against harmful or malicious content online.

Our approach to fighting malware is two-pronged: prevent and disable. The first piece is prevention. One of the best ways to protect users from malware is by preventing them from accessing infected sites altogether. This is why we developed a tool called ''safe browsing.'' It checks any page a user visits against a list of known bad sites. Malicious sites are then clearly identified as dangerous in Google Search results. We were the first major search engine to provide such a warning for search results back in 2006. Today over a billion people use safe browsing.

Safe browsing is also the default for users on Google Chrome, Mozilla Firefox, and Apple Safari browsers, which helps to protect tens of millions of users. When a user attempts to navigate to one of these malicious sites, they get a clear warning advising them to click away.

We are constantly looking at ways to further disseminate safe browsing technology, including by providing public interface for anyone to plug in and review identified malware. We also provide alerts to Web masters who may not be aware that malicious software is hosted on the Web properties.

A second piece of our effort is disabling bad ads. We have always prohibited malware in our ads, and we have a strict suspension policy for advertisers that spread malware. We proactively scan billions of ads each day across platforms and browsers, disabling any we find that have malware.

Our Internet systems have proven to have a very big proven track record. In 2013, we disabled more than 350 million ads. Again, this is only a tiny portion of all advertisements in our platforms, but our systems are constantly evolving to keep up with those bad actors.

While we may be proactive, we are relatively quiet about our technology. Malvertisers are constantly seeking new ways to avoid our detection and enforcement systems, and we want to stay ahead of them and not tip them off to our efforts.

We are not the only ones involved in these efforts. These efforts are a team endeavor. We collaborate closely with others in the Internet community.

Ten years ago, we issued a set of Software Principles, a broad, evolving set of guidelines available online around software installation, disclosure to users, and advertiser behavior. We are a member of StopBadware.org, an nonprofit that offers resources for website owners, security experts, and ordinary users. We own and support free websites like VirusTotal.com and Anti-Malvertising.com to share best practices and investigative resources and to provide checks for malicious content on this topic.

We are in constant communication with other industry players, notifying each of us about new malware attacks and new trends. Just this month, we, along with Facebook, Twitter, AOL, and Yahoo!, co-founded TrustInAds.org, a group that offers guidance to consumers on how to avoid online scams.

Another huge piece is consumer education. A great first place to visit are websites like Google's Online Safety Center or Anti-Malvertising.org to learn more.

Of course, users should always up-to-date anti-virus software, make sure their operating system and browsers are also up to date, and be careful about downloads. If they suspect their computer may be infected, they should use a reputable product to rid it of malware.

We can always use more help in generating awareness among consumers. Malware is a complex problem, but we are tackling it head-on with tools, consumer education, and community partnerships. We believe if we all work together to identify threats and stamp them out, we can make the Web a safer place.

Thank you again for your time and consideration.

Senator LEVIN. Thank you very much, Mr. Salem.

Mr. Spiezle.

STATEMENT OF CRAIG D. SPIEZLE,[1] EXECUTIVE DIRECTOR, FOUNDER, AND PRESIDENT, ONLINE TRUST ALLIANCE, WASHINGTON, DC

Mr. SPIEZLE. Good morning, Chairman Levin, Ranking Member McCain, and Members of the Committee. Good morning and thank you for the opportunity to testify before you today. My name is Craig Spiezle. I am the Executive Director and President of the Online Trust Alliance. OTA is a 501(c)(3) nonprofit with the mission to enhance online trust, empowering users to control their data and privacy, while promoting innovation and the vitality of the Internet.

I am testifying here today to provide context to the escalating privacy and security threats to consumers which result from malicious and fraudulent advertising known as "malvertising."

As outlined in Exhibit A,[2] malvertising incidents increased over 200 percent in this last year to 209,000 incidents which generated over 12.4 billion malicious ad impressions. The impact on consumers is significant.

As referenced, Yahoo! experienced an incident resulting in over 300,000 malicious impressions, of which 9 percent or 27,000 unsuspecting users were compromised. For them, the infection rate was 100 percent.

As noted, this is not an isolated case. Cyber criminals have successfully inserted malicious ads on a range of sites including Google, Microsoft, Facebook, the Wall Street Journal, New York Times, Major League Baseball, and others. The threats are significant. As referenced, the majority and an increasing number are

---

[1] The prepared statement of Mr. Spiezle with attachments appear in the Appendix on page 67.

[2] See Exhibit A or Exhibit No. 1, which appears in the Appendix on pages 75 and 162.

"drive-by downloads," which have increased 190 percent this past year. A drive-by incident is one that when a user simply visits a website, with no interactions or clicking required, is infected.

This threat is not new. Malvertising was first identified over 7 years ago, yet little progress has been made to attack this threat.

The impact ranges from capturing personal information to turning a device into a bot where a cyber criminal can take over a device and use it in many cases to execute a distributed denial-of-service attack, known as a "DDOS," against a bank, government agency, or other organization.

Just as damaging is the deployment of ransomware which encrypts a user's hard drive, demanding payment to be unlocked. Users' personal data, photos, and health records can be destroyed and stolen in just seconds.

In the absence of secure online advertising, the integrity of the entire Internet is at risk. Not unlike pollution in the industrial age, in the absence of regulatory oversight and meaningful self-regulation, these threats continue to grow.

For reference, the development of coal mining and the use of steam power generated from coal is without doubt the most central, binding narrative of the 19th Century. Jobs were created and profit soared, but the environment soon felt the full impact of industrialization in the form of air and water pollution. Today we are at a similar crossroads which are undermining the integrity and trust of the Internet.

So how does malvertising occur? Actually if you would go to Exhibit B,[1] thank you. The most common tactic to run a malicious ad is the cyber criminal going directly to an ad network, selecting a target audience, and paying for an ad campaign. In the absence of any reputational checks or threat reporting among the industry, once detected and shut down by one ad network, the cyber criminal simply "water falls" or goes over to another unsuspecting network to repeat the exploit over and over.

Now on the left there, you see the different tactics of how the malvertising is inserted, and, again, I think it is important to note here in this diagram that consumers are clearly bearing the brunt of it, but also quality, brands, and websites, their image is being tarnished as well.

The impacts of these threats are increasing significantly. Criminals are becoming experts in targeting and timing, taking advantage of the powerful tools and data available to Internet advertisers. They have become what is known as "data-driven marketers" with precision to reach vulnerable segments of society as well as high-net-worth target audiences. They have been able to choose the day and time of the exploits as well as the type of device they choose to exploit.

In the absence of any meaningful policy and traffic quality controls, organized crime has recognized malvertising as the "exploit of choice" offering the ability to remain anonymous and remain undetected for days.

Recognizing the threats, in 2007, DoubleClick, which was later acquired by Google, established a mailing list which today remains

[1] See Exhibit B, which appears in the Appendix on page 76.

one of the primary methods of data sharing. In 2010, OTA established what is now the Advertising and Content Integrity Group, focusing on security and fraud prevention best practices. This group of diverse stakeholders leverages a proven model of threat mitigation and has since published several white papers including a risk evaluation framework and remediation guidelines.

These efforts are a small but first step to combat malvertising, reflecting input from leaders including Google, Microsoft, PayPal, Symantec, Twitter, and others.

As you heard before, last June, StopBadware, a nonprofit funded by Google and others, launched a parallel effort known as the ''Ads Integrity Alliance.'' This past January, this initiative disbanded due to its members' ''desire to refocus their resources on aggressively defending industry practices to policymakers and regulatory bodies.''

In the wake of this group's demise, recently TrustInAds was formed last week. According to the site, its ''focus is public policy and raising consumer awareness of the threats and how to report them.''

It is important to note that, unfortunately, no amount of consumer education can help when a user visits a trusted website that is infected with malvertising. Consumers cannot discern good versus malicious ads or how their device was compromised. Focusing on education after the fact is like the auto industry telling accident victims who to call after an accident from a previously known manufacturing defect, instead of building security features in the cars they sell and profit from.

Other industry efforts have been focused on click fraud, which are fraudulent activities that attempt to generate revenue by manipulating ad impressions. Click fraud is focused on the monetization and operational issues facing the industry. While these efforts are important, please do not be confused: Click fraud is not related to malvertising or any impact that is harmful to consumers.

So what is needed? OTA proposes a holistic framework addressing five important areas: prevention, detection, notification, data sharing, and remediation. Such a framework must be the foundation for an enforceable code of conduct or possible legislation.

In parallel, operational and technical solutions must be explored. I envision a day when publishers would only allow ads from networks that vouch for the authenticity of the ads they serve, and Web browsers would only render such ads that have been signed and verified from trusted sources. It is recognized that such a model would require systemic changes; yet it would increase accountability, and it would protect the long-term vitality of online advertising and, most importantly, consumers.

In summary, as a wired society and economy, we are increasingly dependent on trustworthy, secure, and resilient online services. As observed in almost every area of our Nation's critical infrastructure, we need to recognize that fraudulent businesses, cyber criminals, and State-sponsored actors will continue to exploit our systems.

For some, malvertising remains a ''Black Swan Event,'' rarely seen but known to exist. For others it still remains as the elephant in the room that no one wants to acknowledge or report on. Today companies have no obligation or incentive to disclose their role or knowledge of such an event, leaving consumers vulnerable and unprotected for potentially months or years, during which time untold amounts of damage can occur. Failure to address these threats suggest the needs for legislation not unlike State data breach laws, requiring mandatory notification, data sharing, and remediation to those consumers that have been harmed.

As learned from the Target breach, it is the responsibility of a company and its executives to implement safeguards and to heed the warnings of the community. I suggest that the same standards should apply for the ad industry. We must work together, openly disclose and mediate such vulnerabilities, even at the expense of short-term profits.

It is important to recognize that there is no absolute defense against a determined cyber criminal. In parallel, OTA proposes incentives to companies who have demonstrated that they have adopted such best practices and comply with codes of conduct. They should be afforded protection from regulatory oversight as well as frivolous lawsuits. Perceived antitrust and privacy issues which continue to be raised as the reason why not sharing data must be resolved to aid in the real-time fraud detection and forensics that is required.

Trust is the foundation of every communication we receive, every website we visit, every transaction we make, and every ad we respond to. Now is the time for collaboration, moving from protective silos of information to multi-stakeholder solutions combating cyber crime.

Thank you, and I look forward to your questions.

Senator LEVIN. Thank you very much, Mr. Spiezle.

Senator McCain.

Senator McCAIN. Thank you, Mr. Chairman. I thank the witnesses.

If you put that chart back up about the increase in malvertising,[1] would the witnesses agree that the problem is getting worse rather than better? Would you agree, Mr. Salem?

Mr. SALEM. I do not agree that the problem is getting better. One thing that——

Senator McCAIN. Is it getting worse?

Mr. SALEM. I am sorry. It is not—I do not believe that it is getting worse.

Senator McCAIN. You do not believe that chart then?

Mr. SALEM. I have not seen that chart. I saw that from the report. Our indication where we actually——

Senator McCAIN. So you are saying that chart is not accurate?

Mr. SALEM. That is not the chart—that is not the information that I have, sir.

Senator McCAIN. I see. Maybe you can provide the Subcommittee with the information that you have, Mr. Stamos?

Mr. STAMOS. Sir, our data has been pretty much steady on the kinds of attempts that we have seen coming inbound.

Senator McCAIN. Would you agree that probably the worst attacks come from overseas, specifically Russia?

---

[1] See Exhibit No. 1, which appears in the Appendix on page 162.

Mr. STAMOS. We see attacks from all around. It is usually very difficult to have accurate—to accurately figure out——

Senator McCAIN. Oh, so you have no accurate data as to where it comes from. That is good.

Mr. STAMOS. We have accurate data as to where the IP address——

Senator McCAIN. Well, then, where does it come from?

Mr. STAMOS. We see these kinds of attempts from all around the world. You are right, we do see a lot from Eastern Europe and the former Russian Republics.

Senator McCAIN. Well, thank you for that.

How about you, Mr. Salem?

Mr. SALEM. Yes, we also see a lot of the malware itself will come from servers that are also in Russia and also——

Senator McCAIN. So this is really an international issue as well as a domestic issue, I would argue.

Suppose that some individual is the victim of malware, Mr. Stamos, does Yahoo! have any responsibility for that?

Mr. STAMOS. We absolutely take responsibility for our users' safety, which is why we do all the work we do to protect——

Senator McCAIN. So if someone loses their bank account, you reimburse them?

Mr. STAMOS. Senator, I have always believed that the person who is responsible for committing the crime is the criminal who does it, and it is our responsibility to——

Senator McCAIN. Even though it is using you as a vehicle to commit that crime?

Mr. STAMOS. Senator, we work very hard to fight these criminals, and——

Senator McCAIN. Is that person liable—are you liable for reimbursement for loss of that individual who used—that your services were responsible—were the vehicle for that?

Mr. STAMOS. Senator, we believe that the criminals are liable for their actions.

Senator McCAIN. I see. And you being the vehicle for it, you have no liability, sort of like the automobile that has a problem with it, the maker of the automobile is not responsible because they are just the person who sold it. Is that right?

Mr. STAMOS. No, Senator. I do not think that is a correct analogy.

Senator McCAIN. I see.

Mr. STAMOS. We work very vigorously to protect our users. Every single user is important to us. If a criminal commits a crime, we do everything we can to investigate, figure out how they were able to do that, and then to defeat them the next time.

Senator McCAIN. And you have no liability whatsoever?

Mr. STAMOS. Senator, that is a legal question. I am not a lawyer. I am here to talk about the security side.

Senator McCAIN. I am asking common sense. I am not asking for——

Mr. STAMOS. I think we have a responsibility to our users, and we take that responsibility extremely seriously.

Senator McCAIN. Thank you.

Mr. Spiezle, you have the five recommendations that you make in your testimony. In prevention, you say, "Stakeholders who fail to adopt reasonable best practices and controls should bear the liability and publishers should reject their ads."

Are stakeholders adopting reasonable best practices and controls in your view?

Mr. SPIEZLE. Today that information does not suggest they are doing that. One of the challenges is the reluctance to share information among each other, and it is very isolated right now. Again, recognizing that there is no perfect security, in the absence of taking reasonable steps to protect the infrastructure and consumers from harm, they should be responsible.

Senator McCAIN. How many Americans do you think know that this problem exists?

Mr. SPIEZLE. This information has been kept very quiet. It has been suppressed over years. The executives of some of the trade organizations have actually denied it even exists publicly. So that is a major challenge.

Senator McCAIN. We just saw an example of that, disputing the malvertising facts. Where did you get those facts, by the way, since they do not share your view?

Mr. SPIEZLE. Well, actually, we are very fortunate. There are many players in the industry that see this as a major issue. In fact, just this past week, we had about a dozen companies come to us asking for legislation that are actually in the ecosystem saying they recognize that the absence of this that their businesses are being marginalized and they need help.

Our data comes from multiple sources. It comes from the threat intelligence community. It comes from some of the ad networks themselves who are willing to share this information anonymously. They do not want to be public because of the pressure from the industries and the trade organizations. And we try to normalize it.

I would suggest that this data probably underreports it by at least 100 percent. We do not know and, again, the lack of willingness to share data is impeding the problem today.

Senator McCAIN. Mr. Stamos and Mr. Salem, do you both have the same best practices standard between your two organizations?

Mr. STAMOS. Senator, I believe we use about the same types of technologies and tests.

Senator McCAIN. Do you have the same best standards practices?

Mr. STAMOS. I believe so, yes.

Senator McCAIN. You would not know?

Ms. STAMOS. We work actually very closely with our ad partners to trade notes, and we share a lot of the same technologies.

Mr. SALEM. And I would have to also add that we actually do communicate. We actually do discuss different issues that come up, different malvertising trends.

Senator McCAIN. Do you need liability protection to work more closely together?

Mr. SALEM. We work very closely together. I do not see any——

Senator McCAIN. Then why don't you have the same best practices standards?

Mr. SALEM. We are different organizations, we are different corporations. We basically——

Senator MCCAIN. But you are facing the same problem, Mr. Salem.

Mr. SALEM. Yes, and we communicate about the threats.

Senator MCCAIN. I am glad you communicate. I am asking if you will adopt the same best practices standards.

Mr. STAMOS. Senator, I believe we already do adopt the same practices, but we have diverse implementations. An important part of security is to have a diversity of different ways to combat a single threat.

Mr. SPIEZLE. Senator, if I might add, the OTA has convened several multi-stakeholder workshops offering Chatham House Rules to facilitate the data sharing. And, unfortunately, the response has been—it is being addressed internally. And so, again, we have asked Google multiple times, we have asked Yahoo!, we have asked the other companies to come to the table. And, again, the answer has been, "It is not a problem. It is not one that we really see we need to address."

I will go a step further. The chairman and president of IAB, Interactive Advertising Bureau, in September 2010 publicly stood up and said malvertising is not a problem, it only exists because security vendors want it to be a problem.

Senator MCCAIN. Well, then, I guess we get back to the—Mr. Stamos, do you agree that it is a problem?

Mr. STAMOS. I absolutely agree that this is a problem, but we need to keep in context—when you look at a graph like that, we need to put it next to the overall malware problem, which is honestly the numbers are much, much larger, and there are three parts to that. There are the authors who create malware, which is about creating safe software. There is distribution of which advertising is the part that we are responsible for, but it is honestly a tiny sliver of the distribution problem of malware. And then there is the financial side. And from our perspective, we focus a lot on preventing ourselves from being part of the distribution problem, but then we also fight the entire life cycle, because in the end there is going to be no perfect protection each of those places. What we need to do is decrease the financial incentives for the criminals to attempt to do this in the first place.

Senator MCCAIN. And how do you do that?

Mr. STAMOS. On the software side, the companies that make that software try to make it harder for malware to be created. On the distribution side, we build our analysis systems to make it harder and harder for them to——

Senator MCCAIN. Well, I will look forward to your data on the malvertising since clearly that indicates you have got a lot of work to do. And even though it may be a "tiny sliver," I am not sure that is of some comfort to someone who has their bank account wiped out. Maybe to you, but it is not to them.

Mr. STAMOS. Excuse me, Senator, but every single user is important to us.

Senator MCCAIN. Well, obviously you are downgrading the importance of this issue when you say it is only a tiny sliver. If there are two hundred and some thousand, if I read that right [1]—what is it, Mr. Spiezle?

Mr. SPIEZLE. That is correct, 209,000 identified unique incidents that occurred, that were documented.

Senator MCCAIN. I would say that sliver is a pretty big sliver, Mr. Stamos.

I thank you, Mr. Chairman.

Senator LEVIN. Thank you very much, Senator McCain.

Let me ask you, Mr. Stamos, we have testimony here from Mr. Spiezle on behalf of the Online Trust Alliance that says that, "Ideally we will have solutions where publishers would only allow ads only from networks who vouch for the authenticity of all of the ads they serve, and Web browsers will render only such ads that have been signed and verified from trusted sources. It is recognized that such a model would require systemic changes; yet they would increase accountability, protecting the long-term vitality of online advertising and most importantly the consumers."

Would you support those kind of systemic changes, Mr. Stamos?

Mr. STAMOS. Thank you, Senator. So as to the authenticity issue for ad networks, I can only speak to how Yahoo! does this——

Senator LEVIN. No, not how they do it, but would you support what Mr. Spiezle is recommending?

Mr. STAMOS. So we definitely support the cryptography side. Currently, technology does not exist to sign an ad all the way through, but through our efforts to move to HTTPS encryption, we have moved a great deal of the ad networks in the world to supporting encrypting, and which is really what is supported in browsers right now.

Senator LEVIN. Is their any reason why we cannot require that ads first, before they are put on, be verified that they come from trusted sources? Is there any reason you cannot do that?

Mr. STAMOS. Well, I think right now, Senator, the browser technology does not exist.

Senator LEVIN. Does it exist, Mr. Spiezle?

Mr. SPIEZLE. The browser technology does not exist. I think we are talking about a combination of operational best practices and technical. It is a very complex ecosystem, as Senator McCain stated in his opening comments, with multiple intermediaries. This is a desired state. Again, if we cannot vouch for who the advertise is, we should not accept the ads in the first place, and that is the first part, and that is in the preventative side. But that is operational.

Senator LEVIN. Can that be done now?

Mr. SPIEZLE. I believe it can be done now.

Senator LEVIN. Is it done now?

Mr. STAMOS. Yes, we have agreements with the ad networks we work with to have them pass information through, and if we find that they are problematic, then we get rid of those networks from our——

Senator LEVIN. Do they verify before they put on the ad that it comes from a——

Mr. STAMOS. Senator, I am not sure exactly what each ad network does.

---

[1] See Exhibit No. 1, which appears in the Appendix on page 162.

Senator LEVIN. Mr. Salem, do you do that?

Mr. SALEM. Our ad networks are verified, but they basically can have advertisers that they have direct relationships with, and we do not know what those relationships are.

Senator LEVIN. But do the people that you do have relationships with verify the credibility of their advertisers?

Mr. SALEM. They have a vetting process themselves. I am not exactly sure. I will say, however, that many of the malvertising that we have seen has come from companies or criminals that basically pretend to be legitimate companies. So even if you said that, we are going to vet them. We have seen problems like with Sears.com, with Crosspen.com, they actually may introduce ads with companies that actually appear, create—they appear to be real. Their vetting process appears to be perfect. Yet, again, these criminals have come and made specific companies that look real and——

Senator LEVIN. OK. So let me ask Mr. Spiezle a question. What can be done now practically that is not yet being done by companies like Google and Yahoo!?

Mr. SPIEZLE. Well, I should note, to help address this very specific threat, we held full-day workshops, and in October, we published what we call our "risk evaluation framework," which I have here and it is referenced in my written testimony. It provides a checklist on the onboarding of verifying the reputation. So this was an example of an operational step. We received a lot of——

Senator LEVIN. Has that step been taken by Google and Yahoo!, for instance?

Mr. SPIEZLE. Again, we make them available to anyone——

Senator LEVIN. Do you know whether they have been taken?

Mr. SPIEZLE. I do not know.

Senator LEVIN. Have they been taken, those specific steps?

Mr. SALEM. I do not know.

Senator LEVIN. Do you know, Mr. Stamos?

Mr. STAMOS. I am not sure what exact steps he is talking about.

Senator LEVIN. OK. Well, if you had gone to that meeting, you would have known. How come you did not go to that meeting?

Mr. STAMOS. We are part of a lot of groups that are working on this problem.

Senator LEVIN. Well, let me change to a different part of the testimony here then. "Companies today have little incentive," Mr. Spiezle's testimony, "to disclose their role or knowledge of a security event, leaving consumers vulnerable and unprotected for potentially months or years, during which time untold amounts of damage can occur." And then the suggestion is that there be legislation adopted similar to State data breach laws that require mandatory notification, data sharing, and remediation to those who have been harmed.

Do you support a mandatory notification requirement, Mr. Stamos?

Mr. STAMOS. Mr. Chairman, this is a more complicated issue than breach notification. In the situation you are talking about, malvertising, there is often not a direct relationship with the user, and so there would be no information to know how to notify them.

Also, in a situation where malvertising is caught early before it has an impact, we have to be careful——

Senator LEVIN. Let me get Mr. Spiezle's response to that.

Mr. STAMOS. OK.

Mr. SPIEZLE. So in the context of notification, I agree, it is more—notification to regulatory authorities of an incident occurring, and then obviously depending upon that, in most State data breach——

Senator LEVIN. Let us talk about regulatory authorities. Is there any reason why you should not be required to notify regulatory authorities?

Mr. STAMOS. Mr. Chairman, every day we stop malvertising. So I think it really comes down to the details of whether you talk about an incident. We are talking about two or three incidents today over a multi-year period when every—as Google pointed out, we are talking about finding 10,000 sites a day. They are finding 10,000 sites a day with malware on it.

Senator LEVIN. You are talking about where there are breaches or attempted breaches?

Mr. STAMOS. The 10,000 a day I believe he was talking about are sites that are set up that host malware, and so——

Senator LEVIN. How many breaches a day?

Mr. STAMOS. Mr. Chairman, it is really important for us to use the right terminology here. When you say ''breach''——

Senator LEVIN. So let me ask Mr. Spiezle, please use the right terminology.

Mr. SPIEZLE. So I think the breach is not perhaps the context that I was thinking about. It is more of a confirmed malvertising incident where a network or a site has actually observed and documented malicious ads going through their site and properties and infrastructure. That is what we are referring to.

Senator LEVIN. OK. There you want mandatory notification to the regulator.

Mr. SPIEZLE. And in the absence of that, quite frankly, that is why there is no good data, and that makes it that much harder to go back and find out who is the actually perpetrator.

Senator LEVIN. OK. Putting aside the argument for it, which sounds sensible to me, is there any reason that you cannot do that?

Mr. STAMOS. I would have to get back to you on that, Senator. We would have to see the details of what you call a ''malvertising incident'' and what the reporting looks like.

Senator LEVIN. Mr. Salem.

Mr. SALEM. I personally would be very careful about making a commitment like that. One of the things that we try to do is within a community, discuss what the issues are and make sure that it is not public. As soon as you make things public, you are basically talking about people that have——

Senator LEVIN. I am talking about to the regulator.

Mr. SALEM. But, again, that would be a public document. We would rather not make some of this information public so that the criminals find out how we are detecting them and how we are basically——

Senator LEVIN. Everything you tell a regulator is not necessarily public, by the way. You can have proprietary information, you can have other information that is not made public. Putting aside that problem, any reason why you cannot notify the regulator?

Mr. SALEM. There is no reason.

Senator LEVIN. OK. Would you, Mr. Stamos, get back to us after you study what that recommendation is?

Yahoo!'s privacy policy indicates that you do provide information to partners of certain personal information so that Yahoo! can communicate with consumers about offers from Yahoo! and the marketing partners. Then you say the companies that you deal with, however, those partners, do not have any independent right to share this information.

Is the sharing of that information prohibited?

Mr. STAMOS. Mr. Chairman, while privacy and security are intertwined, we have a dedicated privacy team. So if you want to get into those kinds of details, I will have to take those——

Senator LEVIN. Do you know offhand?

Mr. STAMOS. I do not, sir.

Senator LEVIN. OK. There is a great emphasis here on education, but here is the problem. The business partners, for instance, of Yahoo!—and you provide a list on your website—of these third-party partners, there are over 150 companies that do advertising work alone. You note in your privacy policy that these companies may be placing cookies or Web bugs on our computers as we browse.

How can consumers possibly educate themselves about each of these third parties? There are 150 of them with names like Data Zoo, Daltran, Diligent, companies totally unknown to people outside of this room probably. Do you think it is feasible—and I am going to ask you, Mr. Stamos, and this will be my last question—for consumers to evaluate the security policies and the privacy policies of each of 150 entities? Is that a practical suggestion?

Mr. STAMOS. That is an excellent question, Senator. We are not expecting consumers to go and make the decisions one on one. That is why we provide privacy options for users, and we work with folks like the DAA to provide decisionmaking authority for consumers across multiple partners. And I believe that is where we have to go, is to have the choices up in one place.

Senator LEVIN. Well, but you are suggesting that they educate themselves about each of those partners of yours.

Ms. STAMOS. I am not suggesting that. I am sorry, Mr. Chairman. I am not familiar with the language you are referring to.

Senator LEVIN. OK. Thank you.

Senator Johnson.

Senator JOHNSON. Thank you, Mr. Chairman. I would kind of like to start out just quoting a couple little phrases here to certainly underscore my feeling on this. I think as the Chairman said this has enormous complexity, and I think the Ranking Member said that online Internet advertising plays an indispensable role. I think those are pretty powerful statements in terms of what we are trying to do here. The Internet has been a marvel. It has created all kinds of economic activity, certainly improved people's lives. So we need to understand how enormously complex this situation is, and it is not easy. And the analogy I would use in terms of crime—because we are talking about criminal activity and who is going to be held liable for it.

The analogy I would use would be let us say you have a criminal, that even though you have safeguards in a taxicab, that criminal defeats those safeguards, takes over the cab, and kills somebody. Is the cab company to be held liable for that criminal activity? I think that is probably a more accurate analogy that we are talking about here.

So I think the purpose of this hearing is what can government potentially do to help it, and I think I know who Yahoo! is, I think I know who Google is, I think I know how you guys obtain revenue and make money. I am not too sure about OTA, and there are a couple things that have surprised me in terms of the comments you have made.

So let me first ask you, Mr. Spiezle, who are you? Where do you get your funding? How do you obtain revenue?

Mr. SPIEZLE. Well, thank you for the opportunity to provide clarity. So the OTA, the Online Trust Alliance, got founded, in 2004, as a working group to address and bring forward the anti-spam standards that Yahoo! referenced in their original testimony there through a collaborative effort. And it was recognizing——

Senator JOHNSON. Who funded that effort? I mean, it takes money to do that.

Mr. SPIEZLE. That effort was through companies like Symantec, Microsoft, PayPal, lots of companies that came together—Cisco.

Senator JOHNSON. So do you continue to get funding that way or do you get funding in other ways?

Mr. SPIEZLE. Our funding actually comes from multiple——again, we are a 501(c)(3). We are not a trade organization. We look across the ecosystem. We have a diverse group of sponsors and contributors as well as we receive grants from DHS and others.

So, again, our mission is very clear. We support advertising, but, again, our most important part is improving consumer trust in the vitality of the Internet.

Senator JOHNSON. OK, because here is what sent bells and whistles going off in my head, and I am not sure I heard you say it, but the Chairman said that you talked about the fact that Yahoo! and Google have little incentive—to do what? First of all, is that an accurate statement? So what do they have little incentive to do?

Mr. SPIEZLE. So I think in the context of the question, if I can clarify that incentive, it is an incentive of data sharing, and it is really an industry issue that we have been trying to get people to work on together. And the incentive is data sharing——

Senator JOHNSON. Do you deny the fact that Google and Yahoo! have an enormous free market incentive to make sure that this criminal activity does not occur on the networks?

Mr. SPIEZLE. I think as dominant market players, there is a responsibility in how the lack of data sharing and how it is marginalizing the ecosystem and——

Senator JOHNSON. No, but answer the question. Doesn't Yahoo! and Google, don't they have enormous financial incentives to try and police this and prevent malvertising and malware?

Mr. SPIEZLE. As they have suggested, malvertising is a small percent of the overall ad industry, and so to add the operational friction and to change it is a major change in how they operate today.

Senator JOHNSON. You are still not answering the question.

Mr. SPIEZLE. I do not think there is——

Senator JOHNSON. You really do not think Yahoo! or Google have an enormous financial incentive to try and police this stuff and prevent it from happening?

Mr. SPIEZLE. I think they do. Whether they are——

Senator JOHNSON. OK. Good. That is what I wanted to—because here is the point: What can government do better than what these private companies can do to prevent this? I have sat through hearing after hearing—for example, just this week, we talked about the Defense Department who has been unable to get audit ready in 15 to 20 years.

So my point is: Is there a role the government can play that does not actually do more harm than good?

Now, as I have been investigating this and been involved in Commerce Committee hearings, the first step that we need to take in terms of cybersecurity is information sharing. And the only way we are going to get information sharing is we have to provide some liability protection.

I want to ask all three of you: Is that pretty much the first thing the government has to do, we have to enact some type of information-sharing piece of legislation that provides the kind of liability so that you will actually share information? Let me start with Mr. Stamos.

Mr. STAMOS. Thank you, Senator. We are in support of information sharing as long as there are strong privacy protections for our users, but we are happy to work on the details of that, yes.

Senator JOHNSON. Do you think that is the first step?

Mr. STAMOS. I think that is an important step. I also think something government can do right now is to work on disrupting the financial side of these cyber criminal networks.

Senator JOHNSON. So you are actually talking about enforcement; you are talking about going after criminals and enforcing and penalizing the criminals.

Mr. STAMOS. Yes, penalizing the criminals, but also just making it hard for them to make money. A lot of these guys are actually selling products. They are taking credit cards. They are cashing checks. And so even if we cannot arrest them because they are in a jurisdiction where that is impossible, we can make it difficult for them to profit off of targeting American——

Senator JOHNSON. So would that require more regulation of the banking industry, some targeted actions there?

Mr. STAMOS. Again, I am not a lawyer, so I do not know the exact—I think it is all already illegal. It is really just a focus issue.

Senator JOHNSON. OK. Mr. Salem, again, what can government do? What is the first step?

Mr. SALEM. Senator, you had mentioned basically looking at being allowed information. To be quite clear, my team is the one that does the anti-malvertising, and we are very happy that we could actually speak to our colleagues, at least in the industry, very openly about the different threats and what we can do about it. We actually currently do talk very openly, and some of the other threats that have come out, like we have spoken recently about TrustInAds.org where you have scams basically in the tech support industry. These were terrible for consumers. Some of them had malware installed on their computers under the guise of giving a credit card number to people in India, helping them with their computer.

We are very happy to discuss——

Senator JOHNSON. OK, but that is between companies. What about information sharing with the government so that the government can disseminate some of that information to other people in the industry that you maybe do not have a partnership with? And I guess the other thing I want to get to is some sort of Federal preemption on data breach, so that we have a data breach standard so you are not having to deal with 50 or more, potentially hundreds or thousands of jurisdictions. I mean, is that something pretty important? Is that something the government can do that would be constructive as opposed to hampering your activities?

Mr. SALEM. Yes, it would.

Senator JOHNSON. Because here is my concern, is that we enact some piece of legislation with the best of intentions that actually makes it more difficult, takes your eye off the ball of actually solving the problem as opposed to complying with regulations that are written by people that are not even close to, as agile, as flexible, and as knowledgeable as what your companies are.

Mr. SALEM. Currently today, we are able to do our scanning, look for these bad ads, look for sites, and protect consumers, protect our users, talk to other folks in the industry currently about malvertising, about the malvertising trends. Right now we do not feel like we have problems or that there is anything encumbering us with this communication for the issue of malvertising.

Senator JOHNSON. OK. Part of my concern about some of the answers you are providing in the hearing here is you obviously do not want to alarm your consumers, and I do not want to put words in your mouth, but I am a little concerned that that is—we all know this is a small slice. I mean, this is a big problem, right? And I want you to kind of answer the question I asked Mr. Spiezle about the enormous incentives you have. You mentioned, I think, in your testimony your top priority is users matter, user trust, and user security is a top priority. I think that just makes common sense, but I will give you an opportunity to underscore that point.

Mr. SALEM. For Google, user privacy, user security is No. 1. I mean, honestly we are an Internet business. Our users are one click away from going to our competition, one click away from doing something else. We have to prove that we take this seriously, that when they click on any ad that is a safe ad and that when we deal with our third-party advertisers, that they are vetted partners as well.

Mr. STAMOS. Yes, Senator, we have a huge incentive to maintain user trust. The biggest sites that Yahoo! ads run on are Yahoo! sites, and so to maintain those 800 million people around the world using our sites, we have to maintain the trust of our users, and we have to live up to our responsibility.

Senator JOHNSON. I come from a manufacturing background, so we have gone through ISO certification, which I will have to admit, when I first got into it, I am going, ''Well, this is a pretty good deal for the consultants that do ISO certification.'' But having gone through the process, I became a real believer that this is extremely helpful in terms of providing, not only my company the tools to get our process under control, but to communicate to our customers, to our suppliers that we had our process under control across a whole host of different parts of that standard.

From my standpoint, that kind of certification process would make sense for this particular—and when we are talking about standards, security standards and advertising, is that something that Yahoo! and Google would support, some kind of third-party certification process that would give consumers the comfort that the standards are in place?

Mr. STAMOS. Thank you, Senator. I think we would support self-regulation to set guidelines. From the actual technical standards, this is something that we change and innovate on every single day, so we need to be really careful to not get too prescriptive to where we are living up to a rule and we are not doing what we need to do to——

Senator JOHNSON. Well, that is what I am talking about, a private sector alternative.

Mr. STAMOS. Yes.

Senator JOHNSON. But I want to make sure it is a cooperative one, not potentially somebody who is set up in business and is actually hostile to some of the actors in the room. You really need to have this very cooperative, very flexible, very fast moving, because these standards are going to have to change—what? Daily? I mean, literally what are we talking about in terms of the level of flexibility we are going to need if we are going to have any hope? And all we are going to be able to do is minimize this, right? Probably? I mean, the criminals are going to be one step ahead of us every time. You are going to have to continue to change these standards and what we need to do on an on going basis, correct?

Mr. SALEM. Correct. We need to evolve, and we need to basically be as nimble as possible to make sure that we are one step ahead of those criminals.

Senator JOHNSON. I am out of time.

Mr. SPIEZLE. I might add that the standards that were addressed earlier that industry came together to address spam and deceptive email, DMARC and DKIM and SPF, they are examples of similar technologies that could be employed, so I would actually say that there could be standards that could be developed that could help increase the trustworthiness in advertising.

Senator JOHNSON. Thank you, Mr. Chairman.

Senator LEVIN. Senator McCaskill.

Senator MCCASKILL. Mr. Spiezle, do you know what percentage of all the malware incidents occurred through advertising? I think this is your chart,[1] correct?

Mr. SPIEZLE. Yes, this is a chart——

Senator MCCASKILL. And what percentage of malware incidents are attributable to advertising in the year 2013?

Mr. SPIEZLE. I do not have that specific data.

Senator MCCASKILL. Well, how can you not have that data if you know how many display malvertising there was? Wouldn't you have to know the context of that number?

[1] See Exhibit No. 1, which appears in the Appendix on page 162.

Mr. SPIEZLE. No, this is very specific to documented cases where malicious ads were documented and observed. So we are not looking at click fraud, we are not looking at search ad or fraudulent ad——

Senator McCASKILL. And why not?

Mr. SPIEZLE. Because this is the area, again, that is coming through the pipeline. The critical infrastructure that is impacting us today through malicious advertising where consumers do not have the ability to protect themselves.

Senator McCASKILL. Well, if I have malware on my computer, frankly it does not matter where it came from, and I am trying to get at the whole problem here. This is obviously one small piece of it. Do you all know, Mr. Stamos and Mr. Salem, what percentage of the malware incidents are attributable to advertising?

Mr. SALEM. We do not know that information?

Senator McCASKILL. Does anybody know it?

Mr. SALEM. We do know that the classic way that a consumer will get malware is visiting a site, not necessarily the advertisement on that site. That is the classic way where criminals——

Senator McCASKILL. That is what I am trying to get at. How much of this is site-specific versus ad-specific?

Mr. STAMOS. So the numbers we see, Senator, from other sources on the number of malware infections are in the tens or hundreds of millions. So that is the context in which I would put the hundreds of thousands here.

Senator McCASKILL. OK. So we are talking about less than 1 percent.

Mr. STAMOS. It is real hard to know, Senator, exactly where each malware infection comes from. But I do not think that it is unlikely that it is less than 1 percent.

Senator McCASKILL. OK. Some of the people in this room have heard me say this before—part of the problem here is that consumers were not brought along early in this process to understand the importance of being educated and understanding that what they are getting for free is coming at a price of advertising. I do not think you would argue, Mr. Spiezle, that we would have a much different Internet if it were not for—in fact, the backbone, the foundational backbone of the Internet as we know it and the explosion of economic activity and jobs is all around behavioral marketing, correct?

Mr. SPIEZLE. It is all about advertising, which is great, and we fully agree that advertising supports the services that society and businesses get today.

Senator McCASKILL. So when consumers hear how unfair it is that their data is—that they are seeing ads for outdoor furniture when they have been shopping for outdoor furniture, when they get creeped out about that, they are not making the connection that is why their Internet content is free. You all get that, right? They do not get that connection? And that is all on you. You have not informed them appropriately about the bargain they are striking. And perhaps what would be most helpful in this regard is to figure out what the costs would be if we were to remove—if we were to clamp down in the government on the kind of advertising and the prevalence of advertising on the Internet and the ability to behavioral market on the Internet by knowing what people are interested in as opposed to just like we know that somebody who watches Oprah maybe would—they might want to run an ad for Slim-Fast on Oprah. I mean, that is what happens in advertising. You try to target your audience based on what they are looking at.

Does anybody know what this would cost for people to have an email or to have the search capability they have if it were not for advertising? Has anyone ever tried to quantify that so consumers would understand the bargain they are getting?

Mr. STAMOS. I just have to say, Senator McCain's number, in his opening statement he talked about the overall ecosystem being worth around $43 billion. So I guess that would be the overall cost.

Senator MCCASKILL. OK. What is the one thing the government is supposed to do in this space? I think it is catch criminals, right?

Mr. SALEM. Yes.

Senator MCCASKILL. OK. Mr. Spiezle, why aren't we catching more of these criminals? How much time is your organization spending on the failure of government, both nationally, domestically, Federal, State, local, and internationally, the abject failure we have had at going after—and I know it is really hard because we are talking about IP addresses that disappear in less than that.

Mr. SPIEZLE. Thank you for the question. It is clearly a problem of epidemic proportions, State-sponsored actors and such international here. One of the biggest challenges—and I think we have outlined in every area of security best practices—is data sharing. And it is not just data sharing to government. We also have to remove the barriers and the barriers cited by many of the organizations in this room, for example, antitrust, of sharing this data with each other. That is the first part. In the absence of that, we cannot peel back the onion. Working with the FBI and Secret Service, this is a very difficult problem to go back to and get——

Senator MCCASKILL. So you are saying that the government's failure is because Google and Yahoo! and their colleagues are not sharing information with law enforcement?

Mr. SPIEZLE. I am saying that in general—it is not a government failure. It is in general a failure of the industry sharing data among ourselves and with law enforcement of when these incidents are occurring. But it is a difficult problem. I want to underscore, they are also being victimized, their infrastructure is being victimized as well, and so I certainly recognize that issue that is hurting their businesses. But we have to put in place the measures to protect and prevent it and also to detect it. And when we detect it, then we can notify. But in the absence of data, we cannot notify the other parties to bring down the ads as quickly as possible or to look at the methodology to prevent it from reoccurring.

Senator MCCASKILL. Well, let us try to drill down on that a little bit. Mr. Stamos and Mr. Salem, are you all trying to work in a cooperative and moment-by-moment fashion with law enforcement?

Mr. STAMOS. Yes, Senator, we have a dedicated e-crime team that we are actually in the process of beefing up, that when we see an incident where we believe there is enough information, that we refer that information to law enforcement, that we work with them throughout the investigation. And we have actually had some success in the disruption of several cyber criminal networks.

As Mr. Spiezle said, there is an international component that sometimes make an arrest difficult, but you do not need to arrest them to make it economically infeasible for them to be committing these crimes.

Senator MCCASKILL. Well, I would like more information on that, and I would certainly appreciate anything your organization could bring to that also. I would like to understand why we are not having more robust success in the law enforcement space since your companies are being victimized and consumers are being victimized by criminals.

Mr. SALEM. I can give you a few anecdotes, if you would like, that might help. Google constantly is being asked for information by law enforcement to give information about cyber criminals, and we do that. The few times that we have actually approached law enforcement and said, we have exact IP addresses, we know exactly where these servers are, they are in the United States, one of the things we are asked to give is, ''Well, show us the fraud, show who was fraudulent, the amount of damages.'' We do not have that information.

So that is something where, overall, we have actually had problems approaching law enforcement to actually take action.

Senator MCCASKILL. Do you all feel——

Senator MCCAIN. For the record, would you provide an example of that for us.

Mr. SALEM. I can do that offline, yes.

Senator MCCASKILL. One of the things I think there is a stress for you all, and that is informing consumers as clearly and boldly as many of us believe you should inform them—because a lot of this can be prevented by consumers, as you well know, Mr. Spiezle. If you understand the ecosystem of the Internet and if you understand the concept of cookies and if you understand what your browser is actually doing, if you understand the power of a click, you can avoid a great deal of the danger.

But I am sure some of the stress for your companies is that the more you warn consumers, the more they are going to be afraid to robustly participate in the Internet in terms of accessing ads and doing the things that generate a lot of the income for the overall eco-structure.

So how can you balance this better? I know it is better than it was when I started harping on this several years ago about informing consumers. But the secret about their power, about the individual user's power—I have a great deal of power on this thing. But I have to be honest with you. The only reason I know it is because I have an amazing staff that helps me understand how I can access that power. The average consumer does not have a clue.

It seems to me that is what the organizations that fund you, Mr. Spiezle, ought to be more worried about, is how the consumer becomes more empowered in this environment, because it is the only real way.

Mr. SPIEZLE. If I can respond, I clearly agree that consumers have a shared responsibility here to make sure that they are updating their computers, patching their systems, and practicing safe computing practices, absolutely. But, again, getting back to—I remain that, again, going to a trusted site they know of, they type it in, they do not click on a link, all the things that we tell them not to do, and they go to a trusted site that unsuspectingly deploys a zero-day exploit, an exploit that has never been disclosed to them before, there is no amount of consumer education that can solve that problem.

So we have a shared responsibility across all the stakeholders here—consumers, ad networks, publishers alike here—and that is why I think we are having this discussion today.

Senator MCCASKILL. My final question, Mr. Spiezle, is your organization—I know that probably a lot of the security—I am guessing if I was a company that was selling security projects, I would want to invest in you. I would want to make contributions to you. So I am assuming a lot of your contributors are, in fact, the people who make security products for the Internet.

Mr. SPIEZLE. Actually, to the contrary. Over 50 percent of our funding comes from companies like WebMD, America Greetings Comscore Publishers' Clearinghouse, Twitter, eBay websites and Web properties that are depending on consumers to trust their services. They also include interactive markets including Innouyx, Vivaki, Simplifi, Epsulon, and others.

Senator MCCASKILL. And do you provide the services to these— the workshops you provide, are they free of cost to people who come? Or is part of your income that you actually need the revenues——

Mr. SPIEZLE. Our training workshops are basically at a cost recovery basis, and we hold some throughout the U.S. and Europe as well on a range of subjects.

Senator MCCASKILL. So you do not get any revenue stream from your——

Mr. SPIEZLE. Like I said, they are designed to cover our operating costs of the programs.

Senator MCCASKILL. Thank you.

Senator LEVIN. Thank you, Senator McCaskill.

Senator Portman.

Senator PORTMAN. Thank you, Mr. Chairman, and thanks for holding this hearing.

The chart tells it all. [1] We have seen this dramatic increase in malvertising, so it is appropriate we are talking about it.

I also agree with what Senator Johnson said earlier about how the Internet has really thrived without the heavy hand of government. We want to make sure that continues, critical to our economy.

Earlier we talked about a lot of solutions. And I do not understand enough about the problem to know what the right solutions are, to be frank with you. But verification standards certainly seem to make sense. In your testimony, you talk about information-sharing protocols. Senator McCain rightly talked about the liability protections that are needed to make that work well. I know you guys are not lawyers, but we would like some more information on that, if you could give it to us for the record.

The accountability measures for the ad networks themselves seem to make a lot of sense. We talked about enforcement, and I

---

[1] See Exhibit No. 1, which appears in the Appendix on page 162.

want to ask you about that in a second. But enforcement requires the information, which is important to get at what, Mr. Stamos, you talked about in terms of the financial incentives that are in the system now.

I have a question just to kind of back up so I maybe understand this problem better. Mr. Salem, you are with Google, kind of a big company. And I understand that you scan 100 percent of the ads that enter into your advertising network. Is that true?

Mr. SALEM. We scan 100 percent of the ads eventually. Not every ad is necessarily scanned unless it is hosted by Google. So many of the ads——

Senator PORTMAN. Unless it is what?

Mr. SALEM. Hosted by Google. So we have third parties, and we have Google ads as well. So all of the ads that are Google are scanned immediately before served. A few of the third parties——

Senator PORTMAN. OK. Let us focus on the ads that are Google-hosted. If you are scanning all of those ads, then how did the malvertising that ended up on YouTube earlier this year circumvent that scanning process? I mean, it was a major issue. Everybody was aware of it. How did that happen?

Mr. SALEM. It happened because ads can go bad. So there are a lot of third-party components to ads. There are a lot of Java Script calls. There are potentially, tracking or analytics that happens along with an ad.

When we scan an ad, we scan an ad and the ad looks great. We continually scan ads based on the risk, how often they are shown. These ads went bad before we had a chance to rescan them.

Senator PORTMAN. So the vulnerability was that you did not have a continuous ability to analyze that ad, and it went bad. So what are you doing to address that vulnerability?

Mr. SALEM. So what we have done is we have looked at our risk profile on these ads. We have basically lowered it for many of them, and we are scanning more often for all of these.

Senator PORTMAN. And are you scanning often enough to avoid what happened with the YouTube malware happening again?

Mr. SALEM. We believe so. We scan all of the ads that we host, and we rescan them quite a bit. We have hundreds of thousands of ads we take down continuously. Some of those are based on the websites that they go to that are bad, and some of them are based on the ads themselves that are going bad.

Senator PORTMAN. Your prepared testimony focuses a lot on preventing, which is what this is, and disabling malware. Of course, both are necessary. I get that.

When prevention fails, as it did with this huge incident, what can consumers do to protect themselves from harm inflicted by ads on Google's ad network or any other entity's ad network?

Mr. SALEM. Sure. So just on this incident itself, I would not necessarily call it huge because the website itself was on our safe browsing list. So users that use Chrome, Mozilla, and Safari, they were already covered by this. Also, the specifics were for an unpatched version of Internet Explorer, so this is actually telling you these are the users that actually got the malware or were exposed to the malware. We do not even know how many of them actually downloaded the malware.

Senator PORTMAN. So you do not know what the damage was, but it was not huge?

Mr. SALEM. We know the potential, and when we look at our numbers, we look at what is the potential when an ad goes bad, and we look at our last scan. That is when we consider all that potentially bad advertising.

But that basically shows us that what could protect a user is knowledge that they need to use anti-virus software, that they need to update their browsers, they need to update their operating systems. That in general is best practices, not even just for malvertising but just for malware in general.

Senator PORTMAN. Let me ask a question, if I could, to both of you, Mr. Stamos and Mr. Salem, about consumers, because you talk about how consumers need more information. What can be done to inform people that they have been infected so that they know it without tipping off the cyber criminals involved? Isn't that one area where Senator Johnson was talking about, consumers are going to be key to this. It is impossible for people to know how to react if they do not know that they have been infected. How are you going to let consumers know that?

Mr. STAMOS. Thank you, Senator. As the gentleman from Google said, the cyber criminals are choosing users to attack based on criteria that are not ours and based upon servers that are not ours. So we do not have the exact list of users or even IP addresses for which we are attacked, nor do we have a direct relationship with those users. So direct notification is a difficult issue. That is why we do general notification that we post on our blog, that we have discussion through the press of what happened, and then we have a safety and security website that we refer users back to that gives tips on how they can patch their system and free anti-virus tools to check whether or not that piece of malware was installed.

Senator PORTMAN. Mr. Spiezle, any thoughts on that?

Mr. SPIEZLE. I agree, it is very hard, again, knowing where that ad ran and who it was. There are, obviously, the anti-virus softwares, I agree, that get data on consumers who get notifications from them.

There has been a related effort that actually has been led through the FCC in the CSRIC process with ISP best practices where they detect abnormal behavior coming from an IP address of a residential computer. So there is progress in that front, not related to the ad-specific, but when a device appears to have been compromised and how do you notify. The framework that I identified today and outlined is built on that framework of prevention, detection, notification. So there are parallel efforts, and I raise that because this is an issue that needs us to move out of a silo of one industry and look at what other segments of the industry are doing to solve the problems, similar problems.

Senator PORTMAN. In the Subcommittee's report, it seems to me that Senator Levin's team is saying that you guys do not have the incentive that you would otherwise have because consumers do not know that the malvertising came from you. How do you respond to that? I think if you do not know to attribute to a particular attack, a particular ad network, there might be a disincentive to address it. There would be a much greater incentive if they knew this came from their Yahoo! account, the advertisement that they get on Yahoo!. What is your response to that?

Mr. SALEM. I can actually say something and clear up the misconception. Just because you visited a site and you potentially got an ad from Google, because of the anonymity, we do not necessarily know who you are. So as far as, even being able to let people know, an ad was served to you that potentially had malware, we do not know who you are. It is all anonymous, or pseudo-anonymous, and it is done on purpose that way. That is one of the reasons why someone cannot target you specifically with an ad. They can target, potentially, your gender or your age group based on, you know, some profiling, but that is about it. We do not necessarily know who you are. So that is not even possible.

Senator PORTMAN. Mr. Stamos.

Mr. STAMOS. As to the motivation, obviously if this kind of incident happens, it has an impact on our reputation; it has an impact on the trust our users have in us, and that trust is absolutely the bedrock of our business. And so maintaining user trust is essential, which is why we have a security team, a trust and safety team, an anti-malvertising team, and we are working on this issue 24/7.

Senator PORTMAN. But you cannot tell your customers that they got attacked?

Mr. STAMOS. We cannot tell advertising customers. As Mr. Salem said, we do not have that information. We cannot directly tie Bob Smith to look at this specific advertisement.

Senator PORTMAN. If they could have that connection to a particular ad, wouldn't that make for a more effective enforcement regime? They would know where it came from, and you or the ad networks would then be in a position to respond.

Mr. STAMOS. I believe, Senator, that would be a significant privacy issue that we are also talking about here for us to track individuals looking at——

Senator PORTMAN. Let me ask you about something that I found really interesting in some of the material that was sent to us in advance. It says that some cyber criminals carry out these attacks on weekends and holidays because they figure your guard is down. Is your guard down on weekends and holidays?

Mr. STAMOS. Absolutely not, Senator. Thank you for the question. The systems that do this are automated systems, and you are guilty until proven innocent. So we scan immediately on upload. We scan before an ad is seen. We scan repeatedly afterwards. And if anything is strange, that ad gets immediately pulled, and then our people get paged, and our security team works 24/7, 365 days——

Senator PORTMAN. So consumers should not be worried on weekends or on holidays?

Mr. STAMOS. No, absolutely not.

Senator PORTMAN. OK. I am glad to hear that.

I also had a question about this TrustInAds.com group that I think you all support. Mr. Spiezle, I do not know if your group supports that. But maybe, Mr. Spiezle, you can tell us what to expect from TrustInAds.com in the near future to address this malware problem? How can consumers get information?

34

Mr. SPIEZLE. Well, I cannot really speak to the organization. We have reached out to them. I can only respond to what is on their website, and it is about educating policymakers and notifying consumers what to do when they have been harmed. So the site speaks for itself. I look forward to finding more information from them as well.

Senator PORTMAN. Mr. Salem, do you think it is going to be effective?

Mr. SALEM. Yes, it actually has been effective. We recently just released our study on the tech support vertical, and basically one of the things we were noticing was when Google started clamping down on this terrible scam, the scammers started going to other sites. And what we did was we reached out to our colleagues to make sure that we basically stopped this from happening for everybody.

Senator PORTMAN. Mr. Stamos.

Mr. STAMOS. I totally agree. I think TrustInAds is really focused on the deceptive advertising and the fraud, and one of the reasons it has been put together is it is a single place where you can report those advertisements to make all the companies that are involved are aware so that we can go take them down and ban those advertisers.

Senator PORTMAN. Thank you. Thank you, Mr. Chairman.

Senator LEVIN. Thank you very much, Senator Portman. We thank our participants in this panel very much for your testimony. It has been extremely helpful, and we will now move on to our second panel.

Senator MCCAIN. Mr. Chairman, before you do that—it is a little disturbing when Mr. Salem and Mr. Stamos dispute facts. Ronald Reagan used to say that facts are stubborn things.

I am a bit disturbed by sort of it is somebody else's problem in the testimony today, and it heightens my motivation to both reinvigorate legislation that we had tried before, but also try to make Google and Yahoo! understand that this is a much bigger problem than their testimony indicates they think it is today. And it is a bit disappointing.

Thank you, Mr. Chairman.

Senator LEVIN. Thank you very much.

Senator JOHNSON. Mr. Chairman, just two quick questions?

Senator LEVIN. We have three or four votes in 5 minutes.

Senator JOHNSON. These are actually pretty basic questions.

Senator LEVIN. OK.

Senator JOHNSON. I just want to ask Yahoo! and Google, the technical indications scanning, how many scans are you doing? What percentage of that, if you wanted complete coverage, what are we talking about? Are you able to scan 1 percent, 100 percent?

Mr. SALEM. We scan all ads, so it is 100 percent.

Senator JOHNSON. But you are doing it all, but you are rescanning and rescanning. I mean, what would be complete coverage versus what percent are you—do you understand? Is it an impossible question to answer?

Mr. SALEM. I think that one of the——

Senator LEVIN. Could you give it a try for the record? Would that be all right?

Senator JOHNSON. The other thing I just want to know is how many people in your organization are devoted to cybersecurity, number of people, because I want to ask the government how many they have available.

Mr. STAMOS. As to the last question, we scan every single ad, 100 percent of the ads, and we scan them multiple times, dozens, hundreds of times based upon different risk metrics. And as for the number of people, I would say across the different teams we have over 100 people working on security and trust and safety.

Senator JOHNSON. Thank you. Sorry about that.

Senator LEVIN. That is OK. Mr. Salem, did you want to give an answer to number of people, quickly.

Mr. SALEM. Sure. So Google has over 400 people working specifically on security. We have over 1,000 when it comes down to all of our ad policies and basically making sure that our ads are compliant.

Senator LEVIN. Very good. Thank you. We again thank this panel. You all were very helpful to us, and we appreciate it.

Again, I want to thank Senator McCain for bringing us to this point. I happen to very much agree with his comments and with the thrust of this report.

Let me now call our second panel. Maneesha Mithal, Associate Director of the Division of Privacy and Identity Protection of the Federal Trade Commission in Washington; and Lou Mastria, Managing Director of the Digital Advertising Alliance in New York.

We appreciate both you being here this morning, and we look forward to your testimony. I think you know the rules of the Subcommittee that all who testify here need to be sworn, so we would ask that you both please stand and raise your right hand. Do you swear that the testimony you are about to give to this Subcommittee will be the truth, the whole truth, and nothing but the truth, so help you, God?

Ms. MITHAL. I do.

Mr. MASTRIA. I do.

Senator LEVIN. We are going to get as far as we can into your testimony before these votes start, and then we are going to just have to work around the testimony and the questions, I am afraid. Let us try to do this in 8 minutes each, if you could, and we will put your statements in the record.

So, Ms. Mithal, please start.

STATEMENT OF MANEESHA MITHAL,[1] ASSOCIATE DIRECTOR, DIVISION OF PRIVACY AND IDENTITY PROTECTION, FEDERAL TRADE COMMISSION, WASHINGTON, DC

Ms. MITHAL. Thank you, Chairman Levin, Ranking Member McCain, and Members of the Subcommittee. I am Maneesha Mithal from the Federal Trade Commission. I appreciate the opportunity to present the Commission's testimony on consumer protection issues related to online advertising.

I also thank the Subcommittee for its report that it issued yesterday which highlights online threats to consumers. We look forward to working with you on these important issues.

---

[1] The prepared statement of Ms. Mithal appears in the Appendix on page 79.

The Commission is primarily a civil law enforcement agency, charged with enforcing Section 5 of the FTC Act, which prohibits unfair or deceptive practices. We are committed to using this authority to protect consumers in the online marketplace. For example, we have used Section 5 to take several actions against online ad networks. We also educate consumers and businesses about the online environment and encourage industry self-regulation. In my oral statement, I will discuss our enforcement and education efforts in three areas: privacy, malware, and data security.

First, with respect to privacy, we have brought many enforcement cases against online ad networks. For example, Chitika is an online ad network that offered consumers the ability to opt out of receiving targeted ads. According to our complaint, what they did not tell consumers is that the opt-out lasted only 10 days. We allege this was deceptive under Section 5. Our order requires Chitika to tell the truth in the future, provide consumers with an effective opt-out, and destroy the data they collected while their opt-out was ineffective.

As a more recent example, we obtained a record $22.5 million civil penalty against Google for allegedly making misrepresentations to consumers using Safari browsers. Google placed tracking cookies on consumers' computers and gave them a choice to opt out of these cookies. Google's opt-out instructions said that Safari users did not need to do anything because Safari's default setting would automatically ensure that consumers would be opted out. Despite these instructions, in many cases we allege that Google circumvented Safari's default settings and placed cookies on consumers' computers. Although we generally cannot get civil penalties for violations of Section 5, we were able to get civil penalties in this case because we allege that Google violated a prior FTC order.

The second area I would like to highlight is malware. As you know, malware can cause a range of problems for computer users, from unwanted pop-up ads to slow performance to keystroke loggers that can capture consumers' sensitive information. This is why the Commission has brought several Section 5 cases against entities that unfairly downloaded malware onto consumers' computers without their knowledge. One of these cases, against Innovation Marketing, alleged that the malware was placed on consumers' computers through online ads.

We have also made consumer education a priority. The Commission sponsors OnGuard Online, a website designed to educate consumers about basic computer security. We have created a number of articles, videos, and games that describe the threats associated with malware and explain how to avoid and detect it.

Finally, while going after the purveyors of malware is important, it is also critical that ad networks and other companies take reasonable steps to ensure that they are not inadvertently enabling third parties to place malware on consumers' computers. To this end, online ad networks should maintain reasonable safeguards to ensure that they are not showing ads containing malware.

The Commission has undertaken substantial efforts for over a decade to promote strong data security practices in the private sector in order to prevent hackers and purveyors of malware from harming consumers. We have entered into 53 settlements with on-line and offline businesses that we charged with failing to reason-ably protect consumers' personal information. Our data security cases include actions against Microsoft, Twitter, and more recently Fandango and Snapchat.

In each of our cases, we have made clear that reasonable security is a continuous process of addressing risks, that there is no one-size-fits-all data security program, that the Commission does not require perfect security, and the mere fact that a breach has oc-curred does not mean that a company has violated the law. These principles apply equally to ad networks. Just because malware has been installed does not mean that the ad network has violated Sec-tion 5. Rather, the Commission would look to whether the ad net-work took reasonable steps to prevent third parties from using on-line ads to deliver malware.

In closing, the Commission shares this Subcommittee's concerns about the use of online ads to deliver malware onto consumers' computers, which implicates each of the areas discussed in the Commission's testimony: consumer privacy, malware, and data se-curity. We encourage several additional steps to protect consumers in this area, including more widespread consumer education, con-tinued industry self-regulation, and the enactment of a strong Fed-eral data security and breach notification law that would give the Commission the authority to seek civil penalties for violation.

Thank you, and I would be happy to answer any questions.

Senator LEVIN. Thank you very much.

Mr. Mastria.

STATEMENT OF LUIGI "LOU" MASTRIA,[1] EXECUTIVE DIREC-TOR, DIGITAL ADVERTISING ALLIANCE, NEW YORK, NEW YORK

Mr. MASTRIA. Chairman Levin, Ranking Member McCain, and Members of the Subcommittee, good morning, and thank you for the opportunity to speak at this important hearing. My name is Lou Mastria. I am Executive Director of the Digital Advertising Al-liance.

Companies have every interest to protect the privacy of con-sumers' data, and I am pleased to report to the Subcommittee on the continued success of the DAA's Self-Regulatory Program which provides consumers with privacy-friendly tools for transparency and control of Web viewing data, all of this backed by a growing code of enforceable conduct.

The DAA is a cross-industry nonprofit organization founded by the leading advertising and marketing trade associations. These in-clude the Association of National Advertisers, the American Asso-ciation of Advertising Agencies, the Direct Marketing Association, the Interactive Advertising Bureau, the American Advertising Fed-eration, and the Network Advertising Initiative. These organiza-tions came together in 2008 to develop the Self-Regulatory Prin-ciples for Online Behavioral Advertising, which were then extended in 2011 to cover the collection and use of Web viewing data for pur-

---

[1] The prepared statement of Mr. Mastria appears in the Appendix on page 94.

poses beyond advertising. More recently, the DAA provided guidance for the collection of data in and around mobile environments.

In 2012, the Obama Administration publicly praised the DAA as a model of success for enforceable codes of conduct, recognizing the program as ''an example of the value of industry leadership as a critical part of privacy protection going forward.'' More recently, Commissioner Ohlhausen of the Federal Trade Commission was quoted as calling the DAA ''one of the great success stories in the [privacy] space.''

The DAA administers and promotes these responsible and comprehensive self-regulatory principles for online data collection and use. To provide independent accountability for the DAA, the Council of Better Business Bureaus and the Direct Marketing Association operate collaborative accountability mechanisms independent of the DAA.

To date, there have been more than 30 publicly announced compliance actions through the DAA program. We believe that DAA is a model example of how interested stakeholders can collaborate across an ecosystem to provide meaningful and pragmatic solutions to complex privacy issues, especially in areas as highly dynamic and evolving as online advertising.

The Internet is a tremendous engine of economic growth, as was mentioned earlier, supporting the employment of more than 5 million Americans and contributing more than $500 billion, or 3 percent of GDP. A major part of that includes the data-driven marketing economy which touches every State and contributes nearly 700,000 jobs as of 2012.

Advertising fuels this powerful economic engine. In 2013, Internet advertising revenues reached $43 billion. Because of advertising, consumers access a wealth of online resources at low or no cost. Revenue from online advertising subsidizes content and services that consumers value, such as online newspapers, blogs, social networking sites, mobile applications, email, and phone services. These advertising-supported resources truly have transformed all of our daily lives.

Interest-based advertising is essential to the online advertising model. Interest-based advertising is delivered based on consumers' preferences or interests inferred from data about online activities. Research shows that advertisers pay several times more for relevant ads, and as a result, this generate greater revenue to support free content. Consumers also engage more actively with relevant ads.

Interest-based ads are vital for small businesses as well. They can stretch their marketing budget to reach likely consumers. Third-party ad technologies allow small content providers to sell advertising space to large advertisers, thereby increasing their revenue.

Preserving an advertising ecosystem that meets the needs of both small and large businesses and at the same time provides consumers ways to address their privacy expectations is a reason why so many companies have publicly committed to the DAA principles. The DAA provides consumers choice with respect to collection and use of their Web viewing data, preserving the ability of companies to responsibly deliver services and continue to innovate.

Among other things, the DAA principles call for enhanced notice outside of the privacy policy so that consumers can be made aware of the companies with which they interact while on the net; provision of a choice mechanism giving consumers choice, not companies; education; and strong enforcement mechanisms.

Together these principles increase consumers' trust and confidence in how information is gathered online and how it is used to deliver advertisements based on their interests.

The DAA's multi-site principles, which is one of our three codes of conduct, sets forth clear prohibitions against certain practices, including the use of Web viewing data for eligibility purposes, such as employment, credit, health care treatment, and insurance.

The DAA has developed a universal icon to give consumers transparency and control with respect to intra-space data. The icon provides consumers with notice that information about their online interests are being gathered to customize the Web ads they see. Clicking on the icon takes consumers to a centralized choice tool that enables consumers to opt out of this advertising by participating companies. The icon is currently served more than a trillion times each month globally on or next to ads, websites, digital properties, and tools covered by the program. This achievement represents an unprecedented level of industry cooperation and adoption.

Currently, on the desktop version of the DAA Choice Program, more than 115 third-party platforms participate. The choice mechanism offers consumers a one-click option to opt out of interest-based advertising from all participating platforms.

Consumers are directed to the DAA choice page not only from the DAA icon in and around ads, but also from other forms of website disclosures. Over 3 million unique visitors have exercised choice via our choice page.

We are also committed to consumer education. The DAA launched an educational website at YourAdChoices.com to provide easy-to-understand messaging and informative videos explaining the choices available to consumers, the meaning of the icon, and the benefits derived from online advertising. More than 15 million unique users have visited this site, and to prepare for the introduction of a DAA mobile choice app for mobile environments, which we will release later this year, we have also recently released guidance on how the icons should appear in mobile environments to ensure a consistent user experience in that environment as well.

A key feature of the DAA's Self-Regulatory Program is independent accountability. All of the DAA's self-regulatory principles are backed by robust enforcements administered by the Council of Better Business Bureaus and the Direct Marketing Association. Thirty-three public compliance actions have been announced in the past 2½ years and have included both DAA participants and non-participants alike. We have an obligation to report noncompliance when it happens and cannot be remedied.

The DAA has championed consumer control that both accommodates consumers' privacy preferences and supports the ability of companies to responsibly deliver services desired by consumers. We appreciate the opportunity to be here today. We believe that we have a successful model and can continue to evolve in this area of privacy.

Thank you very much.

Senator LEVIN. Thank you very much, Mr. Mastria.

Senator McCain.

Senator McCAIN. I thank the witnesses. I just have a couple of questions because obviously we have an important vote going on.

Ms. Mithal, you saw the previous chart?[1]

Ms. MITHAL. Yes.

Senator McCAIN. Do you believe that that is an accurate depiction of malvertising?

Ms. MITHAL. I do, and frankly, no matter what the number is, I believe that it is a problem. It is a serious problem, and we are committed to using all of our tools at our disposal to——

Senator McCAIN. Why do you think that the Google and Yahoo! guys would say that it is not accurate?

Ms. MITHAL. I do not know, Senator.

Senator McCAIN. But in your view, this is certainly——

Ms. MITHAL. Well, we have not done our own independent research, but I have no reason to doubt the statistics. And, regardless, even if it happens to one person, it is a significant problem for consumers.

Senator McCAIN. The only other question I have, or comment, it seems to me that consumers are being harmed, whether it be a "sliver," as the other witnesses testified, or whether it is more widespread and on the increase. Would you agree that it is on the increase?

Ms. MITHAL. I do not know, but according to the slide, it looks like it is.

Senator McCAIN. OK. The person, the consumer that is harmed, has no place to go for help or compensation, it appears. Do you agree with that?

Ms. MITHAL. I do.

Senator McCAIN. And so what do we do?

Ms. MITHAL. So I think this is a very serious problem, and it is going to require a multi-pronged solution. I think that, off the top of my head ,I would say three things:

First, increase consumer education, things like updating browsers, patching software, having anti-virus, anti-malware software on their computers.

Second, more robust industry self-regulation. I was heartened to see the Trust-in-Ads announcement last month, and I think that needs to continue.

And third is enforcement, both against the purveyors of malware and against any third parties that are letting these purveyors of malware get through.

Senator McCAIN. Well, it seems to me there should be standards of enforcement, standards of behavior, standards of scanning, standards to do everything they can to prevent the consumer being harmed. And then if they do not employ those practices, they should be held responsible. Does that make sense?

---

[1] See Exhibit No. 1, which appears in the Appendix on page 162.

Ms. MITHAL. It does, Senator. Currently, we have the authority to take action against unfair practices, so the standard is that if a practice causes consumer injury that is not outweighed by the benefits of competition and not reasonably avoidable by consumers, that can be considered a Section 5 violation. And we have brought over 50 cases against companies that have failed to maintain reasonable protections to protect consumers' information. And so that is a tool that we can use, and if Congress chose to give us further tools, we would use them.

Senator MCCAIN. Are you familiar with the legislation that Senator Kerry and I introduced back in 2011?

Ms. MITHAL. I am familiar with it, and I appreciate your leadership.

Senator MCCAIN. Would you do me a favor and look at that again, and if you believe that we need additional legislative tools for you, to look at it, review it, and give us recommendations as to how you think it could be best shaped to protect the consumer and address this issue? And do you believe that it would be helpful if you did have legislation?

Ms. MITHAL. Absolutely, and in particular in the data security area, currently we do not have fining authority. So we have advocated for data security legislation that would give us the authority to seek civil penalties against companies that do not maintain reasonable data security practices.

Senator MCCAIN. All right. I would appreciate it if you would review what we had proposed. It obviously has to be updated, and I will do everything in my power to see if I can get Senator Levin to get engaged as well. He is pretty important in some areas—not others, but some. [Laughter.]

Senator MCCAIN. Thank you.

Senator LEVIN. I am not a tough sell in this area, I want you to know.

Ms. MITHAL. Thank you.

Senator LEVIN. And I am glad that you made reference to the question about whether we need additional strong Federal policy. Your written testimony says that "the Commission continues to reiterate its longstanding, bipartisan call for enactment of a strong Federal data security and breach notification law." And is that still the position of the Commission?

Ms. MITHAL. Absolutely.

Senator LEVIN. Mr. Mastria, do you want to comment? Have you taken a look at the possible—the legislation, for instance, that Senator McCain made reference to?

Mr. MASTRIA. I am generally familiar with it, but as a self-regulatory body, we do not weigh in on legislation. We leave that to our founding trade associations to do that.

Senator LEVIN. All right. Are you done? I am going to try to finish. If not, I will be right back.

Mr. Mastria, the association requires its members to publish the names of parties that do data collection on or for their website and to link to their privacy disclosures. Is that correct? Do you require that of your members?

Mr. MASTRIA. We do require notice and transparency.

Senator LEVIN. No. Do you require your members to publish the names of the parties that do data collection on their website, publish on their website.

Mr. MASTRIA. No. We do require disclosure via a website.

Senator LEVIN. A website.

Mr. MASTRIA. Yes, that is right.

Senator LEVIN. OK. Do they identify on that website which of the parties are not members of your association?

Mr. MASTRIA. So if you go to our choice tool, all of those folks participate with the DAA either directly or indirectly, and so all 115 or 117 that are on there certainly are affiliated with us.

Senator LEVIN. But not necessarily members.

Mr. MASTRIA. We are not a membership organization. Companies have to certify that they abide by our standards.

Senator LEVIN. Everybody on that website that is listed is affiliated.

Mr. MASTRIA. Yes.

Senator LEVIN. OK. There is a provision in there, as I understand it, you have a website called "AboutAds.info," and consumers can visit the page. Again, with a few clicks, they can a list of every participating company that is tracking their browser. Is that correct?

Mr. MASTRIA. It is a list of all participants that are affiliated with the DAA as you characterized that do work to be intermediaries in the advertising space, yes.

Senator LEVIN. All right. And they can opt out of receiving advertisements. Is that correct?

Mr. MASTRIA. There is an opt-out button down at the bottom there that effectively opts out of everybody.

Senator LEVIN. OK. Now, the opting out, as I understand it, prevents consumers from receiving targeted ads based on existing cookies. Is that correct?

Mr. MASTRIA. It is based on cookie technology, yes.

Senator LEVIN. No, but does it prevent consumers from receiving targeted ads?

Mr. MASTRIA. Yes.

Senator LEVIN. Now, when you opt out with one of the participating companies, the companies still, however, is it not correct, have the ability to collect future data about you as you travel the Internet?

Mr. MASTRIA. So the collection——

Senator LEVIN. Is that a yes?

Mr. MASTRIA. So in some cases, yes. But there are prohibitions against the collection of certain data for interest-based advertising.

Senator LEVIN. Well, that is generally true, is it not?

Mr. MASTRIA. Yes.

Senator LEVIN. I am not talking about that. In terms of what is allowed for collection for interest-based advertising, they can continue to collect future information. Is that correct?

Mr. MASTRIA. Yes. I can only speak to what our program covers.

Senator LEVIN. Your program does not prohibit the collection of future information. Is that correct?

Mr. MASTRIA. It does prohibit the collection of future information for interest-based advertising but not necessarily if there is something else going on.

Senator LEVIN. In other words, if you opt out, those companies can no longer collect information for interest-based advertising for you?

Mr. MASTRIA. That is right.

Senator LEVIN. All right. Now, do they have to delete the data that they have already collected on you?

Mr. MASTRIA. Based on the opt-out—the retention policy that we have is tied to—they are allowed to keep it as long as there is a business need, and then that——

Senator LEVIN. That means they are allowed to keep it.

Mr. MASTRIA. Until there is no longer a business need.

Senator LEVIN. Obviously.

Mr. MASTRIA. Yes.

Senator LEVIN. But they are not required to eliminate the data they have already collected——

Mr. MASTRIA. That is right.

Senator LEVIN. Is that correct?

Mr. MASTRIA. But they cannot use it for interest-based ads.

Senator LEVIN. Now, as I understand it, if a consumer clears out all the cookies on his browser, then because this is a cookie-based opt-out, unless an interest-based advertiser technology sees that cookie on the person's computer, they can then send an interest-based ad. Am I stating it correctly?

Mr. MASTRIA. Yes. So the clearing of cookies is an issue, and in 2012 we actually enabled a suite of browser plug-ins which actually solved that issue. It effectively——

Senator LEVIN. So then if you eliminate all your cookies, nonetheless the opt-out will still function.

Mr. MASTRIA. That is right.

Senator LEVIN. All right. So the consumer does not have to continually worry about opting out. Once they have opted out, that will continue to be effective.

Mr. MASTRIA. Using the browser plug-ins effectively creates a hardened cookie the way we sort of jargonly talk about it. Yes.

Senator LEVIN. That is helpful. Thank you.

Have you considered an opt-in approach instead of an opt-out approach?

Mr. MASTRIA. So, Senator, there are certain categories of data for which our codes actually do require opt-in.

Senator LEVIN. How about the interest-based ads?

Mr. MASTRIA. So, generally speaking, if you think about interest-based ads, they work on—as described earlier, there may be an audience that is more interested in outdoor furniture versus——

Senator LEVIN. No, I understand that.

Mr. MASTRIA [continuing]. Indoor furniture.

Senator LEVIN. Have you considered an opt-in approach for interest-based ads?

Mr. MASTRIA. No. The opt-out model seems to work, especially when you are putting consumers in control. The opt-in——

Senator LEVIN. How about asking consumers, ''Would you prefer an opt-in or opt-out model?''

Mr. MASTRIA. We do not ask those questions. What we do is we do ask consumers whether they——

Senator LEVIN. Your members, your associates ask a whole lot of questions.

Mr. MASTRIA. I am sorry. Who?

Senator LEVIN. The people associated with your association, people who you say are not members, they are associated with you. They ask a lot of questions.

Mr. MASTRIA. I am not familiar with those, but I can tell you that——

Senator LEVIN. Is there any reason why you cannot ask consumers whether or not they prefer an opt-in or an opt-out approach to interest-based ads, or why your members could not do that?

Mr. MASTRIA. Well, I think that the reality is that what we give consumers is an ability to opt-out for data that is generally anonymous. For other categories of data, take, for instance, health or financial, there are opt-in procedures——

Senator LEVIN. I am not talking about that other kind of data. I am talking about the kind of data that there is only an opt-out provision for. Is there any reason for why that kind of data could not be subject to a choice, we either want to opt in or opt out? Why couldn't consumers be given that choice? That is my question.

Mr. MASTRIA. Well, it is based on a choice, so——

Senator LEVIN. The choice is opt out of everything or opt out of individual approaches to you. I am saying, Why not give the consumer an opportunity to either opt in or what they currently have, which is to opt out period or opt our specifically?

Mr. MASTRIA. Consumers can, as you noted earlier, decide to clear their cookies and reset all the opt-outs, but that is not the program that we run.

Senator LEVIN. I know that. I guess you are not going to answer my question.

Mr. MASTRIA. I apologize, Senator, but as I said earlier——

Senator LEVIN. You do not think the question is clear?

Mr. MASTRIA. No, no, no. We do not take a position on policy. We simply run the program as it is effectuated.

Senator LEVIN. Don't you have a code?

Mr. MASTRIA. Yes, we have actually three.

Senator LEVIN. Then why not part of the code, make it part of the code to give consumers that option?

Mr. MASTRIA. We do.

Senator LEVIN. No. The option I have just described.

Mr. MASTRIA. That is not part of the code. The code is based on——

Senator LEVIN. Why not change the code to give people that option, give people more choices? Everyone says we want to give consumers choices. I am just adding an important choice.

Mr. MASTRIA. I think——

Senator LEVIN. So you are not bombarded, you are not put in the position you got to go and try to understand what the privacy policy is of 150 different companies, none of which privacy policies are even comprehensible, they are so technical. We are not going to put you in that position. You can opt out on everything. We are giving you that option. You can opt out individually on those advertising companies if you can figure out their advertising policy. Why not give them a third option, an opt-in option to opt in on the type of special interest advertising that you might be interested in? Why not give them that option?

Mr. MASTRIA. So. Senator, the reality is that we do not force people to go look at privacy policies.

Senator LEVIN. OK.

Mr. MASTRIA. One of the key benefits of the DAA program——

Senator LEVIN. Why not urge your members to give people that option in their policy? That is all I am saying.

Mr. MASTRIA. That is not part of the DAA program.

Senator LEVIN. OK. Thank you.

Ms. Mithal, would you for the record give us any suggestions relative to the additional authority which you would like? In addition to commenting on the legislation that Senator McCain made reference to, would you give us any recommendation—we are soliciting recommendations from you as to any legislation that you would recommend to promote greater privacy, greater choice in terms of the Internet and advertising on the Internet? Would you do that?

Ms. MITHAL. Sure, Senator. So I would say that, first and foremost, a Federal——

Senator LEVIN. No, I do not mean right now. I mean for the record.

Ms. MITHAL. Oh, sure. Yes.

Senator LEVIN. Because I have to go vote. I think I have probably missed the first vote already. Thank you both.

Ms. MITHAL. Thank you.

Mr. MASTRIA. Thank you, Senator.

Senator LEVIN. It has been a very useful hearing, and we really appreciate it. Thanks for coming.

We will stand adjourned.

[Whereupon, at 11:41 a.m., the Subcommittee was adjourned.]

APPENDIX

Opening Statement of Senator Carl Levin
Before
Permanent Subcommittee on Investigations
on
Online Advertising and Hidden Hazards
to Consumer Security and Data Privacy

May 15, 2014

For almost a year, the Permanent Subcommittee on Investigations has been investigating hidden hazards to consumers' data privacy and security resulting from online advertising. Our Subcommittee operates in a very bipartisan way, and our practices and rules provide that the Ranking Minority Member may initiate an inquiry, and our tradition is for both sides of the aisle to work on investigations together.

Since this investigation was initiated and led by Sen. McCain, I'd like to call on him to give his opening statement first, after which I will add a few additional remarks. But first I would like to commend Sen. McCain for his leadership and for his staff's hard work in addressing the facts and issues that are the subject of today's hearing. Sen. McCain.

****

Today's hearing is about the third parties that operate behind the scenes as consumers use the internet. In particular, the Subcommittee's report outlines the enormous complexity of the online advertising ecosystem. Simply displaying ads that consumers see as they browse the internet can trigger interactions with a chain of other companies, and each link in that chain is a potential weak point that can be used to invade privacy or host malware that can inflict damage. And those weak links can be exploited although consumers have done nothing other than visit a mainstream website.

The Subcommittee's report also highlights the hundreds of third parties that may have access to a consumer's browser information with every webpage they visit. According to a recent White House report, more than 500 million photos are uploaded by consumers to the internet each day, along with more than 200 hours of video every minute. However, the volume of information that people create about themselves pales in comparison to the amount of digital information continually created about them. According to some estimates, nearly a zettabyte, or 1 trillion gigabytes, are transferred on the internet annually. That's a billion trillion bytes of data.

Against that backdrop, today's hearing will explore what we should be doing to protect people against the emerging threats to their security and privacy as consumers. The report finds that the industry's self-regulatory efforts are not doing enough to protect consumer privacy and safety. Furthermore, we need to give the Federal Trade Commission the tools it needs to protect consumers who are using the internet. Finally, as consumers use the internet, profiles are being created based on what they read, what movies they watch, what music they listen to, on and on. Consumers need more effective choices as to what information generated by their activities on the internet is shared and sold to others.

I'd like to thank all of today's witnesses for their cooperation with this investigation, and I look forward to today's testimony.

# # #

Opening Statement of Senator John McCain
Before
Permanent Subcommittee on Investigations
Hearing On
Online Advertising and Hidden Hazards
to Consumer Security and Data Privacy

May 15, 2014

Thank you, Mr. Chairman. I appreciate you and your staff's cooperation in conducting this important bipartisan investigation. As a longtime advocate for consumer's rights and Internet security, I believe that consumer privacy and safety in the online advertising industry is a serious issue and warrants this Subcommittee's examination.

With the emergence of the Internet and e-commerce, more and more commonplace activities are taking place on the Internet, which has led to major advances in convenience, consumer choice, and economic growth. These advances have also presented novel questions concerning whether consumer security and privacy can be maintained in the new technology-based world. We will examine these issues today specifically in the context of online advertising, where vast data is collected and cyber criminals exploit vulnerabilities in the system and use malware to harm consumers.

As we discuss this complex subject, it's important to keep in mind the following simple idea that I think everyone will agree on: Consumers who venture into the online world should not have to know more than cyber criminals about technology and the Internet in order to stay safe. Instead, sophisticated online advertising companies like Google and Yahoo, whose representatives are here with us today, have a responsibility to help protect consumers from the potentially harmful effects of the advertisements they deliver. Deciding who should bear responsibility when an advertisement harms a consumer can be a technical and difficult question. But, it can't continue to be the case that the consumer alone pays the price when he visits a mainstream website, doesn't even click on anything, but still has his computer infected with malware delivered through an advertisement.

At the same time, online advertising has become an instrumental part of how companies reach consumers. In 2013, online advertising revenue reached a record high of $42.8 billion, surpassing for the first time revenue from broadcast television advertising, which was almost $3 billion less. With the continuing boom in mobile devices, online advertising will become even more lucrative in years to come.

With this hearing, we'll outline the hazards consumers face through online advertisements, how cyber criminals have defeated the security efforts of the online advertising industry, and what improvements could be made to ensure that consumers are protected online and the Internet can remain a safe, flourishing engine for economic growth.

Hazards Facing Consumers

Make no mistake, the hazards to consumers from malware in online advertising are something even a tech-savvy consumer cannot avoid. It is not a matter of simply avoiding shady websites or not clicking on advertisements that look suspicious. For example, in February of this year, an engineer at a security firm discovered that advertisements on YouTube served by Google's ad network delivered malware to visitors' computers. In that case, the user didn't need to click on any ads; just going to YouTube and watching a video was enough to infect the user's computer with a virus. That virus was designed to break into consumers' online bank accounts and transfer funds to cyber criminals. A similar attack on Yahoo in December 2013 also did not require a user to click an advertisement to have his computer compromised.

A consumer whose bank account was compromised by the YouTube ad attack has little recourse under the law as it currently stands. Of course, if an affected consumer managed to track down the cyber criminal who placed the virus, he (or relevant law enforcement agencies) could take legal action against that wrongdoer. But cyber criminals today are normally part of sophisticated professional criminal enterprises, often overseas. Tracking them down is exceedingly difficult—even for professional security specialists. A consumer has essentially no chance whatsoever of recovering funds from cyber criminals.

How can it be that cyber criminals can sneak malware into advertisements under the noses of the most technologically advanced companies in the world? Cyber criminals employ clever tricks to evade the current security procedures used by the online advertising industry. One of those key security procedures is scanning, essentially having a tester visit a website to see if a virus downloads to the test computer. Just as normal online advertisers can target their advertisements to run only in specific locations, cyber criminals can also target by location to avoid scanning. For example, if a cyber criminal knows that the facilities responsible for scanning ads are clustered around certain cities, they can target the malicious advertisement to run in other areas so that the scanners will not see it.

Cyber criminals have used even simpler techniques to bypass security. When law enforcement raided the hideout of a Russian cyber-criminal network, they found calendars marked extensively with U.S. federal holidays and three-day weekends. These cyber criminals were not planning Fourth-of-July picnics, of course; they were planning to initiate malware attacks at times when the security staffing at the ad networks and websites would be at their lowest ebb. Just this past holiday season on Friday, December 27, 2013—two days after Christmas and four days before New Year's Eve—cyber criminals hacked into Yahoo's ad network and began delivering malware-infected advertisements to consumers' computers. The malware seized control of the user's computer and used it to generate "bitcoins", a digital currency that requires a large amount of computer power to create. Independent security firms estimate that around 27,000 computers were infected through this one malware-laden advertisement.

Vulnerabilities Exploited by Cyber Criminals

The result of these cyber-criminal tactics has been countless attacks against consumers online. One major vulnerability in online advertising is that the advertisements themselves are not under the direct control of online advertising companies like Google and Yahoo. Those companies choose not to directly control the advertisements themselves because sending out all of those image or video files would be more expensive. Instead, online advertising companies have the advertiser himself deliver the ad directly to the consumer. While it is cheaper for the companies in the online advertising industry to operate in this way, it can lead to greater hazards for consumers. Malicious advertisers can use their control over advertisements to switch out legitimate ads and put in malware instead. The tech companies who run the online advertising industry frequently do not know when such a switch occurs until after the ad is served. Because those companies don't control the advertisement, their quality control processes are frequently purely reactive, often finding problems after they arise instead of before.

As the online advertising industry grows more and more complicated, a single online advertisement for an individual consumer routinely goes through five or six companies before ultimately reaching the consumer's computer. That fact makes it easier for the various companies in the chain to disclaim responsibility when things go awry.

One instance where that issue was apparent was the attack on Major League Baseball's website in June 2012. In that case, the malicious ad appeared to be for luxury watches and was displayed as a banner at the top of the MLB webpage. The ad was shown to 300,000 consumers before being taken down. In the aftermath of that attack, it was still unclear what entity was responsible for delivery of the malware. One security analyst noted at the time that "the lack of transparency and multiple indirect relationships" in online advertising made assigning responsibility for the attack virtually impossible.

The Complexity of Online Advertising

One way to get an idea of how complicated the online advertising world and online data collection can be is to take a look at what happens when a consumer actually visits a website where advertisements are served by third-party ad companies.

When a user visits a website, that website instantaneously contacts an online advertising company to provide an advertisement. That ad company in turn contacts other Internet companies who help collect and analyze data on the user for purposes of targeting advertisements to him. Each company can, in turn, contact other companies that profit from identifying users and analyzing those users' online activities. Ultimately, hundreds of third-parties can be contacted resulting from a consumer visiting just a single website.

Using special software called "Disconnect", the Subcommittee was able to detect how many third-party sites were contacted when a user visits particular websites. These contacts are represented in a chart. In this first example, we see what happens when a user visits the website of an ordinary business that does not depend heavily on advertising revenues. In this case, our example is TDBank, a company whose website provides online banking services for its existing customers and, more importantly, not to generate income from people visiting the site. For that reason, it does not need to derive a large amount of revenue from online traffic and advertisements.

As you can see, a few third parties were contacted. By contrast, when a consumer visits a website that depends much more heavily on revenue from advertising—based on the number of people who visit their website—the number of third-parties can be enormously higher. For example, this video shows what happens when a consumer visits TMZ.com, a celebrity gossip website.

And, just to make that point even more clear, here are TDBank and TMZ side-by-side.

What these examples illustrate is that consumers generally do not understand the vast, complicated industry that has arisen to analyze their online movements for the purposes of delivering ads online. The websites themselves often don't have relationships with all of the third-parties who are contacted when visitors go to their site, and they often don't know many or all of the advertisers who actually show ads to their visitors.

Even the less complicated aspects of online advertising have proven vulnerable. A number of prominent, popular websites have suffered serious attacks through their own direct sale of advertising space to Internet advertisers. Cyber criminals will often register domain names and email addresses that closely mimic legitimate businesses in order to fool personnel tasked with advertising security. In 2009, *The New York Times* sold Internet space to someone posing as a representative of the phone company Vonage. That supposed representative of the company ran legitimate advertisements on the *Times'* website for several weeks. Then, on a Friday, the legitimate advertisements were replaced with malware-laden advertisements. It took the *New York Times* several days to identify and fix the problem.

Finally, another problem in the current online advertising industry is the lack of meaningful standards for security. The two primary regulators of online advertising are the Federal Trade Commission and self-regulatory groups like the Digital Advertising Alliance and Network Advertising Initiative. The self-regulatory groups have not been active in generating effective guidance or clear standards for online advertising security.

On the privacy side, those self-regulatory groups have worked to respond to concerns of online advertising abuses, but actual enforcement of the privacy-related self-regulatory codes of conduct appears to be lacking in some cases, where even after wrongdoing is detected by academic groups or unrelated security companies, the self-regulatory organizations seem slow to react.

For example, in March 2010, an online advertising company called Epic Marketplace began to engage in "history sniffing", a practice whereby a company can determine a consumer's previous online behavior by examining how the user's browser displays hyperlinks. Through that practice, Epic Marketplace could deduce that users had visited pages relating to, among other things, fertility issues, sensitive medical information, disability insurance, credit problems, and personal bankruptcy. Epic Marketplace then used that information for the purpose of targeting advertisements to those users about those intensely personal issues. Epic Marketplace was a member of a self-regulatory group, the Network Advertising Initiative (NAI), when Epic's behavior came to light. NAI had not discovered Epic's behavior beforehand. Ultimately, Epic Marketplace remained an NAI member and was merely subjected to additional auditing requirements. The fact that a business engaging in such anti-consumer privacy practices could remain a member in good standing suggests that consumers cannot truly rely on a self-regulatory body to guarantee that their information is private and secure.

On the government side, the FTC has brought a number of enforcement actions against companies involved in online advertising for "deceptive" practices pursuant to their authority under Section 5 of the FTC Act. Those cases all involve some specific misrepresentation made by a company rather than a failure to adhere to any general standards. Thus, the easiest thing a company can do to avoid FTC enforcement is not to make specific promises about data privacy or security that could trigger a "deceptive" practices case. The FTC can also bring actions against "unfair" practices, though it has yet to bring any such cases against online advertising companies.

Fixing the Vulnerabilities in the Online Advertising Industry

So, where do we go from here? How can we fix the problems currently facing the online advertising industry and limit the risk of abuse of consumers' privacy and security? First, we must recognize the threat we face. Cybersecurity is a very real and increasing problem, and malware attacks in online advertising are just one technique used by cyber criminals to accomplish objectives ranging from financial gain or disruption of services to industrial espionage. Those attempting to exploit the Internet for criminal purposes are certainly the most culpable, and ensuring law enforcement has the necessary authorities and capabilities to hold criminal actors accountable is an essential element to effective deterrence.

We must also look at the security practices implemented by online advertising companies. Currently, commercial actors have limited incentives to develop and institute security measures for fear of becoming the liable party if something goes wrong. Regulators—both those in government and the self-regulatory bodies in the online advertising industry—need to collaborate to offer guidance on industry best practices for reducing risks. This review is needed to provide greater clarity on what is required of advertising companies to ensure consumer safety, and who should be held responsible when an advertisement harms consumers. This effort appears to be partly underway—just last week, with this hearing on the horizon, several online advertising companies, including Google and Yahoo, announced a new initiative called Trust in Ads that has as its goal the protection of consumers from malicious online advertisements and deceptive practices. The fact that the industry appears to be taking the problem seriously is a step in the right direction, but more needs to be done to protect consumers online.

Some of the advertising companies worry that sharing data and cooperating on security with some companies but not others would raise concerns that they are acting anti-competitively. Recent guidance issued by the Department of Justice and the Federal Trade Commission seemed to clarify that the antitrust laws do not stand in the way of sharing cyber threat information. If there is any lingering uncertainty about the applicability of that guidance to the online advertising context, the DOJ and FTC should make clear that information sharing of online advertising malware threats is not anticompetitive. It is also long past time for legislation allowing for timely and effective information-sharing.

On the question of consumer privacy, there are some guidelines on how much data can be gathered on Internet users and how that data can be used, but these approaches—including verbose privacy notices, "do not track" efforts, and "notice and choice" procedures–have only been partially effective.

A new approach to preventing abuses of consumer data and privacy may be necessary. A few years ago, I introduced "The Commercial Privacy Bill of Rights" with then-Senator Kerry. While updates will be necessary, it provides a framework for how to think about these issues moving forward—one that includes basic rights and expectations consumers should have when it comes to the collection, use, and dissemination of their personal, private information online, and specificity in prohibited practices; a clarified role for the FTC in enforcement; and a "safe harbor" for those companies that choose to take effective steps to further consumer security and privacy. That legislation also envisions a role for industry, self-regulators, and stakeholders to engage with the FTC to come up with best practices and effective solutions.

Consumers deserve to be equipped with the information necessary to understand the risks and to make informed decisions in connection with their online activities. Today, one thing is clear. As things currently stand, the consumer is the one party involved in online advertising who is simultaneously both least capable of taking effective security precautions and forced to bear the vast majority of the cost when security fails. For the future, such a model is not tenable. There can be no doubt that online advertising has played an indispensable role in making innovation profitable on the Internet. But, the value that online advertising adds to the Internet should not come at the expense of the consumer.

Once again, I want to thank the Chairman for agreeing to hold this important hearing and the witnesses for appearing before the Subcommittee today. I look forward to their testimony.

# # #

Written Testimony of
Alex Stamos
Vice President of Information Security
Yahoo! Inc.
Before the Senate Homeland Security and Government Affairs
Permanent Subcommittee on Investigations
"Online Advertising and Hidden Hazards to Consumer Security and Data Privacy"
May 15, 2014

Introduction

Chairman Levin, Ranking Member McCain, and distinguished members of the subcommittee, thank you for convening this hearing and for inviting me to testify today about security issues relating to online advertising. I appreciate the opportunity to share my thoughts and to discuss the user-first approach to security we take at Yahoo.

My name is Alex Stamos, and I am Yahoo's Vice President of Information Security and Chief Information Security Officer. I joined Yahoo in March. Prior to that I served as Chief Technology Officer of Artemis Internet and co-founded iSEC Partners. I have spent my career building and improving secure, trustworthy systems, and I am very proud to work on security at Yahoo.

Yahoo is a global technology company that provides personalized products and services, including search, advertising, content, and communications, in more than 45 languages in 60 countries. We strive to make these daily habits inspire and entertain our users. As a pioneer of the World Wide Web, we enjoy some of the longest lasting customer relationships on the web. It is because we never take these relationships for granted that 800 million users each month trust Yahoo to provide them with Internet services across mobile and web.

One reason I joined Yahoo is that from the top down, the company is devoted to protecting users. Building and maintaining trust through secure products is a critical focus for us, and by default all of our products should be secure for *all* of our users across the globe.

Achieving security online is not an end state; it's a constantly evolving challenge that we tackle head on. At Yahoo, we know that our users rely on us to protect their information. We also see security as a partnership; we want to educate our users to be mindful of their own security habits, and we provide intuitive, user-friendly tools and security resources to help them do so.

Malware is an important issue that is a top priority for Yahoo. While distribution of malware through advertising is one part of the equation, it's important to address the entire malware ecosystem and fight it at each phase of its lifecycle. It is also important to address security more broadly across the Internet.

I outline in my testimony below several specific ways Yahoo is fighting criminals and protecting our users, including: focusing on security in the advertising pipeline and sharing threats; leading the fight on email spam; operating a bug bounty program; and working to fully encrypt 100 percent of Yahoo's network traffic.

Internet Advertising Security and the Fight Against Malware and Deceptive Ads

Internet advertising security is an important focus for us. Yahoo has built a highly sophisticated ad quality pipeline to weed out advertising that does not meet our content, privacy or security standards. In January of this year we became aware of malware distributed on Yahoo sites and immediately took action to remove the malware, investigated how malicious creative copy bypassed our controls, and fixed any vulnerabilities we found. The malware impacted users on Microsoft Windows with out-of-date versions of Java, a browser plugin with a history of security issues, and was mostly targeted at European IP addresses. Users on Macs, mobile devices, and users with up-to-date versions of Java, were not affected.

As I mentioned earlier, the malware ecosystem is expansive and complex. Advertising is only one method of distribution, and distribution is only one part of the problem. Vulnerabilities that allow an attacker to take control of user devices through popular web browsers like Internet Explorer, plugins like Java, office software and operating systems, are large parts of the problem. Malware is also spread by tricking users into affirmatively installing software they believe to be harmless but is, in fact, malicious.

We successfully block the vast majority of malicious or deceptive advertisements with which bad actors attack our network, and we always strive to defeat those who would compromise our customers' security. This means we regularly improve our systems, including continuously diversifying the set of technologies and testing systems to better emulate different user behaviors. Every ad running on Yahoo's sites or on our ad network is inspected using this system, both when they are created and continuously afterward.

Yahoo also strives to keep deceptive advertisements from ever reaching users. For example, our systems prohibit advertisements that look like operating system messages, because such ads often tout false offers or try to trick users into downloading and installing malicious or unnecessary software. Preventing deceptive advertising once required extensive human intervention, which meant slower response times and inconsistent enforcement. Although no system is perfect, we now use sophisticated machine learning and image recognition algorithms to catch deceptive advertisements. This lets us train our systems about the characteristics of deceptive creatives, advertisers and landing sites so we detect and respond to them immediately.

We are also the driving force behind the SafeFrame standard. The SafeFrame mechanism allows ads to properly display on a web page without exposing a user's private information to the advertiser or network. Thanks to widespread adoption, SafeFrame enhances user privacy and security not only in the thriving marketplace of thousands of publishers on Yahoo, but around the Internet.

We also actively work with other companies through our participation in a number of industry groups, including the Interactive Advertising Bureau's (IAB) Ads Integrity Taskforce, which aims to create a higher level of trust, transparency, quality and safety in interactive advertising. We have proudly joined TrustInAds.org, a group of Internet industry leaders that have come together to protect people from malicious online advertisements and deceptive practices. We also participate in groups dedicated to preventing the spread of malware and disrupting the economic lifecycle of cybercriminals, including the Global Forum for Incident Response and Security Teams (FIRST), the Anti-Phishing Working Group, the Underground Economy Forum, the Operations Security Trust Forum (Ops Trust) and the Bay Area Council CSO Forum.

Leading the Fight on Email Spam

While preventing the placement of malicious advertisements is essential, it is only one part of a larger battle. We also fight the rest of the malware lifecycle by improving ways to validate the authenticity of email and by reducing financial incentives to spread malware. Spam is one of the most effective ways malicious actors make money, and Yahoo is leading the fight to eradicate that source of income. For example, one way spammers act is through "email spoofing". The original Internet mail standards did not require that a sender use an accurate "From:" line in an email. Spammers exploit this to send billions of messages a day that feign to be from friends, family members or business associates. These emails are much more likely to bypass spam filters, as they appear to be from trusted correspondents. Spoofed emails can also be used to trick users into giving up usernames and passwords, a technique known generally as "phishing".

Yahoo is helping the Internet industry tackle these issues. Yahoo was the original author of DomainKeys Identified Mail or DKIM, a mechanism that lets mail recipients cryptographically verify the real origin of email. Yahoo freely contributed the intellectual property behind DKIM to the world, and now the standard protects billions of emails between thousands of domains. Building upon the success of DKIM, Yahoo led a coalition of Internet companies, financial institutions and anti-spam groups in creating the Domain-based Message Authentication, Reporting and Conformance or DMARC standard. You can read about this standard and the companies behind it at DMARC.org. DMARC provides domains a way to tell the rest of the Internet what security mechanisms to expect on email they receive and what actions the sender would like to be taken on spoofed messages.

In April of this year, Yahoo became the first major email provider to publish a strict DMARC reject policy. In essence, we asked the rest of the Internet to drop messages that inaccurately claim to be from yahoo.com users. Since Yahoo made this change another major provider has enabled DMARC reject. We hope that every major email provider will follow our lead and implement this common sense protection against spoofed email. DMARC has reduced spam purported to come from yahoo.com accounts by over 90%. If used broadly, it would target spammers' financial incentives with crippling effectiveness.

Incentivizing Sharing: The Bug Bounty Program

Part of keeping our users' data secure is building trustworthy products. To this end, Yahoo operates one of the most progressive bug bounty programs on the Internet, details of which can be viewed at bugbounty.yahoo.com. Our bug bounty program encourages security researchers to report possible flaws in our systems to us via a secure web portal. In this portal we engage researchers and discuss their findings. If their bug turns out to be real, we swiftly fix it and reward the reporter with up to $15,000. In an age where security bugs are often auctioned off and then used maliciously, we believe it is critical that we and other companies create an ecosystem where both burgeoning and established security experts are rewarded for reporting, and not exploiting, vulnerabilities.

Encryption Across Yahoo

Yahoo invests heavily to ensure the security of our users and their data across all of our products. In January, we made encrypted browsing the default for Yahoo Mail. And as of March of this year, domestic and international traffic moving between Yahoo's data centers has been fully encrypted. Our ongoing goal is to enable a secure encrypted experience for **all of our users**, no matter what device they use or from which country they access Yahoo.

Conclusion

I want to restate that security online is not, and will never be, an end state. It's a constantly evolving, global challenge that our industry is tackling head on. Threats that stem from the ad pipeline, or elsewhere, are not unique to any one online company or ad network. And while bad actors pose real threats, we are strongly dedicated to staying ahead of them.

Yahoo fights for user security on multiple fronts. We partner with other companies to detect and prevent the spread of malware via advertising and pioneered the SafeFrame standard to assure user privacy in ad serving. We have led the industry in combating spam in phishing with DKIM and DMARC. We continuously improve our product security with the help of the wider research and security communities. Finally, we are the largest media publisher to enable encryption for our users across the world.

Yahoo will continue to innovate in product security. We will continue to integrate secure development practices into our software lifecycle. We will continue to view user trust and security as top priorities.

Thank you for the opportunity to testify.

Google

Written Testimony of George Salem
Senior Product Manager, Google Inc.
Senate Permanent Subcommittee on Investigations hearing on
"Online Advertising and Hidden Hazards to Consumer Security and Data Privacy"
May 15, 2014

Chairman Levin, Ranking Member McCain, and Senators of the Subcommittee:

Thank you for the opportunity to testify today on Google's efforts to combat malware on the web. My name is George Salem and, as a Senior Product Manager on our Ads Policy team, I develop tools for and support our teams of engineers who fight abuse on our platforms. These teams work to identify bad sites and malware; specific divisions seek to find the root of the malware and combat malicious advertising, also known as "malvertising."

Ensuring our users' safety and security is one of Google's main objectives. One of the biggest threats consumers face on the web is malicious software, known as malware, that can seek to control computers or software programs. Malware allows malicious actors to make money off of innocent victims in various ways. Infected computers can be used to send email spam, support distributed denial-of-service attacks, or extract sensitive user information for means that include identity theft, which has now topped the list of consumer complaints reported to the Federal Trade Commission for thirteen years in a row. Protecting our users against such incursions on their data advances important security and privacy objectives.

Today, I wish to share three main messages:

First, we believe in providing our users the strongest protections against harmful or malicious content. We think about this problem broadly: beyond just malware, we seek to protect our users against any practice that negatively impacts their experience on the web.

Second, we have a two-pronged approach to fighting malware: prevent and disable. Through a combination of sophisticated algorithms and manual review, we prevent users from visiting bad sites and we proactively scan tens of millions of ads each day across multiple platforms and browsers, disabling any ads we find to have malware.

Third, the fight against malware is a team effort, and we collaborate closely with others in the internet community. The online ecosystem is complex and involves many players, particularly when it comes to advertising. Online platforms are in an ever-shifting battle against parties that benefit from malware and are constantly seeking new ways to avoid our detection and enforcement systems. For that reason, we actively contribute best practices, watch lists, and other resources with others to stay ahead of the game.

It's a complex problem, but we are tackling it head on through tools, user education, and community partnerships.

Protecting our users with the strongest protections against harmful or malicious content

Protecting the security of our users and their data is one of our main priorities at Google. Beyond malware, we work to protect our users against what we call 'badware' more generally. Badware encompasses any software that may not be strictly malicious or fraudulent but nonetheless results in an unwanted user experience. Badware may include "trick to click" ads and unwanted system preference downloads. Our business relies on users' trust and ease when using our services, and our goal is to protect against anything that may negatively impact a user's experience in using the web.

Some cybercriminals attempt to use online advertising to distribute malware, a practice known as malvertising. Possible vectors of attack include malicious code hidden within an ad creative (such as a .swf file), embedded on a webpage, or within software downloads. While most ads are safe and legitimate, some bad actors try to find ways to trick consumers by getting harmful and deceptive ads published on reputable sites, exploiting the fact that advertising space may be syndicated to parties who are not known to a web site owner.

Malvertising derails users' faith in the online ecosystem. Advertising has had a tremendous role in the evolution of the web, bringing more products, tools and information to consumers, often free of charge. It has allowed the web economy to flourish — Internet ad revenues surged to a landmark $20.1 billion in the last quarter and the advertising-supported Internet ecosystem employs a total of 5.1 million Americans. Bad ads are bad for everyone, including Google and our users.

Google has a long history of fighting malware, however it is distributed. Ten years ago, we launched a set of Software Principles to protect the broader web against unwanted programs. These principles are a broad, continually evolving set of guidelines around installation, disclosure, behavior and snooping. They state, for example, that applications should not trick our users into installing them; should make it clear when they are responsible for changes to users' experience;

should clearly disclose when they collect or transmit users' personal information, including through an easy to find privacy policy; and should offer easy options for their disabling or removal, should a user desire it. We follow these guidelines with all the products we develop and distribute, and because we strongly believe they are good for the industry and users worldwide, we encourage our current and prospective business partners to adopt them as well.

Our two-pronged approach: Prevent & Disable

Malware and badware are a constantly evolving problem. Google has a two-pronged approach to protecting users from malware online: prevent and disable.

Prevent

One of the best ways to insulate users from the dangers of malware is by proactively preventing them from accessing infected sites altogether. To this end, we developed a tool called Safe Browsing to identify unsafe websites. Safe Browsing creates a continuously updated list of known phishing sites — sites that pretend to be legitimate while trying to trick users into typing in their username and password or sharing other private information — and malware sites. Any page a user visits, as well as all the resources on that page — including pictures and scripts — are checked against this list. Malicious sites we find are then clearly and conspicuously identified as dangerous in Google Search results.

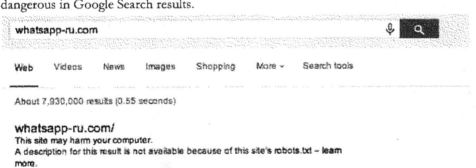

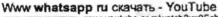

We were the first major search engine to provide this type of warning in search results in 2006, and over a billion people use Safe Browsing today. Every day, we examine billions of URLs, we discover more than 10,000 new dangerous websites, and we show clear and conspicuous warnings on up to 14 million Google search results and 300,000 malicious downloads.

We help tens of millions of people every week protect themselves from harm by making safe browsing the default setting to users of Google Chrome, Mozilla Firefox and Apple Safari browsers and when users attempt to navigate to a site that would steal their personal information or install software designed to take over their computers they get a warning. Whether a user navigates directly to a compromised site or is directed to it through other means, such as an advertisement, they will instead see an unambiguous interstitial — a page inserted before the user's intended destination site loads — alerting them to the presence of malicious content and advising them to click away from that site. We want to help protect all Internet users, not just those using Google services.

We not only make Safe Browsing data and lists available for others to use for free, but we also provide an interface for others to plug in and review identified malware: our Safe Browsing API. An API is an application programming interface that details how certain software should work together. This API enables client applications to check website addresses against Google's constantly updated list of suspected phishing and malware sites, extending Safe Browsing protection to tens of millions of people every week.

We learned from our Safe Browsing data that most sites containing malicious code have been compromised by malware authors without the knowledge of the webmaster. Consequently, we encourage webmasters to sign up with Google's Webmaster Tools so they can receive notifications when we find security problems on their site. We send thousands of notifications to webmasters every day and provide them with resources to help them fix their issues. Once notified, most of them take action to clean up their sites within 30 days.

In addition, Safe Browsing Alerts for Network Administrators allow Autonomous System (AS) owners to receive early notifications for malicious content found on their networks. A single network or ISP can host hundreds or thousands of different websites. Although network administrators may not be responsible for running the websites themselves, they have an interest in the quality of the content being hosted on their networks. With this additional level of information, administrators can help make the Internet safer by working with webmasters to remove malicious content and fix security vulnerabilities.

Disable

While we work very hard to prevent users from coming into contact with malware on the web in general, we work just as hard to disable and keep malware out of our advertising products and services. We have always prohibited malware in our ads and we have strict suspension policies for partners that spread malware or badware. When an account is suspended, we stop running ads related to that account and we may also suspend any related accounts. We do allow advertisers to appeal a suspension if they fix the violations in the account and send us a report of the changes they have made. For those who we have found to repeatedly violate our policies or who have not resolved their violations, the account will be permanently suspended along with any new account setups the advertiser tries to create in the future.

In 2006, to fight the proliferation of malvertising, we built a dedicated system to scan our Ads platforms and disable any account that distributes malware or badware. Today, we proactively scan billions of ads for malware on all aspects of our advertising services, which includes search and display ads on multiple platforms and browsers. We subsequently re-scan the ads that pose greatest risk to our users to make sure malware has not been introduced into an advertisement after our initial vetting. It should be noted that the vast majority of ads served by Google are good, and most of the ads we disable are hosted by third parties.

Our internal systems have a proven track record in disabling malvertising. In 2013, we disabled more than 350 million bad ads, disapproved more than three million applications from joining our networks due to possible malware, blacklisted more than 200,000 publishers, banned over 270,000 advertisers, and disabled advertising from more than 400,000 websites hiding malware. In fact, we disabled 400,000 ads in the last 30 days for malware policy violations.

While we are very proactive in our efforts against malware, we are often silent to the public about our internal scanning technologies and other specific initiatives. Malware and badware are pushed by bad actors who are sophisticated and dynamic, constantly seeking ways to avoid detection and enforcement by internet platforms. Our goal is to stay one step ahead of malvertisers and not tip them off to our activities even as we share tips and best practices with our users and with the broader Internet community.

We work very hard to prevent malware in our system, but bad actors are very sophisticated and sometimes incidents of malvertising do occur. In 2010, a malware threat called JS:Prontexi was widely publicized. This was one of the first published accounts where an advertising malware threat occurred with no user interaction or clicks. What was not publicized was that Google had become aware of the issue and moved quickly before the reports made it to press. By that time, we were actively scrubbing existing and new ads, already disabling over 10,000 bad ads. The remaining few hundred malware distributing ads were found quickly thereafter.

Earlier this year, a rogue advertiser began serving malware infected ads to users in YouTube. Like many attacks, this began on a Friday afternoon. Days earlier, we had disabled the malware serving site with Safe Browsing. So users of browsers that subscribe to safe browsing - Chrome, Firefox, and Safari - were protected when the attack began. Bromium, the operation publishing the threat, worked with Google directly to identify the exact ads. Since this attack, our teams took the appropriate steps to resolve the issue and beefed up our dynamic tests to prevent such events from occurring again. These are a good examples where like-minded industry partners worked together, behind the scenes, to protect all of our users.

We work with industry and share best practices

The anti-malware teams at Google study malware distribution and work closely with the security community to identify malware on the web and share the information more broadly.

To further disseminate helpful information on how to protect users' security, last year we incorporated data on Safe Browsing into our Transparency Report. The site provides information on how many people see Safe Browsing warnings each week, where malicious sites are hosted around the world, how quickly websites become reinfected after their owners clean malware from their sites, and additional information. By providing details about the threats we detect and the warnings we show, we hope to shine some light on the state of web security and encourage safer web security practices.

We are a member of StopBadware.org, an anti-malware nonprofit organization run by the Berkman Center at Harvard Law School that offers resources for website owners, security experts and ordinary users. The site hosts the Search Badware Website Clearinghouse, a searchable database of badware URLs that is voluntarily submitted by StopBadware's partners, sponsors, and users. StopBadware uses the data to analyze and report trends in web-based infections, provide the public with research tools such as the Top 50 Networks list, and assist web hosting companies and other network providers with identifying badware sites on their networks.

We also own VirusTotal, a free web service that provides checks for viruses, worms, trojans and other kinds of malicious content. It uses 51 anti-virus products and scan engines to evaluate user-uploaded files or URLs, and it also offers a free public API. While the service helps identify malicious content, it may also be used as a means to spot false positives — innocuous resources detected as malicious by one or more scanners.

Furthermore, we created an email alias connecting vetted industry players and we use it to notify them directly of malware compromises and trends. Parties on the alias include the anti-malvertising teams from various ad-serving and tech companies. Additionally, we have industry contacts within companies that utilize Google ad products to provide direct feedback.

In 2009 we created Anti-Malvertising.com, a website that provides best practices and investigative resources for publishers and ad operations teams, as well as tips for users. The site includes a custom search engine to run quick background checks on advertisers: one can enter an advertiser's name, company name, or ad URL and access information to help determine whether said advertiser is trustworthy. Anti-Malvertising.com fits into our broader goal to help and encourage all members of the online advertising ecosystem to take an active role in malvertising prevention. It's one part of Google's commitment to educating our customers, improving the industry as a whole, and making the Internet a safer place for everyone.

More recently, we co-founded the Trust in Ads group with Facebook, Twitter and AOL to protect users from malicious online advertisements and deceptive practices. We kicked off this effort by identifying abusive practices in the tech support advertising space. Scam advertisers often present themselves as official representatives of companies of products for which users seek support. Under the disguise of paid assistance, these advertisers trick users into special downloads and installs that that may contain malicious software. Trust in Ads offers guidance on how to avoid these scams in the first in a series of trend reports on bad ads. The site also has a dedicated page at trustinads.org/report with information on how users can easily report any kind of suspicious ad on the group's founding companies' platforms.

Conclusion

The Internet is a driver of innovation, communication, and entrepreneurship, which underscores the importance of implementing policies and procedures that protect our users' data. We are committed to developing technology to protect users across the web, contributing research, and facilitating industry initiatives and conversations. We believe that if we all work together to identify threats and stamp them out, we can make the web a safer place for everyone. We look forward to working with this Subcommittee on additional ideas and initiatives to keep users safe online.

Thank you again for your time and consideration.

Statement of

Craig D. Spiezle

Executive Director & Founder

Online Trust Alliance

Testimony before the

Senate Committee on Homeland Security & Government Affairs

Senate Permanent Subcommittee on Investigations

Emerging Threats to Consumers

within the Online Advertising Industry

May 15, 2014

Chairman Levin, Ranking Member McCain, and members of the Committee, good morning and thank you for the opportunity to testify before you today.

My name is Craig Spiezle. I am the Executive Director and President of the Online Trust Alliance. OTA is a 501c3 non-profit, with the mission to enhance online trust, empowering users to control their data and privacy, while promoting innovation and the vitality of the internet.

I am testifying to help provide context to the escalating privacy and security threats to consumers resulting from malicious and fraudulent advertising known as malvertising.

As outlined in Exhibit A, malvertising increased over 200% in 2013 to over 209,000 incidents generating over 12.4 billion malicious ad impressions.[1] The impact on consumers is significant. This past January Yahoo experienced an incident resulting in over 300,000 malicious impressions in a single hour. Approximately 9% or 27,000 unsuspecting users were compromised. For these consumers, the infection rate was 100%.

This is not an isolated case. Cybercriminals have successfully inserted malicious ads on a range of sites including Google, Microsoft, Facebook, Wall Street Journal, New York Times, Expedia, Major League Baseball, (MLB) and others.[2, 3, 4]

The threats are significant, with the majority known as "drive by downloads". A drive by is malicious software which runs when a user innocently visits a web site – with no

---

[1] OTA data analysis based on incidents reported via data providers including RiskIQ, Zedo, The Media Trust, DoubleClick malvertising group and other sources, factoring in daily site traffic and life of exploit.

[2] http://www.webroot.com/blog/2014/02/14/doubleclick-malvertising-campaign-exposes-long-run-beneath-radar-malvertising-infrastructure/

[3] http://blog.trendmicro.com/trendlabs-security-intelligence/malicious-banners-target-expediacom-and-rhapsodycom/

[4] http://www.scmagazineuk.com/major-league-baseball-website-hit-by-malvertising-that-may-potentially-impact-300000-users/article/246503/

interaction or clicking required.[5] This threat is not new; malvertising was first identified over seven years ago, yet to-date, little progress has been made.

The impact of malvertising ranges from capturing personal information to turning a device into a bot where essentially a cybercriminal can take over that device and use it in many cases to execute a distributed denial-of-service attack (DDoS) against a bank, government agency or other organization. [6] Just as damaging is the deployment of ransomware which encrypts a user's hard drive, demanding payment to be unlocked. Users' personal data, family photos and health records can be destroyed and stolen in seconds.

In the absence of secure online advertising, an impossibly task given today's fragmented advertising ecosystem, the integrity of the internet is at risk. Not unlike pollution in the industrial age, in the absence of regulatory oversight and meaningful self-regulation, these threats continue to grow. The development of coal mining and the use of steam power generated from coal is without doubt the central, binding narrative of the nineteenth century. Jobs were created and profit soared, but the environment soon felt the full impact of industrialization in the form of air and water pollution. Today we are approaching similar cross roads which are undermining the integrity of the internet.

Facing the onslaught of threats, a disturbing trend has emerged with enterprises opting to block all third-party advertising viewed by their employees. This follows users who have been installing ad blockers such as Ad Block Plus and No Script to similarly block all ads.[7, 8] While these tools may help maximize security and privacy, they marginalize the vitality of advertising which supports the sites and services which consumers and business depend on.

---

[5] A drive by download is malicious code which executes against a device by simply visiting a site, with no interaction and installs malware. A social engineered exploit is in the form of a pop up or dialog box which attempts to convince a user to take action including downloading a fraudulent update.

[6] http://en.wikipedia.org/wiki/Ransomware_(malware)

[7] https://adblockplus.org/en/internet-explorer

[8] http://noscript.net/

How does malvertising occur?

Since the first banner ads appeared twenty years ago, online advertising and complexity has progressed exponentially.[9] The industry has moved from sites having independent ad sales teams to a complex ecosystem of ad sellers, aggregators and buyers. Stakeholders include advertisers and ad agencies who create ads through a complex arbitrage of ad exchanges, ad networks and demand side platforms (DSP), where ultimately the display ad or ad banner is served through programmatic ad buying. (Exhibit B)[10][11] A typical ad goes through five or six such intermediaries before being served.

The most common tactic to run a malicious ad is the criminal going directly to an ad network, selecting a target audience and paying for an ad campaign. In the absence of reputational checks or threat reporting among the industry, once detected and shut down by one ad network, they simply "water fall" or roll over to other unsuspecting networks to repeat variations of similar exploits.

Other tactics are illustrated in Exhibit C. They include impersonating legitimate advertisers or ad agencies, taking over an employee's user account, actions by rogue employees and the hacking of ad servers compromising existing ads and directly inserting malicious ads.[12]

Increasingly ads are purchased through an automated process as illustrated in Exhibit D. These systems without human inaction have increased from 38% of total display advertising in 2012 to a forecast of 73% in 2015. While this automation offers significant efficiencies, it lacks robust circuit breakers to detect fraudulent advertisers.[13][14]

---

[9] http://www.wired.com/2010/10/1027hotwired-banner-ads/

[10] If browser or device cookies are disabled or if a user has enabled anti-tracking mechanisms, they will be served a contextual ad versus one based on the browser habits or profile. If a user turns on "Do Not Track" and the site respects the setting, they would most likely receive contextual based ads.

[11] http://onlineadvertisingecosystem.com/

[12] http://www.tripwire.com/state-of-security/vulnerability-management/analyzing-cve-2013-4211-openx-ad-server-remote-code-execution-vulnerability/

[13] http://cmsummit.com/behindthebanner/

[14] http://www.adotas.com/2014/05/watch-200-milliseconds-the-life-of-a-programmatic-ad-impression/

The impact of these threats has increased significantly. Criminals are becoming experts in targeting and timing, taking advantage of the powerful tools and data available to internet advertisers. They are data driven marketers with precision to reach vulnerable segments of society or high net worth audiences. This have been enabled to choose the day and time of exploits as well as the type of device they choose to target.

In the absence of policy and traffic quality controls, organized crime has recognized malvertising as the "exploit of choice" offering the ability to be anonymous and remain undetected for days.

Industry & Self-Regulatory Efforts

Recognizing the threats of malvertising, in December 2007, DoubleClick, later acquired by Google, established a mailing list which remains today as one of the primary methods of malvertising data sharing. In 2010, OTA established what is now the Advertising and Content Integrity Group, (ACIG), focused on security and fraud prevention best practices. This group of diverse stakeholders leverages a proven model of threat mitigation.[15] This group has since published white papers including a risk evaluation framework and remediation guidelines.[16, 17] These efforts are a small but first step to combat malvertising, reflecting input from leaders including Google, Microsoft, PayPal, Symantec, Twitter and interactive advertisers, web sites and ad agencies.

Last June, StopBadware, a non-profit organization, launched a parallel effort known as the Ads Integrity Alliance. In January 2014, this initiative disbanded due to its members' "desire to refocus their resources on aggressively defending industry practices to policy groups and regulatory bodies".[18]

---

[15] https://otalliance.org/resources/botnets/index.html
[16] https://otalliance.org/resources/malvertising.html
[17] https://otalliance.org/docs/Advertising%20Risk%20Evaluation%20Framework.pdf
[18] https://www.stopbadware.org/blog/2014/01/20/stopbadware-steps-down-as-leader-of-the-ads-integrity-alliance

In the wake of this group's demise, TrustInAds.org was launched last week. According the site, its focus is public policy and raising consumer awareness of the threats and how to report them.[19]

Unfortunately no amount of consumer education can help when users visit trusted web sites that are serving malvertising. Consumers cannot discern good vs malicious ads or how their device was compromised. Focusing on education after the fact is like the auto industry telling accident victims whom to call after an accident from a previously known manufacturing defect, instead of building security features in the cars they sell and profit from.

Other industry efforts have been focused on click fraud, fraudulent activities that attempt to generate revenue by manipulating ad impressions. Click fraud is focused on the monetization and operational issues facing the industry. While efforts to address these issues are underway, do not be confused—click fraud is not related to malvertising's harmful impact on consumers. Click fraud affects websites and advertisers. Malvertising affects consumers.

What is Needed?

OTA proposes a holistic framework addressing five key areas: Prevention, Detection, Notification, Data Sharing and Remediation. Such a framework should be the foundation for an enforceable code of conduct or possible legislation.

1.   Prevention – Focused on the development and adoption of controls, systems and safeguards. Networks need to know who their advertisers are and have methods do identify outliers who may have malicious or fraudulent intent. Stakeholders who fail to adopt reasonable best practices and controls should bear the liability and publishers should reject their ads.

---

[19] http://trustinads.org/index.html

2. <u>Detection</u> – There is no perfect security, but circuit breakers must be in place to help detect abnormal ad behavior. Continuous monitoring is required with 24 /7 incident response teams and abuse desks to both detect and notify stakeholders.

3. <u>Notification & Data Sharing</u> - Escalation paths are needed to share threat intelligence, report abuse and take down threats. Standardized abuse reporting formats and metrics need to be established not unlike those used in the anti-spam and online abuse communities.

4. <u>Remediation</u> – Resources need to be allocated to taking down threats, including addressing any security vulnerabilities in the ecosystem and the user's device that have been compromised.

5. <u>Recovery</u> - Assistance to be provided to users whose devices and accounts have been compromised.

In parallel, operational and technical solutions need to be explored. Ideally we will have solutions where publishers would only allow ads only from networks who vouch for the authenticity of all of the ads they serve, and web browsers will render only such ads that have been signed and verified from trusted sources. It is recognized that such a model would require systemic changes; yet they would increase accountability, protecting the long term vitality of online advertising and most importantly the consumers.

In summary, as a wired society and economy we are increasingly dependent on trustworthy, secure and resilient online services. As observed in every area of our nation's critical infrastructure, we need to recognize that fraudulent businesses, cybercriminals and state sponsored actors will continue to exploit our systems.

For some, malvertising remains a "Black Swan Event", rarely seen but known to exist. For others it is the elephant in the room that no one wants to acknowledge.

Today, companies have little if any incentive to disclose their role or knowledge of a security event, leaving consumers vulnerable and unprotected for potentially months or years, during which time untold amounts of damage can occur. Failure to address these threats suggest the needs for legislation not unlike State data breach laws, requiring mandatory notification, data sharing and remediation to those who have been harmed.

As learned from the Target breach, it is the responsibility of a company and its executives to implement safeguards and to heed the warning of the community. The same standards should apply for the ad industry. We must work together, and openly disclose and mediate known vulnerabilities, even at the expense of short-term profits.

It is important to recognize there is no absolute defense against a determined criminal. OTA proposes incentives to companies who adopt best practices and comply with codes of conduct. They should be afforded protection from regulatory oversight as well as frivolous lawsuits. Perceived anti-trust and privacy issues must be resolved to facilitate data sharing to aid in fraud detection and forensics.

Trust is the foundation of every communication we receive, every web site we visit, every transaction we make and every ad we view. Now is the time for action and collaboration, moving from protective silos of information to multi-stakeholder solutions combating cybercrime.

I look forward to your questions.

Thank You

Exhibit A – Malvertising Trends

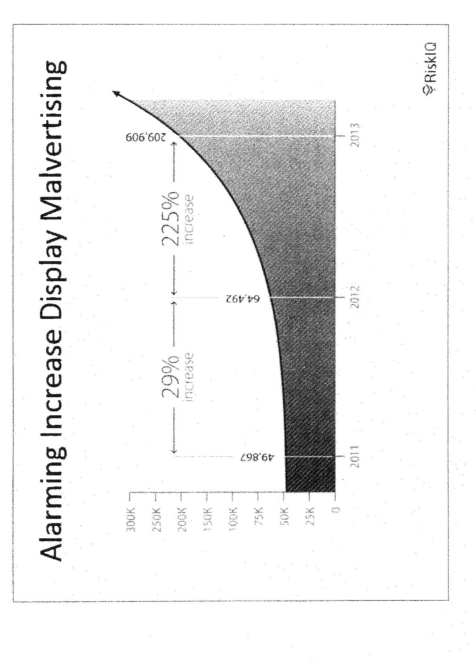

Exhibit B – Interactive Advertising Ecosystem

Exhibit C – How Malvertising Works

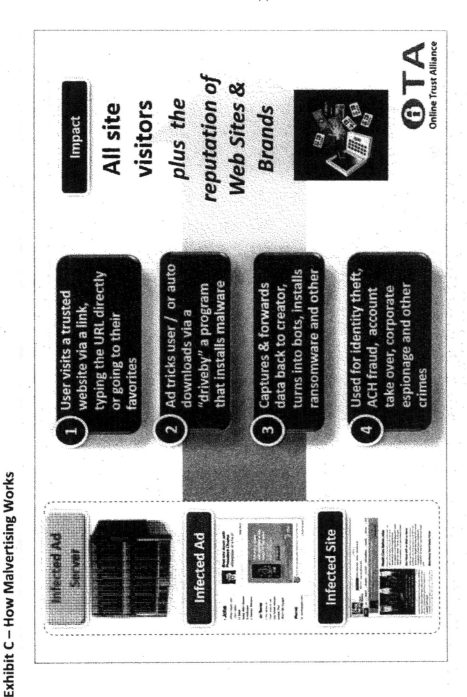

Exhibit D – Programmatic Ad Buying

MediaCrossing

200MS: The Life of a Programmatic RTB Ad Impression

200 MILLISECONDS
The Life of a Programmatic RTB Ad Impression

0 — Jane Doe™ clicks on a URL, and the publisher's content begins to load in browser.

10 — Publisher may find information it has stored on Jane Doe, possibly in its Data Management Platform (DMP).

30 — Publisher sends available information to its ad server asking ad server whether an ad campaign is available that would target Jane Doe. If there is a campaign matching Jane Doe's profile, an ad is served.

40 — If no campaign targets Jane Doe, the server seeks to match the impression programmatically requesting response from selected traders, ad networks and supply side platforms (SSPs).

65 — If the impression is not cleared, the server may seek to clear the impression in a programmatic direct way via private exchanges. If the impression is not cleared, the request is sent to an open ad exchange in hopes of achieving liquidity.

75 — Open ad exchange sends a bid request containing information on Jane Doe's browser, website URL and ad type to multiple bidders including traders, ad networks and demand side platforms (DSPs).

100 — Each bidder processes bid request, overlays it with additional user data and marketers' targeting and budget rules. Each bidder's algorithm evaluates the request, selects the creative and sends it along with optimal bid price to ad exchange.

125 — Ad exchange selects winning bid from bidder responses through second price auction.

150 — Ad exchange sends winning bid and price from winning bid to Publisher's ad server which tells Jane Doe's browser which ad to display.

175 — Jane Doe's browser pulls ad from winning bidder's ad server and sends matching ad to browser. Browser displays web page including matching ad.

200 — Winning bidder's ad server receives ad tag data on Jane Doe's initial interaction experience.

PREPARED STATEMENT OF

THE FEDERAL TRADE COMMISSION

on

Emerging Threats in the Online Advertising Industry

Before the

COMMITTEE ON HOMELAND SECURITY AND GOVERNMENTAL AFFAIRS

PERMANENT SUBCOMMITTEE ON INVESTIGATIONS

UNITED STATES SENATE

Washington, D.C.

May 15, 2014

I. INTRODUCTION

Chairman Levin, Ranking Member McCain, and members of the Subcommittee, I am Maneesha Mithal, Associate Director of the Division of Privacy and Identity Protection at the Federal Trade Commission ("FTC" or "Commission").[1] I appreciate the opportunity to present the Commission's testimony on consumer protection issues involving the online advertising industry.

Online advertising offers many benefits to consumers. It helps support a diverse range of online content and services that otherwise might not be available, or that consumers would otherwise have to pay for – services such as blogging, social networking and instant access to newspapers and information from around the world. It also can be used to tailor offers for products and services most relevant to consumers' interests.

But online behavioral advertising, which entails collecting information about consumers' online activities across websites in order to serve them personalized advertising, can also raise a number of consumer protection concerns. For example, some consumers may be uncomfortable with the privacy implications of being tracked across the websites they visit, or may be unaware that this practice is even occurring. And, without adequate safeguards in place, consumer tracking data may fall into the wrong hands or be used for adverse unanticipated purposes, including transmission to other third parties. These concerns are exacerbated when the tracking involves sensitive information about, for example, children, health, or a consumer's finances. Finally, online advertising can be used to deliver spyware and other malware to cause a host of problems to consumers' computers.

---

[1] This written statement presents the views of the Federal Trade Commission. My oral statements and responses to questions are my own and do not necessarily reflect the views of the Commission or of any Commissioner.

As the nation's consumer protection agency, the FTC is committed to protecting consumers in the online marketplace. The Commission is primarily a civil law enforcement ageney, and its main operative statute is Section 5 of the FTC Act, which prohibits unfair or deceptive acts or practices in or affecting commerce.[2] A company acts deceptively if it makes materially misleading statements or omissions.[3] A company engages in unfair acts or practices if its practices cause or are likely to cause substantial injury to consumers that is neither reasonably avoidable by consumers nor outweighed by countervailing benefits to consumers or to competition.[4] The Commission uses its enforcement authority under Section 5 to take action against online advertising companies and others engaged in unfair or deceptive practices. It also educates consumers and businesses about the online environment and encourages industry self-regulation.

This testimony will discuss the Commission's work to address three consumer protection issues affecting the online advertising industry: privacy, malware, and data security. It will then provide some recommendations for next steps in this area.

II. CONSUMER PROTECTION ISSUES AFFECTING THE ONLINE ADVERTISING INDUSTRY

A. PRIVACY

Since online privacy first emerged as a significant issue in the mid-1990s, it has been one of the Commission's highest consumer protection priorities. The Commission has worked to address privacy issues in the online marketplace, particularly those raised by online advertising networks, through consumer and business education, law enforcement, and policy initiatives.

---

[2] 15 U.S.C. § 45(a). The Commission also enforces numerous specific statutes.

[3] *See* Federal Trade Commission Policy Statement on Deception, appended to *Cliffdale Assocs.. Inc.*, 103 F.T.C. 110, 174 (1984).

[4] *See* 15 U.S.C. § 45(n); Federal Trade Commission Policy Statement on Unfairness, appended to *Int'l Harvester Co.*, 104 F.T.C. 949, 1070 (1984) ("FTC Unfairness Statement").

Throughout the last decade, the FTC has examined the privacy implications of online behavioral advertising through a number of workshops and reports.[5] In March of 2012, the Commission released its Privacy Report, which set forth best practices for businesses -- including the online advertising industry – to protect consumer privacy while ensuring that companies can continue to innovate.[6] The report called on companies to provide simpler and more streamlined choices to consumers about their data, through a robust universal choice mechanism for online behavioral advertising.[7]

The Commission has also engaged in a number of privacy enforcement actions involving the online advertising industry. For example, in its first online behavioral advertising case, the Commission alleged that online advertising network Chitika violated the FTC Act's prohibition on deceptive practices when it offered consumers the ability to opt out of the collection of information to be used for targeted advertising – without telling them that the opt-out lasted only ten days.[8] The Commission's order prohibits Chitika from making future privacy

---

[5] *See. e.g.*, FTC Press Release, *Staff Proposes Online Behavioral Advertising Policy Principles* (Dec. 20, 2007), *available at* http://www.ftc.gov/news-events/press-releases/2007/12/ftc-staff-proposes-online-behavioral-advertising-privacy; FTC Town Hall, *Ehavioral Advertising: Tracking, Targeting, & Technology* (Nov. 1-2, 2007), *available at* http://www.ftc.gov/news-events/events-calendar/2007/11/ehavioral-advertising-tracking-targeting-technology; FTC Workshop, *Protecting Consumers in the Next Tech-Ade* (Nov. 6-9, 2006), *available at* http://www.ftc.gov/news-events/events-calendar/2006/11/protecting-consumers-next-tech-ade; FTC Staff Report, *Self-Regulatory Principles for Online Behavioral Advertising* (Feb. 2009), *available at* http://www.ftc.gov/sites/default/files/documents/reports/federal-trade-commission-staff-report-self-regulatory-principles-online-behavioral-advertising/p085400behavadreport.pdf.

[6] FTC Report, *Protecting Consumers in an Era of Rapid Change: Recommendations for Businesses and Policymakers* (Mar. 2012) ("Privacy Report"), *available at* http://www.ftc.gov/sites/default/files/documents/reports/federal-trade-commission-report-protecting-consumer-privacy-era-rapid-change-recommendations/120326privacyreport.pdf. Commissioner Ohlhausen and Commissioner Wright were not members of the Commission at that time and thus did not participate in the vote on the report.

[7] In the Privacy Report, the Commission articulated five essential elements of a robust do-not-track mechanism: universal, persistent, easy to find and use, effective, and that the mechanism provide control over the collection of information, not just the delivery of targeted ads. *Id.* at 53.

[8] *Chitika, Inc.*, No. C-4324 (F.T.C. June 7, 2011) (consent order), *available at*

misrepresentations. It also requires Chitika to provide consumers with an effective opt-out mechanism, link to this opt-out mechanism in its advertisements, and provide a notice on its website for consumers who may have opted out when Chitika's opt-out mechanism was ineffective. Finally, the order required Chitika to destroy any data that can be associated with a consumer that it collected during the time its opt-out mechanism was ineffective.

Online ad network ScanScout also settled FTC charges that it deceptively claimed that consumers could opt out of receiving targeted ads by changing their computer's web browser settings to block cookies.[9] In fact, ScanScout used Flash cookies, which browser settings could not block. Under the terms of the order, ScanScout is prohibited from misrepresenting the company's data collection practices and consumers' ability to control collection of their data. It also requires ScanScout to improve disclosure of its data collection practices and to provide a user-friendly mechanism that allows consumers to opt out of being tracked.

Epic Marketplace, an online ad network, settled charges that it used "history sniffing" to secretly and illegally gather data from millions of consumers about their interest in sensitive medical and financial issues ranging from fertility and incontinence to debt relief and personal bankruptcy.[10] As explained in the complaint, Epic Marketplace is a large advertising network with a presence on 45,000 websites. Consumers who visited any of the network's sites received a cookie, which stored information about their online practices including sites they visited and the ads they viewed. The cookies allowed Epic to serve consumers behaviorally targeted ads. Despite claims that it would collect information only about consumers' visits to sites in its

---

http://www.ftc.gov/enforcement/cases-proceedings/1023087/chitika-inc-matter.

[9] *ScanScout, Inc.*, No. C-4344 (F.T.C. Dec. 14, 2011) (consent order), *available at* http://www.ftc.gov/enforcement/cases-proceedings/102-3185/scanscout-inc-matter.

[10] *Epic Marketplace, Inc.*, No. C-4389 (F.T.C. Mar. 13, 2013), *available at* http://www.ftc.gov/enforcement/cases-proceedings/112-3182/epic-marketplace-inc.

network, Epic was employing "history-sniffing" technology that allowed it to collect data about sites outside its network that consumers had visited, including sites relating to personal health conditions and finances. The FTC alleged that the history sniffing was deceptive and allowed Epic to determine whether a consumer had visited any of more than 54,000 domains, including pages relating to fertility issues, impotence, menopause, incontinence, disability insurance, credit repair, debt relief, and personal bankruptcy. The order imposed similar relief to the other cases in this area.

Finally, in 2012 Google agreed to pay a record $22.5 million civil penalty to settle charges that it misrepresented to Safari browser users that it would not place tracking cookies or serve targeted ads to them,[11] violating an earlier privacy order with the Commission.[12] In its complaint, the FTC alleged that for several months, Google placed a certain advertising tracking cookie on the computers of Safari users who visited sites within Google's DoubleClick advertising network, although Google had previously told these users they would automatically be opted out of such tracking, as a result of the Safari browser default settings. Despite these promises, the FTC alleged that Google placed advertising tracking cookies on consumers' computers, in many cases by circumventing the Safari browser's default cookie-blocking setting.[13] According to the complaint, Google's misrepresentations violated an earlier FTC order, which barred Google from – among other things – misrepresenting the extent to which consumers can exercise control over the collection of their information.

---

[11] *United States v. Google, Inc.*, No. 512-cv-04177-HRL (N.D. Cal. Nov. 16, 2012), *available at* http://www.ftc.gov/enforcement/cases-proceedings/google-inc.

[12] *Google, Inc.*, No. C-4336 (F.T.C. Oct. 13, 2011), *available at* http://www.ftc.gov/enforcement/cases-proceedings/102-3136/google-inc-matter.

[13] Google used an exception to the browser's default setting to place a temporary cookie from the DoubleClick domain. Because of the particular operation of the Safari browser, that initial temporary cookie opened the door to all cookies from the DoubleClick domain, including the Google advertising tracking cookie that Google had represented would be blocked from Safari browsers.

B.   SPYWARE AND OTHER MALWARE

Spyware and other malware can cause substantial harm to consumers and to the Internet as a medium of communication and commerce. When downloaded without authorization, including through online ads, spyware and other malware can cause a range of problems for computer users, from nuisance adware that delivers pop-up ads, to software that causes sluggish computer performance, to keystroke loggers that capture sensitive information.

The Commission has sought to address concerns about spyware and other malware through law enforcement and consumer education. Since 2004, the Commission has initiated a number of malware-related law enforcement actions, which reaffirm three key principles. The first is that a consumer's computer belongs to him or her, not to the software distributor, and it must be the consumer's choice whether or not to install software. This principle reflects the basic common-sense notion that Internet businesses are not free to help themselves to the resources of a consumer's computer. For example, in *FTC v. Seismic Entertainment Inc.*,[14] and *FTC v. Enternet Media, Inc.*,[15] the Commission alleged that the defendants unfairly downloaded spyware to users' computers without the users' knowledge, in violation of Section 5 of the FTC Act. And, in its case against CyberSpy Software LLC, the FTC alleged that the defendants unfairly sold keylogging software to others that could be downloaded to users' computers without their knowledge or consent.[16]

The second principle is that buried disclosures of material information necessary to

---

[14] *FTC v. Seismic Entertainment Productions, Inc., et al.*, No. 04-377-JD (D.N.H. 2006), *available at* http://www.ftc.gov/enforcement/cases-proceedings/042-3142-x05-0013/seismic-entertainment-productions-inc-et-al.

[15] *FTC v. Enternet Media Inc. et al.*, No. CV 05-777 CAS (C.D. Cal. 2006), *available at* http://www.ftc.gov/enforcement/cases-proceedings/052-3135-x06-0003/enternet-media-inc-conspy-co-inc-et-al.

[16] *FTC v. CyberSpy Software, LLC*, No. 6:08-cv-1872-ORL-31GJK (M.D. Fla. 2010), *available at* http://www.ftc.gov/enforcement/cases-proceedings/082-3160/cyberspy-software-llc-trace-r-spence.

correct an otherwise misleading impression are not sufficient in connection with software downloads, just as they have never been sufficient in more traditional areas of commerce. Specifically, burying material information in an End User License Agreement will not shield a malware purveyor from Section 5 liability. This principle was illustrated in *FTC v. Odysseus Marketing, Inc.*[17] and *Advertising.com, Inc.*[18] In these two cases, the Commission alleged (among other violations) that the companies failed to disclose adequately that the free software they were offering was bundled with harmful software programs.

The third principle is that, if a distributor puts a program on a computer that the consumer does not want, the consumer should be able to uninstall or disable it. This principle is underscored by the FTC's cases against Zango, Inc.[19] and DirectRevenue LLC.[20] These companies allegedly provided advertising programs, or adware, that monitored consumers' Internet use and displayed frequent, targeted pop-up ads – over 6.9 billion pop-ups by Zango alone. According to the Commission's complaints, the companies deliberately made these adware programs difficult for consumers to identify, locate, and remove from their computers, thus thwarting consumer efforts to end the intrusive pop-ups. Among other relief, the consent orders require Zango and DirectRevenue to provide a readily identifiable means to uninstall any adware that is installed in the future, as well as to disgorge $3 million and $1.5 million, respectively.

[17] *FTC v. Odysseus Marketing, Inc.*, No. 05-CV-330 (D.N.H. 2006), *available at* http://www.ftc.gov/enforcement/cases-proceedings/042-3205-x050069/odysseus-marketing-inc-walter-rines.

[18] *Advertising.com, Inc.*, No. C-4147 (F.T.C. Sept. 12, 2005) (consent order), *available at* http://www.ftc.gov/enforcement/cases-proceedings/042-3196/advertisingcom-inc-et-al-matter.

[19] *Zango, Inc. f/k/a 180 Solutions, Inc.*, No. C-4186 (F.T.C. Mar. 7, 2007) (consent order), *available at* http://www.ftc.gov/enforcement/cases-proceedings/052-3130/zango-inc-fka-180solutions-inc-et-al-matter.

[20] *DirectRevenue LLC*, No. C-4194 (F.T.C. June 26, 2007) (consent order), *available at* http://www.ftc.gov/enforcement/cases-proceedings/052-3131/directrevenue-llc-et-al.

In addition to engaging in law enforcement, the FTC has made consumer education on malware issues a priority. The Commission sponsors OnGuard Online, a website designed to educate consumers about basic computer security. [21] OnGuard Online and its Spanish-language counterpart, Alerta en Línea,[22] average more than 2.2 million unique visits per year. The comprehensive web site has general information on online safety, as well as sections with detailed information on a range of topics, including spyware. And, the FTC also has created a number of articles, videos, and games available to consumers on both its website[23] and OnGuard Online to describe the threats associated with spyware and malware as well as provide consumers with information about how to avoid and detect such malicious software.

C. DATA SECURITY

While taking action against the purveyors of malware is important, it is also critical to ensure that companies are taking reasonable steps to ensure that they are not inadvertently enabling third parties to place malware on consumers' computers. To this end, online advertising networks should maintain reasonable safeguards to ensure that they are not displaying advertisements containing malware that can slow down consumers' computers, expose them to unwanted content such as pop-up ads, and gain unauthorized access to their personal information.

The Commission has undertaken substantial efforts for over a decade to promote strong data security practices in the private sector in order to prevent hackers and purveyors of malware from harming consumers. In addition to enforcing Section 5 of the FTC Act, discussed above, the Commission enforces several specific statutes and rules that impose obligations upon

---

[21] *See* http://www.onguardonline.gov.

[22] *See* http://www.alertaenlinea.gov.

[23] *See generally* http://www.consumer.ftc.gov.

businesses to protect consumer data. The Commission's Safeguards Rule, which implements the Gramm-Leach-Bliley Act, for example, provides data security requirements for non-bank financial institutions.[24] The Fair Credit Reporting Act requires consumer reporting agencies to use reasonable procedures to ensure that the entities to which they disclose sensitive consumer information have a permissible purpose for receiving that information,[25] and imposes safe disposal obligations on entities that maintain consumer report information.[26] The Children's Online Privacy Protection Act requires reasonable security for children's information collected online.[27] Reasonableness is the foundation of the data security provisions of each of these laws.

The FTC conducts its data security investigations to determine whether a company's data security measures are reasonable and appropriate in light of the sensitivity and volume of consumer information it holds, the size and complexity of its data operations, and the cost of available tools to improve security and reduce vulnerabilities. The Commission's 53 settlements with businesses that it charged with failing to provide reasonable protections for consumers' personal information have halted harmful data security practices; required companies to provide strong protections for consumer data; and raised awareness about the risks to data, the need for reasonable and appropriate security, and the types of security failures that raise concerns.[28]

In its most recent data security case, the FTC announced a settlement with Snapchat, Inc., a company that markets a popular mobile application ("app") that allows consumers to send and receive photo and video messages known as "snaps."[29] According to the complaint, Snapchat

---

[24] 16 C.F.R. Part 314, implementing 15 U.S.C. § 6801(b).

[25] 15 U.S.C. § 1681e.

[26] *Id.* at § 1681w. The FTC's implementing rule is at 16 C.F.R. Part 682.

[27] 15 U.S.C. §§ 6501-6506; *see also* 16 C.F.R. Part 312 ("COPPA Rule").

[28] *See* Commission Statement Marking the FTC's 50th Data Security Settlement, Jan. 31, 2014, *available at* http://www.ftc.gov/system/files/documents/cases/140131gmrstatement.pdf.

[29] *Snapchat, Inc.*, No. 132-3078 (F.T.C. May 8, 2014) (proposed consent agreement), *available at*

misrepresented that its app provided a private, short-lived messaging service, claiming that once the consumer-set timer for a viewed snap expired, the snap "disappears forever." Snapchat's app has a "Find Friends" feature that allows consumers to find and communicate with friends who use the Snapchat service. However, unbeknownst to users, the Find Friends feature collected the names and phone numbers of all contacts in a user's mobile device address book and had major security flaws. The complaint alleges that Snapchat violated Section 5 by misrepresenting the disappearing nature of messages sent through its app and the amount of personal information that its app would collect for the Find Friends feature.

The complaint also charges that despite its claims regarding reasonable security, Snapchat failed to adequately secure the Find Friends feature, which led to significant misuse and unauthorized disclosure of consumers' personal information. For example, the complaint alleges that numerous consumers complained that they had sent snaps to someone who impersonated a friend. In fact, because Snapchat failed to verify users' phone numbers during registration, these consumers were actually sending their personal snaps to complete strangers who had registered with phone numbers that did not belong to them. Moreover, in December 2013, Snapchat's failures allowed attackers to compile a database of 4.6 million Snapchat usernames and phone numbers, which could have subjected consumers to costly spam, phishing and other unsolicited communications.

The FTC also recently entered into settlements with Credit Karma, Inc.[30] and Fandango, LLC.[31] to resolve allegations that the companies misrepresented the security of their mobile apps.

---

http://www.ftc.gov/enforcement/cases-proceedings/132-3078/snapchat-inc-matter.

[30] *Credit Karma, Inc.*, No. 132-3091 (F.T.C. Mar. 28, 2014) (proposed consent agreement), *available at* http://www.ftc.gov/enforcement/cases-proceedings/132-3091/credit-karma-inc.

[31] *Fandango, LLC*, No. 132-3089 (F.T.C. Mar. 28, 2014) (proposed consent agreement), *available at* http://www.ftc.gov/enforcement/cases-proceedings/132-3089/fandango-llc.

Credit Karma's mobile app allows consumers to monitor and access their credit scores, credit reports, and other credit report and financial data, and has been downloaded over one million times. Fandango's mobile app allows consumers to purchase movie tickets and has over 18.5 million downloads. According to the complaints, despite claims that the companies provided reasonable security to consumers' data, Credit Karma and Fandango did not securely transmit consumers' sensitive personal information through their mobile apps. In particular, the apps failed to authenticate and secure the connections used to transmit this data, and left consumers' information vulnerable to exposure – including Social Security numbers, birthdates, and credit report information in the Credit Karma app, and credit card information in the Fandango app. The Commission's settlements prohibit Credit Karma and Fandango from making misrepresentations about privacy and security, and require the companies to implement comprehensive information security programs and undergo independent audits for the next 20 years.

Finally, the FTC announced a case against TRENDnet, Inc., which involved a video camera designed to allow consumers to monitor their homes remotely.[32] The complaint alleges that TRENDnet marketed its SecurView cameras for purposes ranging from home security to baby monitoring. Although TRENDnet claimed that the cameras were "secure," they had faulty software that left them open to online viewing, and in some instances listening, by anyone with a camera's Internet address. This resulted in hackers posting 700 consumers' live video feeds on the Internet. Under the FTC settlement, TRENDnet must maintain a comprehensive security program, obtain outside audits, notify consumers about the security issues and the availability of software updates to correct them, and provide affected customers with free technical support for

---

[32] *TRENDnet, Inc.*, No. C-4426(F.T.C. Jan. 16, 2014) (consent order), *available at* http://www.ftc.gov/enforcement/cases-proceedings/122-3090/trendnet-inc-matter.

the next two years.

In each of its 53 data security cases, the Commission has examined a company's practices as a whole and challenged alleged data security failures that were multiple and systemic. Through these settlements, the Commission has made clear that reasonable and appropriate security is a continuous process of assessing and addressing risks; that there is no one-size-fits-all data security program; that the Commission does not require perfect security; and that the mere fact that a breach occurred does not mean that a company has violated the law. These principles apply equally to advertising networks. Just because malware has been installed does not mean that the advertising network has violated Section 5. Rather, the Commission would look to whether the advertising network took reasonable steps to prevent third parties from using online ads to deliver malware.

III. RECOMMENDATIONS FOR NEXT STEPS

The Commission shares this Committee's concerns about the use of online advertisements to deliver malware onto consumers' computers, which implicates each of the areas discussed in this testimony – consumer privacy, malware, and data security. We encourage several additional steps to protect consumers in this area.

The first is more widespread consumer education about how consumers can protect their computers against malware. The FTC materials discussed in this testimony are available at www.OnguardOnline.gov and www.ftc.gov. We encourage businesses, advocacy organizations, and other government agencies at the state, local, and federal levels to use these materials and tailor them to their particular constituencies and concerns.

The second is continued industry self-regulation to ensure that ad networks are taking reasonable steps to prevent the use of their systems to display malicious ads to consumers. Just last week, Facebook, Google and Twitter publicly unveiled TrustInAds.org, a new organization aimed at protecting people from malicious online advertisements.[33] The companies report that they will bring awareness to consumers about online ad-related scams and deceptive activities, collaborate to identify trends, and share their knowledge with policymakers and consumer advocates. In addition, the Online Trust Alliance has published guidelines for companies in this area, along with a risk evaluation tool.[34] The Commission applauds these groups for taking steps to address this issue.

Finally, the Commission continues to reiterate its longstanding, bipartisan call for enactment of a strong federal data security and breach notification law. Reasonable and appropriate security practices are critical to preventing data breaches and protecting consumers from identity theft and other harm. Despite the threats posed by data breaches, many companies continue to underinvest in data security. For example, the Commission's settlements have shown that some companies fail to take even the most basic security precautions, such as updating antivirus software or requiring network administrators to use strong passwords. With reports of data breaches on the rise, and with a significant number of Americans suffering from identity theft, having a strong and uniform national data security requirement would reinforce the requirement under the FTC Act that companies must implement reasonable measures to ensure that consumers' personal information is protected. Although most states have breach notification laws in place, having a strong and consistent national breach notification requirement would simplify compliance by businesses while ensuring that all consumers are protected.

Among other things, such legislation would supplement the Commission's existing data

---

[33] *See generally* http://www.trustinads.org.

[34] *See generally* Online Trust Alliance, *Advertising & Content Publishing Supply Chain Integrity* (Apr. 1, 2014), *available at* https://otalliance.org/resources/malvertising.html.

security authority by authorizing the Commission to seek civil penalties in appropriate circumstances against companies that do not reasonably protect consumers' data. Providing the Commission with authority to seek civil penalties in these cases would help deter unlawful conduct, including using malware to gain access to consumers' personal information – such as through keystroke loggers. Such legislation could provide the Commission with an important consumer protection tool.

VI. CONCLUSION

Thank you for the opportunity to provide the Commission's testimony on consumer protection issues involving the online advertising industry. We look forward to continuing to work with the Subcommittee and Congress on this important issue.

94

BEFORE THE

U.S. SENATE PERMANENT SUBCOMMITTEE ON INVESTIGATIONS

HEARING ON

ONLINE ADVERTISING AND HIDDEN HAZARDS TO CONSUMER SECURITY AND DATA PRIVACY

MAY 15, 2014

TESTIMONY OF

LUIGI MASTRIA, CIPP, CISSP

EXECUTIVE DIRECTOR

DIGITAL ADVERTISING ALLIANCE

Chairman Levin, Ranking Member McCain, and Members of the Subcommittee, good morning and thank you for the opportunity to speak at this important hearing.

My name is Lou Mastria. I am Executive Director of the Digital Advertising Alliance ("DAA") and I am pleased to report to the Committee on the substantial progress of our Self-Regulatory Program that is providing consumers transparency and choice.

The DAA is a non-profit organization led by the leading advertising and marketing trade associations including the Association of National Advertisers ("ANA"), the American Association of Advertising Agencies ("4As"), the Direct Marketing Association ("DMA"), the Interactive Advertising Bureau ("IAB"), the American Advertising Federation ("AAF"), and the Network Advertising Initiative ("NAI"), in consultation with the Council of Better Business Bureaus ("CBBB"). These organizations came together in 2008 to start developing the Self-Regulatory Principles for Online Behavioral Advertising, which were extended in 2011 beyond advertising to cover the collection and use of Multi-Site Data across non-Affiliate sites over time, and then again extended in July 2013 to provide guidance for data collection in mobile environments. The DAA was formed to administer and promote these responsible and comprehensive Self-Regulatory Principles for online data collection and use.

The DAA is a model example of how interested stakeholders can collaborate to provide flexible, market-driven solutions to complex privacy issues. In my testimony, I will describe the benefits of online advertising and how the industry through the DAA provides consumer-friendly privacy standards in a way that also ensures the continued vibrancy of the Internet and our nation's place as the global leader in the data-driven economy.

I. Benefits of Online Advertising

The Internet is a tremendous engine of economic growth. It has become the focus and a symbol of the United States' famed innovation, ingenuity, inventiveness, and entrepreneurial spirit, as well as the venture funding that follows. Simply put: the Internet economy and the interactive advertising industry create jobs. A 2012 study found that the Internet economy supports the employment of more than five million Americans, contributing an estimated $530 billion, or approximately 3%, to our country's GDP.[1] There is Internet employment in every single state.[2] Another recent study, commissioned by DMA's Data-Driven Marketing Institute ("DDMI") and conducted independently by Professors John Deighton of Harvard Business School and Peter Johnson of Columbia University, and entitled "The Value of Data: Consequences for Insight, Innovation & Efficiency in the U.S. Economy" ("Value of Data"), quantifies the value data has to our economy. The Value of Data study found that the Data-Driven Market Economy ("DDME") added $156 billion in revenue to the U.S. economy and fueled more than 675,000 jobs in 2012 alone. The study also found that an additional 1,038,000 jobs owe part of their existence to these DDME jobs. The study estimated that 70% of the value of the DDME – $110 billion in revenue and 475,000 jobs nationwide – depends on the ability of firms to share data across the DDME.

Advertising fuels this powerful Internet economic engine. The support provided by online advertising is substantial. In 2013, Internet advertising revenues reached a new high of $43 billion, an impressive 17% higher than 2012's full-year number.[3]

---

[1] Professor John Deighton, Harvard Business School, *Economic Value of the Advertising-Supported Internet Ecosystem*, at 81 (September 2012), available at http://www.iab.net/media/file/iab_Report_September-24-2012_4clr_v1.pdf (last visited May 12, 2014).

[2] *Id.* at 66.

[3] Interactive Advertising Bureau 2013 Internet Advertising Report (April 2014) (reporting results of PricewaterhouseCoopers study), available at http://www.iab.net/AdRevenueReport (last visited on May 12, 2014).

Because of advertising, consumers can access a wealth of online resources at low or no cost. Revenue from online advertising enables e-commerce and subsidizes the cost of content and services that consumers value, such as online newspapers, blogs, social networking sites, mobile applications, email, and phone services. These advertising-supported resources have transformed our daily lives.

Interest-based advertising is an essential form of online advertising. Interest-based advertising is delivered based on consumer preferences or interests as inferred from data about online activities. Consumers are likely to find interest-based advertisements more relevant to them, and advertisers are more likely to attract consumers that want their products and services.

Interest-based advertising is especially vital for small businesses because it is efficient. Smaller advertisers can stretch their marketing budgets to reach consumers who may be interested in their offerings. Smaller website publishers that cannot afford to employ sales personnel to sell their advertising space, and may be less attractive to large brand-name advertising campaigns, can increase their revenue by featuring advertising that is more relevant to their users. In turn, advertising-supported resources help other small businesses to grow. Small businesses can use free or low-cost online tools, such as travel booking, long-distance calling, and networking services, to help them run their companies.

II. The DAA

As the DAA was convened, its goal was to provide greater transparency and control to consumers with respect to their Web viewing data while preserving these incredible benefits to consumers and our economy. Since 2008, the DAA has worked with a broad set of stakeholders with significant input from businesses, consumers, and policy makers to develop a program governing the responsible collection and use of Web viewing data. This work led to the development of the groundbreaking *Self-Regulatory Principles for Online Behavioral Advertising* ("Principles"), released in 2009.

The DAA approach provides consumers choice with respect to collection and use of their Internet viewing data while preserving the ability of companies to responsibly deliver services and continue innovating. This approach allows consumers to enjoy the incredibly diverse range of Web sites by preserving the responsible data flows that support these offerings and that fuel our nation's economy.

The DAA Principles apply broadly to the diverse set of actors that work interdependently to deliver relevant advertising intended to enrich the consumer digital experience, and to foster consumer-friendly privacy standards that are to be applied throughout the ecosystem. The Principles were developed over a year-long period in which broad consensus was reached among the key constituencies of the Internet community. These Principles call for (1) enhanced notice outside of the privacy policy so that consumers can be made aware of the companies they interact with while using the Internet, (2) the provision of choice mechanisms, (3) education, and (4) strong enforcement mechanisms. Together, these Principles increase consumers' trust and confidence in how information is gathered online and in mobile environments and how it is used to deliver advertisements based on their interests.

A. Consumer Disclosure through the DAA Icon

The DAA program has developed a universal icon to give consumers transparency and control with respect to interest-based ads. The icon provides consumers with notice that information about their online interests is being gathered to customize the Web ads they see.

Clicking the icon also takes consumers to a centralized choice tool that enables consumers to opt out of this type of advertising by participating companies.

The icon is served globally more than *one trillion times each month* on or next to Internet display ads, websites, and other digital properties and tools covered by the program. This achievement represents an unprecedented level of industry cooperation and adoption.

B. Consumer Control

At DAA's *www.aboutads.info* website and accessible from the companion *www.YourAdChoices.com* website, the DAA program makes available a choice mechanism that unites the opt-out mechanisms provided by more than 115 different third-party advertisers participating in the program. The choice mechanism offers consumers a "one-click" option to request opt outs from all participants or allows a user to make choices about specific companies. Consumers are directed to aboutads.info not only from DAA icon-based disclosures on or around ads, but from other forms of website disclosure. In 2012, the DAA also introduced a suite of browser plug-ins to help ensure the persistency of these choices.

Since program launch, there have been more than 30 million unique visitors to the DAA program Web sites. *Over three million unique users* have exercised choice using the integrated opt-out mechanism provided at AboutAds.info. Many users visit DAA program Web sites, learn about their choices, and ultimately choose not to opt out. This shows that once consumers understand how online advertising works, many prefer to receive relevant ads over irrelevant ads. Research supports this proposition. A recent poll of U.S. consumers shows that 68 percent of Americans prefer to get at least some Internet ads directed at their interests and 40 percent of Americans prefer to get all their ads directed to their interests.[4]

---

[4] Interactive Survey of U.S. Adults commissioned by the DAA (April 2013), *available at* http://www.aboutads.info/DAA-Zogby-Poll.

C. Consumer Education

The DAA is also committed to consumer education. The DAA launched a dedicated educational site at *www.YourAdChoices.com* to provide easy-to-understand messaging and informative videos explaining the choices available to consumers, the meaning of the DAA icon, and the benefits they derive from online advertising. Companies participating in the DAA program have donated voluntarily more than four billion impressions to support an educational campaign for *www.YourAdChoices.com*. More than *15 million unique users* have visited this site. This site also provides access to the DAA's user choice mechanism. The combination of the educational campaign and the ubiquitous availability of the DAA icon have significantly increased consumer usage of the DAA program tools.

D. Accountability

For the past 40 years, the advertising industry has distinguished itself through its self-regulatory systems for independent oversight of compliance and public reporting of enforcement actions. In keeping with this tradition, a key feature of the DAA Self-Regulatory Program is accountability. All of the DAA's Self-Regulatory Principles are backed by the robust enforcement programs administered by the Council of Better Business Bureaus ("CBBB") under the policy guidance of the Advertising Self-Regulatory Council (ASRC), and by the DMA under its Guidelines for Ethical Business Practice. In addition to the oversight provided by the CBBB and DMA compliance programs, the NAI also has a strong compliance program. The NAI's compliance program, like the CBBB and DMA programs, helps members to comply with their self-regulatory obligations, and to hold them accountable.[5] A more detailed description of how these programs work is included in Appendix I.

---

[5] NAI Enforcement Page (providing Compliance Reports from 2009-2013), *available at* http://www.networkadvertising.org/code-enforcement/enforcement.

E. Application of Self-Regulatory Principles to Data Collected on Mobile Devices

The DAA Self-Regulatory Program has adapted over time and we expect this evolution to continue with changes in the marketplace driven by technological advancements and evolving consumer preferences. In July 2013, the DAA issued new implementation guidance addressing operation across a variety of channels including mobile. The guidance explains how the Self-Regulatory Principles apply to certain data practices that may occur on mobile or other devices.

Stakeholders representing all major elements of the mobile ecosystem participated in the development of this guidance. The guidance describes how the Self-Regulatory Principles apply to the mobile web environment and to the application environment, which DAA calls "Cross-App" data – data collected from a device across non-Affiliated applications over time. The DAA has now turned its work with DAA stakeholders to develop and implement a companion choice mechanism for Cross-App Data. This new tool will offer consumers an unprecedented level of control over data collection across applications on a device.

The successful approach taken by the DAA led to an event in February 2012 at the White House where the Chairman of the Federal Trade Commission ("FTC"), the Secretary of Commerce, and White House officials publicly praised the DAA's cross-industry initiative. The White House recognized our Self-Regulatory Program as "an example of the value of industry leadership as a critical part of privacy protection going forward." Since the White House event, the DAA's further work in releasing the Self-Regulatory Principles for Multi-Site Data (November 2011) and guidance on the Application of Self-Regulatory Principles to the Mobile Environment (July 2013) has garnered additional praise, including from FTC Commissioner Ohlhausen who has stated that the DAA "is one of the great success stories in the [privacy] space."

III. Conclusion

The DAA has championed consumer control that both accommodates consumers' privacy expectations and supports the ability of companies to responsibly deliver services desired by consumers and continue innovating. We appreciate the opportunity to be here today. We believe our successful model can continue to effectively evolve in the privacy area and can also be replicated in other areas.

I am pleased to answer any questions that you may have.

* * *

APPENDIX I: ACCOUNTABILITY PROGRAMS

The CBBB Accountability Program builds on the successful track records of the other ASRC programs: the National Advertising Division, operating since 1971; the Children's Advertising Review Unit, operating since 1974; and the Electronic Retailing Self-Regulation Program, operating since 2004. These programs feature independent monitoring; public reporting of decisions; and referral to government agencies, often to the FTC, of any uncorrected non-compliance. They have extremely high voluntary compliance rates. In fact, over 90 percent of companies voluntarily adopt the recommendations of these programs. Those companies that fail to comply or refuse to participate in the self-regulatory enforcement process are referred publicly to the appropriate government agency for further review.

The CBBB administers its Interest-Based Advertising Accountability Program under the ASRC self-regulatory policy guidance and procedures. Because of the highly complex, technical and interdependent nature of interest-based advertising, the Accountability Program receives a weekly privacy dashboard report based on independent data about more than 250 companies' compliance with various requirements of the Principles. The Accountability Program's technical staff analyzes these data and independently performs further research to determine whether there may be a violation of the Principles warranting formal inquiry. Like other ASRC programs administered by the CBBB, the CBBB Accountability Program also finds potential cases through its own staff monitoring and investigation, by analysis of consumer complaints and reviews of news stories and technical reports from academics and advocacy groups. Where there is a potential compliance issue, the CBBB initiates formal inquiries and works to ensure the company understands the Principles and voluntarily implements the requirements of the Principles. At the end of the process, the CBBB Accountability Program issues a public decision, which details the nature of the inquiry, the Accountability Program's conclusions, any recommendations for correction, and includes a statement from the company in question regarding its implementation of the recommendations. A press release is also issued.

The CBBB's Accountability Program has brought 33 cases since November 2011. The CBBB Accountability Program has focused its inquiries on the key concepts of transparency and choice under the DAA's Self-Regulatory Principles. In its initial round of cases, the Accountability Program investigated whether companies were correctly and reliably providing consumers with an effective choice mechanism. Cases involved defective links to opt-out mechanisms and transparency that was deficient or otherwise lacking.

The DMA's enforcement program likewise builds on a long history of proactive and robust self-regulatory oversight. The DMA's longstanding Guidelines for Ethical Business Practice ("Guidelines") set out comprehensive standards for marketing practices, which all DMA members must follow as a condition of membership. The DAA Self-Regulatory Principles are incorporated into these Guidelines.

The DMA's Committee on Ethical Business Practice examines practices that may violate DMA Guidelines. To date, the DMA Guidelines have been applied to hundreds of marketing cases on a variety of issues such as deception, unfair business practices, personal information protection, and online behavioral advertising. In order to educate marketing professionals on acceptable marketing practices, a case report is regularly issued which summarizes questioned direct marketing promotions and how cases were administered. The report also is used to educate regulators and others interested in consumer protection issues about the DMA Guidelines and how they are implemented.

The Committee on Ethical Business Practice works with both member and non-member companies to gain voluntary cooperation in adhering to the guidelines and to increase good business practices for direct marketers. The DMA Corporate Responsibility team and Ethics Committee receive matters for review in a number of ways: from consumers; member companies; non-members; or, sometimes, consumer protection agencies. Complaints are reviewed against the Guidelines and Committee members determine how to proceed. If a potential violation is found to exist, the company will be contacted and advised on how it can come into full compliance.

Most companies work with the Committee to cease or change the questioned practice. However, if a member company does not cooperate and the Committee believes there are ongoing Guidelines violations, the Committee can recommend that action be taken by the Board of Directors and can make case results public. Board action could include censure, suspension or expulsion from membership, and the Board may also make its actions public. If a non-member or a member company does not cooperate and the Committee believes violations of law may also have occurred, the case is referred to federal and/or state law enforcement authorities for review.

The CBBB and DMA programs demonstrate the success of self-regulation and its many benefits, including the ability for the regulatory apparatus to evolve to meet new challenges. Importantly, accountability under the Principles applies to all members of the advertising ecosystem, not merely "members" of the various organizations.

United States Senate
PERMANENT SUBCOMMITTEE ON INVESTIGATIONS
Committee on Homeland Security and Governmental Affairs

Carl Levin, Chairman
John McCain, Ranking Minority Member

ONLINE ADVERTISING AND HIDDEN HAZARDS TO CONSUMER SECURITY AND DATA PRIVACY

MAJORITY AND MINORITY STAFF REPORT

PERMANENT SUBCOMMITTEE ON INVESTIGATIONS

UNITED STATES SENATE

RELEASED IN CONJUNCTION WITH THE PERMANENT SUBCOMMITTEE ON INVESTIGATIONS' MAY 15, 2014 HEARING

SENATOR CARL LEVIN
Chairman

SENATOR JOHN McCAIN
Ranking Minority Member

PERMANENT SUBCOMMITTEE ON INVESTIGATIONS

ELISE J. BEAN
Staff Director and Chief Counsel
DANIEL J. GOSHORN
Counsel
ANGELA MESSENGER
Detailee

HENRY J. KERNER
Staff Director and Chief Counsel to the Minority
JACK THORLIN
Counsel to the Minority
SCOTT WITTMANN
Research Assistant to the Minority

MARY D. ROBERTSON
Chief Clerk

SAMIRA AHMED
Law Clerk
KYLE BROSNAN
Law Clerk to the Minority

Permanent Subcommittee on Investigations
199 Russell Senate Office Building – Washington, D.C. 20510
Majority: 202/224-9505 – Minority: 202/224-3721
Web Address: http://www.hsgac.senate.gov/subcommittees/investigations

ONLINE ADVERTISING AND HIDDEN HAZARDS TO CONSUMER SECURITY AND DATA PRIVACY

TABLE OF CONTENTS

ONLINE ADVERTISING AND HIDDEN HAZARDS TO CONSUMER SECURITY AND DATA PRIVACY

I. EXECUTIVE SUMMARY

For the past year, the Permanent Subcommittee on Investigations of the U.S. Senate Homeland Security and Governmental Affairs Committee has been examining issues central to consumer privacy and security on the Internet and in the broader online economy. Central to this segment of the economy is the online advertising industry, which continues to grow in importance. In 2013, U.S. online advertising revenue for the first time surpassed that of broadcast television advertising as companies spent $42.8 billion to reach consumers.[1]

The online advertising ecosystem is highly complex. Online advertisers do far more than merely disseminate text, graphic, or video advertisements. Underlying the work of online advertisers are sophisticated systems that are able to identify and target specific consumer groups with relevant advertising, as well as state-of-the art security practices to monitor the integrity of these ad delivery systems. The ability to target advertising is a key function of online ad delivery systems, and advertisers are willing to pay a premium of between 60 and 200 percent for these services.[2] With the continuing boom in mobile devices, the importance, and complexity, of digital advertising is likely to continue increasing in years to come.[3]

Although consumers are becoming increasingly vigilant about safeguarding the information they share on the Internet, many are less informed about the plethora of information created about them by online companies as they travel the Internet. A consumer may be aware, for example, that a search engine provider may use the search terms the consumer enters in order to select an advertisement targeted to his interests. Consumers are less aware, however, of the true scale of the data being collected about their online activity. A visit to an online news site may trigger interactions with hundreds of other parties that may be collecting information on the consumer as he travels the web. The Subcommittee found, for example, a trip to a popular tabloid news website triggered a user interaction with some 352 other web servers as well. Many of those interactions were benign; some of those third-

---

[1] Press Release, Interactive Advertising Bureau, 2013 Internet ad Revenues Soar to $42.8 billion, Hitting Landmark High & Surpassing Broadcast Television For First Time—Marks 17% Rise Over Record-Setting Revenues in 2012 (Apr. 10, 2014) http://www.iab.net/about_the_iab/recent_press_releases/press_release_archive/press_release/pr-041014.

[2] J. Howard Beales and Jeffrey Eisenach, *An Empirical Analysis Of The Value Of Information Sharing in the Market for Online Content*, Navigant Economics, 2014, https://www.aboutads.info/resource/fullvalueinfostudy.pdf.

[3] *Id.*

parties, however, may have been using cookies or other technology to compile data on the consumer. The sheer volume of such activity makes it difficult for even the most vigilant consumer to control the data being collected or protect against its malicious use.

Furthermore, the growth of online advertising has brought with it a rise in cybercriminals attempting to seek out and exploit weaknesses in the ecosystem and locate new potential victims. Many consumers are unaware that mainstream websites are becoming frequent avenues for cybercriminals seeking to infect a consumer's computer with advertisement-based malware, or "malvertising." Some estimates state that malvertising has increased over 200% in 2013 to over 209,000 incidents generating over 12.4 billion malicious ad impressions.[4] According to a recent study by the security firm Symantec, more than half of Internet website publishers have suffered a malware attack through a malicious advertisement.[5]

The Subcommittee seeks to highlight this specific aspect of online security. The Internet as a whole, as well as all the consumers who visit mainstream websites, is vulnerable to the growing number of malware attacks through online advertising. While there are many other significant vulnerabilities on the Internet, malware attacks delivered through online advertising are a real and growing problem.

The complexity of the online advertising industry makes it difficult to identify and hold accountable the entities responsible for damages resulting from malware attacks. Those attempting to exploit the Internet for criminal purposes are certainly the most culpable, and ensuring the government has adequate criminal enforcement authority is critical to deterring this activity. Yet, if responsibility for malware attacks is laid solely on cybercriminals, commercial actors may have reduced incentives to develop and institute security measures for fear of becoming the liable party if something goes wrong. The Subcommittee's investigation shows that lack of accountability within the online advertising industry may lead to overly lax security regimes, creating serious vulnerabilities for Internet users. Such vulnerabilities could grow worse in the absence of additional incentives for the most capable parties on the Internet to work with consumers and other stake holders to take effective precautionary measures.

---

[4] Written Testimony of Craig D. Spiezle before the Senate Committee on Homeland Security & Government Affairs Permanent Subcommittee on Investigations, May 15, 2014.
[5] Leelin Thye, *"Danger: Malware Ahead!-Please, Not My Site"*, SYMANTEC (Jan. 17, 2013), http://www.symantec.com/connect/blogs/danger-malware-ahead-please-not-my-site.

3

a. Subcommittee Investigation

With this investigation the Subcommittee seeks to highlight malvertising, a growing threat to consumers and the online industry. The threat malware poses to consumers is not new, and the sources of malware and the vulnerabilities it exploits are often well documented. Malware can exploit malicious code in pirated software,[6] or vulnerabilities in mainstream software and operating systems. Although malware is most commonly hosted on websites with little or no security oversight, or even completely fraudulent websites visited by consumers, each year more consumers are delivered malware through mainstream websites that may have been compromised or are unwittingly serving malicious advertising.[7]

Several legislative proposals to strengthen Internet privacy and security have stalled, and there currently is no sector-specific federal data privacy law for Internet companies.[8] Self-regulatory standards set by the online industry, while having significant privacy guidance, do not outline comprehensive security standards. Furthermore, the FTC has brought no cases related to malware transmitted through advertisements, and has not issued comprehensive regulations to curb deceptive or unfair practices in online advertising, including setting minimum safeguards on consumer data collection practices or establishing liability for damages caused by advertisements that transmit malware attacks on Internet users.[9] To address privacy issues in online advertising, in February 2012, President Obama urged the industry to implement a "Do Not Track" button that would allow users to control the extent to which they are tracked on the Internet for online advertising purposes.[10] However, the Do Not Track initiative has stalled, with advertisers and consumer groups unable to agree on even a definition of what constitutes "tracking."[11]

The Subcommittee conducted an investigation focusing specifically on the features and vulnerabilities in the online advertising industry that invite malware attacks. The Subcommittee also sought to

---

[6] White Paper, *"The Link Between Pirated Software and Cybersecurity Breaches, How Malware in Pirated Software is Costing the World Billions"* (Mar., 2014), http://www.microsoft.com/en-us/news/downloads/presskits/dcu/docs/idc_031814.pdf.

[7] Cisco, *"2013 Annual Security Report"*
(2013), https://www.cisco.com/web/offer/gist_ty2_asset/Cisco_2013_ASR.pdf.

[8] See, e.g. Commercial Privacy Bill of Rights Act of 2011 S. 799, 112th Cong. (2011).

[9] As opposed to, for example, the Health Insurance Portability and Accountability Act's Privacy Rule for health information.

[10] Press Release, The White House, We Can't Wait: Obama Administration Unveils Blueprint for a "Privacy Bill of Rights" to Protect Consumers Online (February 23, 2012)
http://www.whitehouse.gov/the-press-office/2012/02/23/we-can-t-wait-obama-administration-unveils-blueprint-privacy-bill-rights.

[11] David Goldman, *Do Not Track proposal is DOA*, CNN (July 16, 2013),
http://money.cnn.com/2013/07/16/technology/do-not-track/.

4

highlight the potential hazards to private consumer information which result from consumer visits to even mainstream websites. The Subcommittee surveyed Internet participants and interviewed representatives from major ad networks, ad exchanges, data brokers, self-regulatory bodies, the Federal Trade Commission, consumer protection groups, and other participants in the online advertising industry to identify the vulnerabilities that have led to significant hazards to consumer safety and loss of consumer privacy online. Every entity contacted by the Subcommittee cooperated with requests for information.

b. Investigation Overview

In December 2013, an Internet user visited a popular, mainstream website. Without any further action on her part, her computer was infected with a virus: all the personal information, usernames, and passwords she used on her device could have been stolen, and her computer hijacked.[12] The owners of the website she visited had no idea that the attack had taken place because the virus came not from the website itself, but from an embedded online advertisement managed by the Internet company Yahoo's online advertising network.[13] The user did not need to click on the advertisement—indeed, if the mainstream website she visited had time to load onto her computer before the malware was delivered, the frame where the advertisement would have gone would have been empty because the cybercriminals didn't even bother putting an image in.[14] The owners of the website where the advertisement ran did not even know who had delivered the malware because, in today's complex online advertising industry, websites often have no direct relationship with the entities that advertise on their sites. Although Yahoo reacted promptly to the attack, as many as 2 million consumers may have been exposed to the covert advertising malware.[15]

In February 2014, cybercriminals launched a similar attack on YouTube through an advertisement delivered by Google.[16] As in the Yahoo attack, the user did not need to click on the advertisement in

---

[12] Edward Moyer, *Yahoo says malware attack farther reaching than thought*, CNET (Jan. 11, 2014), http://www.cnet.com/news/yahoo-says-malware-attack-farther-reaching-than-thought/; Lance Whitney, *Yahoo malware turned PCs into Bitcoin miners*, CNET (Jan. 9, 2014), http://news.cnet.com/8301-1009_3-57616958-83/yahoo-malware-turned-pcs-into-bitcoin-miners/

[13] Whitney, *supra.*

[14] Interview with Yahoo, in Wash., D.C. (Jan. 16, 2014).

[15] Alex Hern, *Yahoo malware turned European Computers into bitcoin slaves*, THE GUARDIAN (Jan. 8, 2014), http://www.theguardian.com/technology/2014/jan/08/yahoo-malware-turned-europeans-computers-into-bitcoin-slaves.

[16] McEnroe Navaraj, *The Wild Wild Web: YouTube ads serving malware*, BROMIUM LABS CALL OF THE WILD BLOG (Feh. 21, 2014), http://labs.bromium.com/2014/02/21/the-wild-wild-web-youtube-ads-serving-malware.

question.[17] Google also responded quickly to that attack. Similar attacks have struck across many online advertising platforms.

As it turned out, in the December 2013 attack, Yahoo's network was compromised by a hacker who had stolen a Yahoo employee's credentials, not through any structural weakness unique to Yahoo. But cybercriminals have numerous methods to evade security measures. For example, cybercriminals time their attacks carefully, often picking U.S. holidays or Friday afternoons when they believe online traffic will be high and there will be fewer security personnel available to react. The practice is so pervasive that when law enforcement personnel raid cyber-criminal residences and offices in Russia and other foreign countries, they find calendars extensively marked with U.S. federal holidays and three-day weekends.

These incidents demonstrated the importance of educating the public on the threat of malvertising. The Subcommittee discovered no evidence to suggest Google or Yahoo's ad network is any more vulnerable to malware attacks than any other major online ad network. Yahoo and Google appear to follow standard industry practice. However, the industry as a whole remains vulnerable to these forms of attack.

The prevalence of vulnerabilities in the online advertising industry has made it difficult for individual industry participants to adopt effective long-term security countermeasures. Many entities use "scanning" to search for malicious advertisements, an automated process that mimics loading each advertisement onto a webpage on test machines to see if malware is transmitted. However, this scanning is rendered increasingly ineffective by cybercriminals who endeavor to, in essence, learn the geographic location of the scanners and then direct malicious advertisements away from those scanners. In other instances, cybercriminals change the nature of an advertisement after it has been scanned and cleared, turning an initially benign advertisement into malware

Beyond scanning, most protective measures for consumers and their data come from industry-led voluntary compliance regimes and the contractual relationships between entities in the advertising ecosystem. But those voluntary compliance regimes and contractual arrangements are often incomplete, unreliable, or poorly enforced. As the online advertising industry grows increasingly complex, it is also becoming more difficult to ascertain responsibility when consumers are hurt by malicious advertising or data collection. A cautious citizen can avoid becoming a victim of crime in real life by, for example, avoiding bad

---

[17] *Id.*

6

neighborhoods and keeping a wary eye on the street traffic. But, online, a visit to even a reputable website can now result in thousands of dollars in damage to the consumer and the compromise of private information at the hands of actors most consumers don't know are present.

Vulnerabilities in online advertising stem from the fact that advertisements online differ in nature from advertisements broadcast on radio or television. On radio or television, the content of the advertisement is transmitted by the same party that hosts the rest of the content on the station. A radio station, for example, may play a recording of an advertisement on the same frequency and equipment it uses for playing songs. A television station may broadcast commercials from the same studio that is transmitting the evening news. By contrast, if a user visits a mainstream website, the server that hosts the website is often not the server that selects and delivers an advertisement that runs on the website.

Host websites most commonly sell ad space on their sites through an intermediary, most often an ad platform operated by well-known tech companies.[18] These intermediary companies manage "real estate" on the host websites, filling the spaces set aside by the host with advertisements. These intermediary companies also typically gather data on Internet users for the purpose of individually targeting online advertisements to those users when they visit partner websites. Through a complicated series of Internet transactions, the intermediary companies—often referred to as ad networks or exchanges—ultimately direct an Internet user's browser to display an advertisement from a server controlled by neither the ad network nor the original host website.

Separating the party who delivers the online advertisement from the party who runs the host website means that the consumer who visits the host website is forced to trust her data and security to a party unknown to her. While a consumer might think visiting an online news site is safe because of the mainstream trustworthiness of the entity, the consumer's computer and personal information are actually at the mercy of dozens, or even hundreds, of other businesses and individuals that such websites may not even be aware of or have a direct relationship with.

The Subcommittee's investigation has revealed that host websites often do not select and cannot predict which advertisements will be delivered by the intermediary ad networks that rent space on their websites. They may not know what entities are running advertisements on their site until they receive feedback from ad networks after the fact. In fact, many host websites rely on ad networks, exchanges, supply-side

---

[18] For instance, Yahoo, Google, and Microsoft all operate ad networks.

platforms (SSPs) and demand-side platforms (DSPs) to handle security and quality control. In some cases, host websites are not consulted about what kind of cookies are used, what types of consumer data are being collected, or what vulnerabilities for malicious software are contained in the advertisements being run on their websites.

Today, most ad networks and exchanges also have limited control over the actual content of the advertisements whose placement they facilitate. While many do robust scanning to detect malware, the ad networks and exchanges do not control the server that ultimately delivers the advertisement to the host website. Sometimes, a malicious advertiser will initially appear benign, but change its advertisement once it has passed through initial scans. On other occasions, a malicious party will infiltrate the ad network itself and pass malware on to unsuspecting consumers.

Despite the difficulty in eliminating bad actors from the online advertising ecosystem, ad networks are currently engaged in multiple industry-led efforts to set best practices guidelines. While the ad networks uniformly force advertisers to agree to follow codes of conduct drawn up by voluntary self-regulatory agencies like the Network Advertising Initiative (NAI) or the Digital Advertising Alliance (DAA), the scope of the codes of conduct and the oversight of company compliance with these standards can be limited. For example, NAI has just seven employees reviewing or auditing 91 companies.[19] The codes themselves are predominantly oriented toward privacy concerns, and do not comprehensively address online advertising malware security.

The complex interactions underlying the online advertising industry that make it vulnerable to malware attacks also underscore the difficulties in enforcing restrictions on the collection and use of sensitive consumer data. Multiple companies told the Subcommittee that, while they do scan for malware, there is no scanning or automated process in place to check for compliance on the part of advertisers who limit the operation of cookies used to collect consumer data. While self-regulatory codes or particular contracts might require advertisers or ad networks to limit their collection of consumer data to non-personally identifiable information (non-PII), there is little systematic oversight to ensure that practice conforms to the contractual obligations.

Self-regulation in the online advertising industry has worked in some areas, but needs strengthening in some key respects. On the privacy side, self-regulatory groups such as the DAA and NAI have created guidelines and standards widely adopted by online advertising companies. Detection of deviation of those standards and punishment

---

[19] Subcommittee interview with NAI (Jan. 31, 2014).

for noncompliance has sometimes been weak, as examples in this report indicate, but there are enforcement mechanisms that do hold companies accountable in some cases. Comparable standards and enforcement mechanisms have not materialized for online advertising security, however. A new industry effort to address fraudulent advertising called Trust in Ads was launched on May 8, 2014.[20] While the existence of such an effort is a positive development, further efforts to create real self-regulation on security in online advertising will be needed to make meaningful progress.

At this time, government rules regarding online advertising also fail to comprehensively safeguard consumers or level the playing field for companies working to prevent advertising malware. The Federal Trade Commission (FTC), the key government agency overseeing online activities, has brought over 100 enforcement actions related to online data privacy and security problems. However, most of the FTC's online enforcement actions have been brought under the auspices of statutes prohibiting companies from engaging in "deceptive" practices, although the FTC also has enforcement authority to stop "unfair" practices.[21] In deceptive practice cases, a company typically has made a specific promise not to engage in a particular practice, but does so anyway. Such cases, while egregious, can only be brought when a company makes a specific representation and then fails to follow it. While the FTC has brought cases against some companies under its authority to regulate "unfair" practices, industry participants claim not to have a clear understanding of what practices are actually forbidden.[22] In addition, although the FTC has pursued Internet security cases, those cases have focused primarily on improper storage of personal information. Congress has not passed legislation on this topic, and the FTC has brought no cases related to malware transmitted through advertisements, and has not issued comprehensive regulations to curb deceptive or unfair practices in online advertising, including setting minimum safeguards on consumer data collection practices or establishing liability for damages caused by advertisements that transmit malware attacks on Internet users.[23]

The online advertising industry can be complex and difficult to understand. In such an environment, determining responsible parties when things go wrong can be difficult. What is clear, however, is that the one party who is least capable of monitoring and regulating

[20] *Internet Industry Leaders Offer Tips for Consumers to Avoid Tech Support Advertising Scams,* TRUSTINADS.ORG BLOG (May 7, 2014), http://blog.trustinads.org/2014/05/internet-industry-leaders-offer-tips.html.
[21] See The Federal Trade Commission Act, 15 U.S.C. §45(a), Section 5 in particular.
[22] Interview with Marc Groman, President and CEO, Network Advertising Initiative, in Wash., D.C. (Jan. 31, 2014).
[23] As opposed to, for example, the Health Insurance Portability and Accountability Act's Privacy Rule for health information.

advertising—the consumer—is the party who currently bears the full brunt of the losses when the system fails.

c. Findings and Recommendations

Findings. Based on the Subcommittee's investigation, the Report makes the following findings of fact.

1. **Consumers risk exposure to malware through everyday activity.** Consumers can incur malware attacks without having taken any action other than visiting a mainstream website. The complexity of the online advertising ecosystem makes it impossible for an ordinary consumer to avoid advertising malware attacks, identify the source of the malware exposure, and determine whether the ad network or host website could have prevented the attack.

2. **The complexity of current online advertising practices impedes industry accountability for malware attacks.** The online advertising industry has grown in complexity to such an extent that each party can conceivably claim it is not responsible when malware is delivered to a user's computer through an advertisement. An ordinary online advertisement typically goes through five or six intermediaries before being delivered to a user's browser, and the ad networks themselves rarely deliver the actual advertisement from their own servers. In most cases, the owners of the host website visited by a user do not know what advertisements will be shown on their site.

3. **Self-regulatory bodies alone have not been adequate to ensure consumer security online.** Self-regulatory codes of conduct in the online advertising field do not comprehensively address consumer security from malware. In addition, the self-regulatory efforts in online security to date have been dependent upon online ad networks for their funding and viability, creating a potential conflict of interest in their dual roles as industry advocates and standard-setting bodies. The self-regulatory bodies prioritize industry representatives over consumer advocates in the standard-setting process.

4. **Visits to mainstream websites can expose consumers to hundreds of unknown, or potentially dangerous, third parties.** Subcommittee analysis of several popular websites found that visiting even a mainstream website exposes consumers to hundreds of third parties. Each of those third parties may be capable of collecting information on the consumer and, in extreme scenarios, is a potential source of malware.

5. **Consumer safeguards are currently inadequate to protect against online advertising abuses, including malware, invasive cookies, and inappropriate data collection.** Cybercriminals are constantly finding new ways to evade existing security methods. Self-regulatory codes do not significantly address online advertising security, and data collection protections are often limited in scope, and underutilized. Current FTC safeguards are insufficient to comprehensively protect consumers from online advertising abuses.

6. **Current systems may not create sufficient incentives for online advertising participants to prevent consumer abuses.** Because responsibility for malware attacks and inappropriate data collection through online advertisements is undefined, online advertising participants may not be fully incentivized to establish effective consumer safeguards against abuses.

Recommendations. Based upon the Subcommittee's investigation, the Report makes the following recommendations.

1. **Establish better practices and clearer rules to prevent online advertising abuses.** Under the current regulatory and legislative framework, legal responsibility for damages caused through malvertising usually rests only with the fraudulent actor in question. Since such actors are rarely caught and even less frequently able to pay damages, the harm caused by malicious advertisements is ultimately born by consumers who in many cases have done nothing more than visit a mainstream website. While consumers should be careful to keep their operating systems and programs updated to avoid vulnerability, sophisticated commercial entities, large and small, should take steps to reduce systemic vulnerabilities in their advertising networks. If sophisticated commercial entities do not take steps to

further protect consumers, regulatory or legislative change may be needed so that such entities are incentivized to increase security for advertisements run through their systems.

2. **Strengthen security information exchanges within the online advertising industry to prevent abuses.** Some online advertising companies claim they do not share information about security hazards with other companies, because of fears they will be accused of violating antitrust laws by cooperating with competitors. The Department of Justice and the Federal Trade Commission recently issued joint guidance suggesting that the sharing of cyber threat-related information would not trigger antitrust liability. Those agencies should clarify the extent to which online advertising participants may exchange information about security hazards without incurring antitrust or other liability. If necessary, Congress should pass legislation that removes legal impediments to the sharing of actionable cyber-threat related information and creates incentives for the voluntary sharing of information.

3. **Clarify specific prohibited practices in online advertising to prevent abuses and protect consumers.** Self-regulatory bodies should endeavor to develop comprehensive security guidelines for preventing online advertising malware attacks. In the absence of effective self-regulation, the FTC should consider issuing comprehensive regulations to prohibit deceptive and unfair online advertising practices that facilitate or fail to take reasonable steps to prevent malware, invasive cookies, and inappropriate data collection delivered to Internet consumers through online advertisements. Greater specificity in prohibited or discouraged practices is needed before the overall security situation in the online advertising industry can improve.

4. **Develop additional "circuit breakers" to protect consumers.** Given the complexity of the online advertising ecosystem, more "circuit breakers" should be incorporated into the online advertising system, systems that introduce check-points that ensure malicious advertisements are caught at an earlier stage before transmission to consumers. Online advertising industry participants should thoroughly vet new advertisers and

12

perform rigorous and ongoing checks as often as feasible to ensure that advertisements that appear legitimate upon initial submission remain so.

II. BACKGROUND

In order to understand some of the hazards consumers face in the online advertising industry, it is necessary to understand two different processes: (1) how data is collected on Internet users by third parties and (2) how online advertisements are delivered while making use of that data. The online advertising industry has evolved to make extensive use of those two processes, presenting challenges to consumer safety and privacy today.

a. Data Collection in the Online Advertising Industry

1. Cookies

Since the inception of the Internet, cookies have been the primary tools by which companies transmit information about Internet users.[24] Best conceptualized as an identity card for a particular machine that accesses the Internet, cookies are small text files placed on an Internet user's computer hard drive or browser that store information about a user's interactions with a particular website.[25] When an Internet user visits a website, the user's browser sends a request to the website's server to load the page in question. In addition to the request for the page, the user's browser is programmed to send along information from any cookies placed by the website's server. If there are no such cookies—either because the user has never visited the website before or because she has deleted the cookies on her hard drive—the website's server may assign a new cookie for use in the current session and potentially on subsequent visits.

The most basic function a cookie serves is to identify a device. With a cookie, websites can know how many unique machines—and, by extension, roughly how many unique visitors—come to their site. By allowing a website to identify individual visitors, cookies can help websites provide useful services to visitors. For example, many anti-fraud provisions are cookie-based, and most online "shopping cart" functions need a cookie to confirm that the user who added one item to their cart is the same user who has navigated to a different part of the website.

2. First-Party vs. Third-Party Cookies

A cookie that is placed by the website a user actually visits is called a first-party cookie. If a user visits an online shopping website,

---

[24] *See, e.g.*, Network Advertising Initiative, *Understanding Online Advertising: How Does it Work?*, https://www.networkadvertising.org/understanding-online-advertising/how-does-it-work.
[25] *Id.*

she might have a cookie placed on her machine so that the company can recognize the user when she move to another page on the site and remember what she put into her online shopping cart.

By contrast, a third-party cookie is one placed by a website other than the one the user directly accessed. If a user visits most ordinary websites (e.g., a newspaper website or a blog), some third party (or third parties) will likely place a cookie on that user's computer. Almost every website examined by the Subcommittee called some third party or parties who operated cookies on that website.[26] As discussed above, a cookie is placed in response to a browser's request to load a page. When a user visits a website that runs a third-party cookie, the host website instructs the user's browser to contact the third-party. The third party sends back whatever content the user's browser requested, as well as a cookie. This interaction can be displayed schematically as follows:

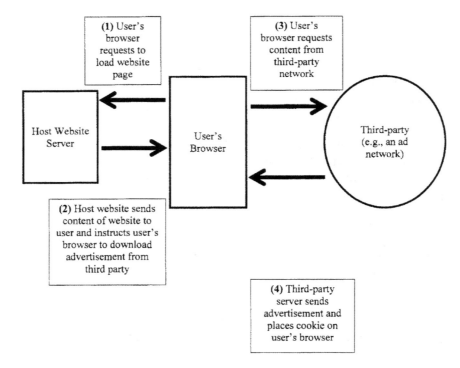

Figure 1: Third-party cookie placement on a user's machine.

---

[26] The Subcommittee detected third-party activity using the "Disconnect Private Browsing" application on a Chrome web browser. As explained on its website, Disconnect "detects when your browser tries to make a connection to anything other than the site you are visiting." *See* https://disconnect.me/disconnect/faq#what-is-disconnect-private-browsing. According to DoubleClick's website, "DoubleClick sends a cookie to the browser after any impression, click, or other activity that results in a call to the DoubleClick server." Since, in our example, there was a call to DoubleClick's server detected by Disconnect, we can infer that a cookie was placed through that interaction.

3. Tracking Users Through Cookies

While cookies themselves simply identify machines, Internet companies can use cookies as a proxy for a single user's online activities. An ad network's cookie might note, to use a fictitious example, that one unique user first visited "www.FreshCooking.com", then "www.FreshCooking.com/vegan." The ad network can read the webpage uniform resource locators (URLs) and, of course, access the content on FreshCooking.com itself and infer that the user in question is interested in cooking.[27] It can cross-reference that information with any other recent website visits by that user that it detected through its cookie network (say, a visit to "www.MeatFree.com").[28] Knowing even only some of the user's browsing history can allow an ad network to conclude with a high degree of certainty that the user in question is a vegetarian. It can then use that information to deliver targeted advertisements to that user.

4. Data Collection and Advertising

Ad networks are the most prominent third-party cookie users because (a) they directly benefit from the collection of user information and (b) they have a built-in opportunity to deliver cookies every time they deliver an ad. As discussed in a later section in the report, ad networks use the data they collect from cookies to target advertisements as precisely as possible to particular users, trying to infer as much information as they can about each user's location, interests, and demographic information. The more data these ad networks can collect from different websites on a particular user, the better the inferences they can draw.

The built-in opportunity to deliver a cookie stems from the fact that the host website's server has to contact the ad network every time it needs an ad. While the ad network does not deliver the advertisement itself—a distinction which will become vitally important in the context of malware—the host website's server's call to the ad network allows the ad network to place a cookie.

Ad networks are not the only companies that operate cookies across multiple websites. Data brokers like Acxiom and BlueKai, who collect information on consumers in order to facilitate the targeting of advertisements, have also contracted to place and access their cookies across multiple websites. As discussed above, third parties can deliver a cookie because some part of the host website draws upon content from

---

[27] *See*, Fed. Trade Comm'n., *Cookies: Leaving a Trail on the Web* (Nov. 2011) https://www.consumer.ftc.gov/articles/0042-cookies-leaving-trail-web.
[28] *Id.*

the third-party server. In the context of advertising, the third-party content requested by the host website is the advertisement itself. A call from the host website opens the door for a cookie to be placed by the third party whose content was called for. However, the third-party content displayed on the host website can be almost invisible—it is very often a single pixel on the screen.[29] Because the host website requested some nominal amount of content from the third-party—even if the content is just a single pixel—the third-party can now deliver its cookie to the user's browser as well. Thus, data brokers or other entities that deliver no real content to the host website can still deliver cookies by contracting with the host website to place a single pixel on their website.[30]

5. Cookie Controversies

The ability to place cookies is highly valuable to ad networks. In fact, advertisers are willing to pay a premium of between 60 and 200 percent for targeted advertisements based on cookies.[31] The privacy implications are equally clear. Cookies can in theory be used to infer damaging personal information about particular users, such as the fact that a user has a certain medical condition. Even less immediately controversial inferences, like the age of a user, can enable criminals to target the very young or elderly with fraudulent advertisements.

Generally, a browser's default settings leave cookies active, since many benign web functions consumers have come to expect are cookie based. A privacy minded (and tech-savvy) user can avoid all cookie-based tracking if she so chooses. However, very few Internet users actually alter default browser settings that prioritize consumer privacy.[32] The default browser setting therefore makes a tremendous difference in the use of cookies, and consequently how much data is gathered on Internet users.

Furthermore, despite some interest by browser developers to block certain types of cookies, this does not always lead to better consumer privacy. For example, when Apple announced that its Safari browser's default setting would block third-party cookies, Google used a "workaround" that enabled it to place cookies despite the default setting. Google ultimately agreed to pay a $22.5 million fine to the FTC for that

---

[29] *See, e.g.,* BlueKai, *Privacy Policy,* http://bluekai.com/privacypolicy.php.

[30] The arrangement whereby placing one pixel can allow a third party to place a cookie is called a "pixel tag." *See Id.*

[31] J. Howard Beales and Jeffrey Eisenach, *An Empirical Analysis Of The Value Of Information Sharing in the Market for Online Content,* Navigant Economics, 2014, https://www.aboutads.info/resource/fullvalueinfostudy.pdf.

[32] Charles Arthur, *Why the default settings on your device should be right first time,* THE GUARDIAN (Nov. 30, 2013), http://www.theguardian.com/technology/2013/dec/01/default-settings-change-phones-computers.

"deceptive" practice.[33] Mozilla also announced that it would block third-party cookies by default in its Firefox browser, but actual implementation has been delayed several times and the online advertising industry has voiced strong disapproval of the measure.[34]

b. How Online Advertisements are Delivered

1. Simplified Process of Ad Delivery

Online advertisements may appear to be part of the host website that a user visits, just like images in an article online, but they are different in several important respects. First, and most crucially, the advertisements delivered through ad networks are generally not under the control of the host website at the time of delivery. The ads usually do not physically reside on the same server as the main content of the website. Second, while an advertisement in a newspaper is just a static picture, online advertisements can deliver files and whole programs to a user even if the advertisement itself appears to be just an image.

When a user visits a website that uses an ad network to deliver its ads, the host website instructs the user's browser to contact the ad network. The ad network, in turn, retrieves whatever user cookie identifiers it can. Using those identifiers, the ad network can access its own database to see what other information about the user's history it has in order to identify the user's interests and demographic information. The ad network can then decide which advertisement would be best to serve that particular user.

Though the ad network decides which advertisement should be sent, it often does not deliver the actual advertisements. Instead, the ad network instructs the user's browser to contact a server designated by the actual advertiser. The server that delivers the advertisement is most often called a content delivery network (CDN). It is most often a separate, stand-alone entity, and thus represents another potential vulnerability within the advertising delivery process.

The advertiser's designated server then delivers the actual image or video to the user's browser. All of those steps cumulatively occur over the course of about one second.

---

[33] Press Release, Fed. Trade Comm'n, Google Will Pay $22.5 Million to Settle FTC Charges It Misrepresented Privacy Assurances to Users of Apple's Safari Internet Browser (Aug. 9, 2013), http://www.ftc.gov/news-events/press-releases/2012/08/google-will-pay-225-million-settle-ftc-charges-it-misrepresented.

[34] James Temple, *Mozilla anticookie tool plans crumbling*, S.F. GATE (Nov. 5, 2013), http://www.sfgate.com/technology/dotcommentary/article/Mozilla-anticookie-tool-plans-crumbling-4958045.php.

18

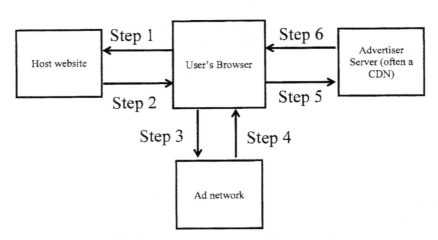

Figure 2*: A simplified depiction of the ad delivery process.*

Two caveats must be made about this summary. First, the actual delivery process can end up being far more complicated. The ad network can go through any number of exchanges and other online advertising companies which exist to help ad networks target a user as precisely as possible. Several experts told the Subcommittee that the actual number of intermediary companies between the host website and the advertiser averages around 5 or 6 in many cases. Those other online advertising companies are discussed at length in another section. For purposes of this section of the report, it is sufficient to note that the ad network (or other companies) that chooses which advertisement to deliver does not control the actual delivery of that ad, which is a source of a great deal of security vulnerability in the industry. Second, this depiction obviously applies only to typical third-party delivered advertisements, not direct sales or other variations that might be found within the online advertising industry.

2. *The Role of Ad Tags in the Online Ad Delivery Process*

Another important aspect of ad delivery is the complicated manner in which the user's browser, the host website, the ad network, and the advertiser communicate with each other. That communication is ultimately achieved through "ad tags," which are hypertext markup language (HTML) code sent between online advertising entities, which will ultimately call up the correct advertisement to be delivered to a user.[35] That HTML code conveys information about the advertisement space to be filled. The ad tag includes basic details about the size of the space to be filled as well as cookie-based identifiers to facilitate targeting of the ad. The functioning of ad tags explains how online

---

[35] *See,* Appnexus, *Ad Tags: an Introduction,* https://wiki.appnexus.com/display/industry/Ad+Tags.

advertising companies can send advertisements to users' browsers without the advertising companies actually directly knowing what that advertisement is.

Ad tags are the messages that tell online advertising companies what ad to deliver without actually having to send the advertisement itself between multiple companies. When a user visits a website, that host website sends an ad tag out to its ad network. That tag will contain some form of cookie identification so that the ad network will recognize the user. The host website does not need to know anything about the user in order to facilitate data collection; all it must do is notify the ad network of the user's cookie identifier.[36] The ad network's server will then rapidly call up all available data on the user and decide which advertisement to deliver (or call upon another outside party to decide which advertisement to deliver). The ad network will then send an ad tag back through the user's browser, telling it to retrieve the proper advertisement at a URL that the advertiser (the customer of the ad network) has specified.

This is where a key vulnerability in the online advertising system lies. The ad network often performs some manner of initial quality control on the advertisement by examining what happens when it calls the particular URL of the advertiser. However, the actual file at that URL can be quietly changed after that initial quality control check so that when a user actually encounters the ad, an innocuous and safe ad may have been transformed into a vehicle for malware.[37]

3. Direct Sale Advertisements vs. Ad Network Advertisements

Not all online advertisements are delivered through ad networks. Some websites still sell many of their own advertisements directly. Most "floating" ads, where an advertisement obscures the content of a website, are sold directly.[38] Because such advertisements are highly intrusive, websites are reluctant to entrust ad networks to choose advertisements that could reflect poorly on the website.

Most direct sales of advertisements are made by popular websites to large advertisers whose products are directly complementary to the website's focus. Because of the complementary nature of the product and the website, there is less need for targeting ads in the way an ad network can. For example, CNN, a news site, can directly sell

---

[36] Interview with Craig Spiezle, Executive Director and President, Online Trust Alliance, in Wash., D.C. (Mar. 19, 2014).

[37] Id.

[38] Interview with Mike Zaneis, Executive Vice President, Public Policy and General Counsel, Interactive Advertising Bureau, in Wash., D.C. (Apr. 23, 2014).

advertisements to HBO for its parody news program "Last Week Tonight" and coordinate banner, sidebar, and interactive components of the same advertisement.[39]

Figure 3. *Example of direct-sale advertisement, where CNN coordinated the sale of multiple ad-spaces to HBO. Note the ads for "Last Week Tonight" on the left, right, top, and middle of CNN's front page.*

While direct sales minimize user data transmission because they are often untargeted, they also remove the quality-control processes available to ad networks. The host websites are sometimes less technologically sophisticated than ad networks, which can lead to additional vulnerabilities, as will be discussed at length in Part III of this report.

c. Evolution of the Online Advertising Industry

The online advertising ecosystem has significantly evolved over the years to reflect the intricate expansion of the Internet. Today, the online advertising ecosystem is more than just an exchange of advertisements and money – it is an exchange of information that continues to grow as more users access the Internet and either knowingly or unknowingly share their personal data with an attentive and vibrant online advertising market.

Originally, advertisements were exchanged online between an advertiser (or an ad agency) and a publisher (a website). The advertiser directly bought ad space or inventory from a publisher and then transmitted its advertisement to the publisher's website(s) for public

---

[39] CNN (Apr. 27, 2014), http://www.cnn.com. The Subcommittee has not confirmed that this particular sale was direct, but the coordination across different sections of the same website is emblematic of direct sales.

display, much like a billboard near a highway. Each time a particular advertisement was displayed, it was called a single impression.[40]

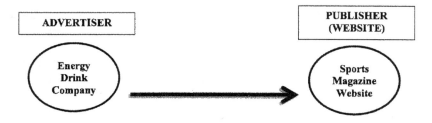

Figure 4. Depiction of an advertiser directly buying ad space from a publisher.

1. The Rise of Ad Networks

As publishers created more websites and the opportunity for online advertising increased, advertisers wanted to expand their presence on the Internet and buy more ad space, or "inventory" for specific audiences (based on age, gender, interests, location, etc.). However, it was difficult for advertisers to reach target audience members because, according to online industry experts, Internet audiences were "incredibly fragmented, splitting their online time between many different websites."[41] Advertisers needed a neutral party to analyze the increasing amount of advertising space from publishers to be able to transmit their advertisements to the right users despite audience fragmentation.[42] At the same time, publishers needed a way to efficiently sell their inventory and fill in their ad spaces.[43]

Thus, in 1997, ad networks were established to serve as a conduit between the advertisers and the publishers.[44] Originally, ad networks would receive inventory from publishers like sports magazines or news websites and aggregate or "package" this data into different categories based on age, gender, interests, etc.[45] Ad networks would sell these "packages" to advertisers based on the type of audience the advertiser was targeting.

---

[40] Description of Impressions, GOOGLE, https://support.google.com/adwords/answer/6320?hl=en (last visited May 2, 2014).
[41] White Paper, *Ad Network vs Ad Exchanges: How do they Compare?*, OPENX at 2 (Oct. 3, 2013), http://openx.com/whitepaper/ad-exchange-vs-ad-network-how-do-they-compare (hereinafter "OpenX White Paper").
[42] *Id.*
[43] Video, *The Evolution of Online Display Advertising*, INTERNET ADVERTISING BUREAU UK (Nov. 11, 2012), http://www.iabuk.net/video/the-evolution-of-online-display-advertising.
[44] OpenX White Paper, *supra* note 41 at 2.
[45] Webinar, *Ad Networks vs. Ad Exchanges*, OPENX, http://openx.com/webinars/ad-networks-vs-ad-exchanges.

22

For example, in the figure below a shoe company and its ad agency may want to run a campaign targeted at male sports fans ages 18 to 24. The shoe company would send this request to an ad network. The ad network, which contracts with publishers, has acquired and packaged ad space, or "inventory", and offers to sell the shoe company inventory packages. The shoe company reviews these packages and buys inventory that best matches its ad campaign's audience segment. Based on the type of inventory package the shoe company purchased, the ad network then transmits the shoe company's advertisement to the publisher providing the selected inventory – a newspaper website in this example.

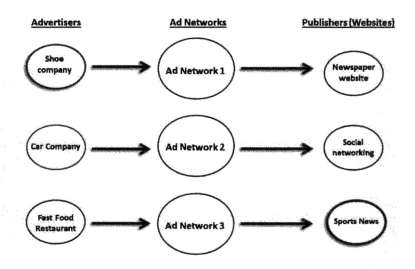

Figure 5. Depiction of online advertising process through ad networks.

2. The Weaknesses of Ad Networks

While the ad networks provided advertisers an opportunity to target specific audience segments, the process in which the ad networks bought, packaged, and sold inventory created challenges for advertisers and publishers alike.[46] Ad networks often offered advertisers little insight into where advertisements were ultimately placed.[47] This resulted in advertisers often having to buy inventory "blindly" and then

---

[46] *Id.*
[47] *Id.*

wait, sometimes for several months, to see whether their ad campaign was effective.[48]

Additionally, ad networks did not place value on specific ad space and only provided advertisers a set price for an inventory package that contained millions of ad spaces.[49] This resulted in advertisers purchasing ad spaces in bulk that might not necessarily attract viewers that are the best match for their ad campaign.[50] Thus, advertisers were essentially spending money on a package of ad spaces that were only partially on target.[51]

Furthermore, in some cases advertisers would buy inventory packages from an ad network that might not collect or sell inventory data from a publisher that would be the best match for the advertiser's targeted audience. In the example above, the shoe company's preferred target audience frequently visits the sports news website. However, the shoe company's ad network may not collect or sell inventory data from the sports news website, which could deal solely with a different ad network. Thus, even though the shoe company's advertisements are ultimately displayed online to some members of its target audience who visit the newspaper website, the shoe company would be unable to reach members of its target audience who access the sports news website.

In order to avoid this challenge, advertisers would contract with multiple ad networks in an attempt to ensure that their advertisements would eventually reach as many targeted audience segments as possible. However, this method also proved problematic since advertisers were now blindly buying inventory packages from multiple ad networks without insight into where their advertisements were displayed. In some cases, advertisers were buying the same audience segment more than once.[52]

Publishers also faced great difficulties with the ad network process. Ad networks did not offer publishers a way to identify the best advertisers for their websites. Additionally, publishers would usually work with a series of ad networks in case one would fail to sell its inventory.[53] This resulted in many different parties taking a cut from the publisher's ad space revenue.[54]

---

[48] *Id.*

[49] *Id.*

[50] *Id.*

[51] *Id.*

[52] Video, INTERNET ADVERTISING BUREAU UK, *supra* note 43.

[53] Webinar, OPENX, *supra* note 45.

[54] *Id.*

24

Use of the ad networks was meant to simplify the exchange of information between and among advertisers and publishers by aggregating data into unique inventory packages. However, due to the ad networks' lack of transparency and their imprecise valuations of ad space, the online advertising industry desperately needed a new business model to promote and efficiently advance the exchange of data in a way that was beneficial to both advertisers and publishers.[55]

3. A New Business Model: The Ad Exchanges

In 2005 the online advertising industry saw the birth of the ad exchanges—a new online advertising business model that would solve many of the problems created by the ad networks.[56] Whereas the ad networks forced advertisers into buying ad spaces in bulk (via inventory packages), the ad exchanges offered advertisers the chance to buy ad space individually.[57] On an ad-by-ad basis, advertisers could choose where they wanted their advertisement to be displayed and how much they were willing to pay for a particular ad space.

As shown in the figure below, when a person visits a publisher's website (Step One), that publisher will send out a request to an ad exchange to fill the website's ad space with advertisements that will be displayed to that particular user (Step Two).[58] In its request to the ad exchange, the publisher will provide the user's unique cookie identifier and information on the type of ad space available (e.g., ad space size).[59] Next, the ad exchange passes along the publisher's advertisement criteria as well as information the exchange has collected on the user to participating advertisers in the exchange (Step Three).[60] At this time, advertisers bid against one another in real time for this particular ad space to be displayed to this particular user (Step Four).[61] This process is called "real-time bidding."[62] To give a sense of the scale of online advertising, the typical cost for a thousand ad impressions (views of an individual ad) ranges from about $0.50 to $17 depending on the subject of the advertisement and the quality of the host website.[63] The ad exchange will then select the highest bidder (Step Five) and send that advertisement to the publisher's website (Step Six) where the ad space is

---

[55] Video, INTERNET ADVERTISING BUREAU UK, *supra* note 43.
[56] Webinar, OPENX, *supra* note 45.
[57] *Id.*
[58] OpenX White Paper, *supra* note 41 at 5.
[59] *Id.*
[60] *Id.*
[61] *Id.*
[62] Webinar, OPENX, *supra* note 45.
[63] *See,* Michael Johnston, *What Are Average CPM Rates in 2014?*, MONETIZE PROS (Jan. 27, 2014), http://monetizepros.com/blog/2014/average-cpm-rates.

filled with the ad image (Step Seven) and finally displayed to the user (Step Eight).[64] This entire process usually takes less than a second.[65]

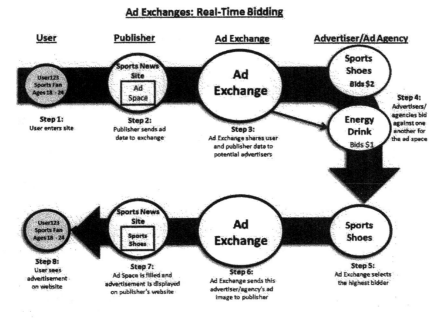

Ad Exchanges: Real-Time Bidding

Figure 6. Depiction of the online advertising process with ad exchanges.

The ad exchanges offer valuable information to publishers and advertisers alike. On the advertising side, the ad exchange can offer advertisers insight into what ads are performing well and where those ads are being displayed so advertisers can adjust their campaigns to maximize the impact of their ads.[66] On the publishing side, the ad exchange can provide valuable information to publishers on what advertiser or ad agency is buying that publisher's inventory and how much they are paying for it.[67] This level of insight offered by the ad exchanges is a major improvement from former ad network models.[68]

Additionally, since advertisers buy impressions (views of an ad) individually as opposed to "packaged" deals (as offered by ad networks), they are able to buy specific ad space at much higher prices since they can buy only the impressions they specifically want.[69] As a result of advertisers only buying impressions that they deem valuable, the level of competition for each ad space drives up the price for each impression on

---

[64] OpenX White Paper, *supra* note 41 at 5.
[65] *Id.*
[66] Webinar, OPENX, *supra* note 45.
[67] *Id.*
[68] *Id.*
[69] *Id.*

a website, with advertisers willing to pay a premium of between 60 and 200 percent,[70] which ultimately results in more revenue for the publishers, compared to the noncompetitive environment of the ad network model.[71]

4. The Weakness of Ad Exchanges

While ad exchanges offer many improvements to ad network structures, both are still similar in the sense that advertisers can only bid on ad space from a finite amount of publishers that contract with a particular ad exchange. Thus, since advertisers are limited in the amount of publishers they can reach, they are equally limited in the amount of users they can access as well. Essentially, the ad exchange model alone still leaves advertisers requiring a way to be able to reach across the entire online advertising industry and participate in real-time bidding on ad space from publishers in and outside their ad exchange.

5. Reaching Across the Online Advertising Industry: Demand-Side Platforms

Demand-side platforms (DSPs) are companies that allow advertisers to extend their "virtual" reach across the online advertising ecosystem. Instead of participating with a single ad exchange, advertisers contract with a DSP, which then enters multiple ad exchanges on behalf of the advertiser. This allows advertisers more access to users who view websites owned by different publishers that contract with different ad exchanges.

In the example below, the shoe company might have an advertisement targeted toward sports fans aged 18-24. The shoe company would send this information to a DSP, which then scans the ad exchanges for bids on websites viewed by sports fans aged 18-24. The DSP may find two ad exchanges that are currently auctioning ad space on the sports news website and a sporting goods store's website respectively, which have just been accessed by members of the shoe company's target audience. The DSP enters a bidding process on behalf of the shoe company and wins the ad space in both ad exchanges. The shoe company's advertisement is then transmitted and displayed to the particular users on the sports news website and the sporting goods store's website, which both meet the shoe company's target audience criteria. Supply-side platforms work in the same manner, but on the publisher side instead of the advertiser side. They enter multiple exchanges for publishers in order to find the highest-bid advertiser.

---

[70] J. Howard Beales and Jeffrey Eisenach, *An Empirical Analysis Of The Value Of Information Sharing in the Market for Online Content*, NAVIGANT ECONOMICS, 2014, https://www.aboutads.info/resource/fullvalueinfostudy.pdf.
[71] Webinar, OPENX, *supra* note 45.

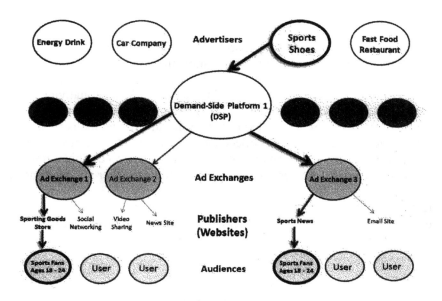

Figure 7. Online advertising process with a demand-side platform.

d. The Role of Self-Regulatory Groups

Although the FTC can and does bring enforcement actions against individual companies, self-regulatory groups currently generate the most specific standards for the behavior of companies in the online advertising industry. Many online advertising companies adhere to standards generated by the Digital Advertising Alliance (DAA) and Network Advertising Initiative (NAI) that govern behavioral advertising and data collection.

Each of those organizations has put forward a code with general guidelines for companies that engage in online advertising. These codes are predominately written and approved by major industry players, with varying, but limited, levels of consumer input.[72] Those organizations do not deal in large part with security issues pertaining to malware in online advertising.

---

[72] In an interview with the Subcommittee, NAI noted that while consumers have ability to comment on proposed rule changes, ultimate approval authority feel to NAI's Board of Directors, comprised of industry representatives. IAB also told the Subcommittee that consumers have a limited role in their rulemaking process. Interview with Marc Groman, President and CEO, Network Advertising Initiative, in Wash., D.C. (Jan. 31, 2014).

e. Data Brokers

The FTC has defined "data brokers" as "companies that collect information, including personal information about consumers, from a wide variety of sources for the purpose of reselling such information to their customers for various purposes, including verifying an individual's identity, differentiating records, marketing products, and preventing financial fraud."[73] In the context of the online advertising industry, the information that data brokers collect and then resell to online businesses (advertisers, ad networks, ad exchanges, publishers, etc.) can help those companies compile data on particular users and then better target online advertisements to those individuals. Yet, many concerns have been raised about the lack of transparency regarding the practices of data brokers, specifically the data brokers' ability to collect a wealth of information on consumers without the consumer ever knowing that this collection is taking place.[74]

In December 2013, the U.S. Senate Committee on Commerce, Science, and Transportation released a Majority Staff Report that focused on the data broker industry and highlighted data broker activities regarding the collection, use, and sale of consumer data for marketing purposes.[75] The staff report found that data brokers collect a vast amount of detailed information on millions of consumers including data points on people's financial status, what type of car they drive, what types of pets they have, and even whether the consumer is suffering from a medical condition.[76] Additionally, the staff report found that many data brokers, without any consumer permission or knowledge, create profiles of consumers that are financially vulnerable and sell that information to other businesses that are targeting individuals in need of quick cash, loans, or other financial products.[77]

The report found that data brokers combine information on consumers collected both online and "offline" in order to compile the most complete set of data points about a particular person. Essentially, in addition to collecting consumer information online from sources on the Internet, data brokers also store and sell information on consumers

---

[73] Fed. Trade. Comm'n., PROTECTING CONSUMER PRIVACY IN AN ERA OF RAPID CHANGE, at 68 (Mar. 2012), http://www.ftc.gov/sites/default/files/documents/reports/federal-trade-commission-report-protecting-consumer-privacy-era-rapid-change-recommendations/120326privacyreport.pdf (hereinafter "FTC 2012 Privacy Report").
[74] *Id.*
[75] Majority Staff of S. Comm. on Commerce, Science, and Transportation, A REVIEW OF THE DATA BROKER INDUSTRY: COLLECTION, USE, AND SALE OF CONSUMER DATE FOR MARKETING PURPOSES, (Dec. 2013), http://op.bna.com/der.nsf/id/sbay-9ehtxt/$File/Rockefeller%20report%20on%20data%20brokers.pdf (hereinafter "Sen. Commerce Committee Data Broker Report").
[76] *Id* at ii.
[77] *Id.*

29

concerning their activities offline including purchases and interests.[78] There is little a consumer can do to "opt-out" of their offline activities. Moreover, given the "veil of secrecy" behind which data brokers operate, it is unclear the extent to which consumers can limit data brokers' access to their personal information that is compiled and eventually sold without consumer consent or knowledge.[79]

---

[78] *Id* at 30.

[79] *Id* at iii.

III. ONLINE ADVERTISING AND HIDDEN HAZARDS TO CONSUMER SECURITY AND DATA PRIVACY

Through its investigation, the Subcommittee identified a number of hidden hazards to consumers in the online advertising industry. Prominent among these hazards is malicious software ("malware") delivered through online advertising without any clicks or interaction by a user. Furthermore, the data collection that makes online advertising possible also allows cybercriminals to target their activities against vulnerable users. As the online advertising industry becomes more and more complex and fragmented, there may be less accountability for individual participants. Although the companies themselves also suffer reputational or other damage from these attacks, consumers are often left with little, if any, meaningful remedy for their damages. Self-regulatory bodies could provide stronger oversight to ensure safety in the online advertising arena from these sorts of hazards.

a. Case Studies: Emerging Dangers in Online Advertising

The Subcommittee's investigation revealed a number of dangers to online users which have already caused significant damage to consumers. For each vulnerability, Subcommittee staff identified actual cases where the vulnerability has already been exploited.

> *1. Malware From Online Advertising Can Do Damage Without Clicks: YouTube/Google Ad Attack, February 2014*

Two of the most important facts discovered by the Subcommittee in its investigation are (1) that malware in online advertising often does not require any clicking on ads by the user, and (2) malware delivered through advertising is found on the most reputable, most popular sites on the Internet and can be delivered through the biggest, most technologically sophisticated ad networks. One incident that highlights both points was a malware attack through Google's ad network that was delivered to users on YouTube.[80]

In February 2014, a security engineer discovered that a YouTube link was hosting malware. When she followed up on the lead, she discovered that the malware was actually delivered via an advertisement.[81] A user did not actually need to click on any ads on YouTube; just watching a video was enough to lead to an infection.[82]

---

[80] McEnroe Navaraj, *The Wild Wild Web: YouTube ads serving malware*, BROMIUM LABS CALL OF THE WILD BLOG (Feb. 21, 2014), http://labs.bromium.com/2014/02/21/the-wild-wild-web-youtube-ads-serving-malware.
[81] *Id.*
[82] *Id.*

The malware in question would examine a consumer's computer and, when it found whatever machines fit its criteria, it would release a "banking Trojan" virus—designed to break into online bank accounts and transfer funds to a cybercriminal's account.[83] That malware was designed to target users with unpatched versions of Internet Explorer. Google worked with the security engineer to identify the exact ads in question and took steps to prevent a recurrence of similar attacks.[84]

An unwitting consumer who visited YouTube and encountered this malware would have no opportunity to protect herself from potential financial ruin. If she suffered an attack, she would have little recourse unless she managed to track down the cybercriminal who launched the attack, an almost impossible task for security professionals and completely beyond the capabilities of an ordinary consumer.

2. *The Complexity of the Online Advertising Industry Leads to Multiple Points of Vulnerability: Major League Baseball's Website Delivers Malware, June 2012.*

The vision of the online advertising industry as companies that simply connect website publishers and advertisers does not reflect the multiple layers of complexity that have been added over the past decade. A routine advertisement often goes through five or six intermediaries before ending upon a user's browser. The advertiser will often work through a separate advertising agency, marketer, ad exchange, demand-side platform, *and* ad network before an ad actually reaches the user's browser. Each time one of those entities passes along a call for an advertisement, there is an opportunity for the introduction of malware. With more opportunities for bad software to enter the system, each participant has a better case to make that it is not responsible for system-wide security, and it becomes that much more difficult to determine where along the chain something went wrong.

One incident where this point was made clear was the website of Major League Baseball (MLB) in June 2012.[85] Many visitors to MLB's popular website MLB.com were exposed to a malicious advertisement that, when clicked on, downloaded a virus to the user's computer.[86] This malicious ad, which had the potential to impact 300,000 users, was delivered to MLB.com through a compromised ad network that began

---

[83] *Id.*

[84] Interview with Google in Wash., D.C (May 12, 2014).

[85] The Subcommittee did not speak with Major League Baseball and based its analysis on expert testimony and publicly available information.

[86] Evan Keiser, *MLB.com distributing Fake AV Malware via compromised Ad Network*, SILVERSKY ALTITUDE BLOG (Jun. 18, 2012), https://www.silversky.com/blog/mlbcom-distributing-fake-av-malware-compromised-ad-network.

distributing malware.[87] The ad in question was an advertisement for luxury watches that was displayed as a banner at the top of the MLB webpage.

Figure 8. A screenshot of MLB.com which shows the malicious ad at the top of the webpage.[88]

According to reports, when users clicked on the ad, they were prompted to download fake anti-virus software that "pretends to scan the victim's computer, find files it claims are infected, and then attempts to get the victim to purchase the 'Full Version' to remove the non-existent threats for the low, low price of $99.99."[89]

This malware attack only came to light after it was discovered by an online security company, Perimeter's Security Operations Center. Researchers from that company suspected that this attack was a result of an infected ad network that distributed the malicious ad to MLB.com. Evan Keiser, a security analyst at Perimeter described vulnerabilities in the online advertising industry that resulted in the MLB malvertising attack:

> "Sadly, this has become an extremely common issue: well-known and respected websites inadvertently distribute malware due to one of their hosted syndicated ads being compromised... The website operator provides a spot [...] where an ad network loads its ads. Many of these ad networks, in turn, load content from syndication partners and from other ad networks. At some point down the chain, one of these partners source the web ad from the advertiser's web server. Because of the multiple layers of syndication between the website and originating ad server, it can be often very hard to understand exactly where the ad actually originated. It's only a

---

[87]Dan Raywood, *Major League Baseball website hit by malvertising that may potentially impact 300,000 users*, SC MAGAZINE UK (Jun. 20, 2012), http://www.scmagazineuk.com/major-league-baseball-website-hit-by-malvertising-that-may-potentially-impact-300000-users/article/246503.
[88] Fahmida Y. Rashid, *MLB.com Serving Fake Antivirus Via Malicious Online Ads*, SECURITY WATCH (Jun. 19, 2012), http://securitywatch.pcmag.com/none/299326-mlb-com-serving-fake-antivirus-via-malicious-online-ads.
[89] Keiser, *supra* note 86.

slight exaggeration to say that the lack of transparency and multiple indirect relationships can be so complicated that the average ad network makes the Fulton Fish Market look like the New York Stock Exchange by comparison."[90]

The fact that the source of an attack can remain a mystery even after detection further highlights the lack of accountability within the online advertising industry. Incentives to provide security are weakened by the fact that many malware attacks are either never discovered or never publicly attributed to a particular ad network or other online advertising entity.

3. Online Advertising Malware Attack Coordinated to Hit at Vulnerable Times: Yahoo Malware Attack, December 2013-January 2014

As anyone who works in an office can attest, Friday afternoons can sometimes bring a lull in activity. Federal holidays are another time when office staffing is minimized. Cybercriminals who exploit the online advertising industry are aware of those facts as well. They deliberately coordinate their attacks to commence at a time when they believe there are as few quality-control personnel at the various advertising companies as possible. Law enforcement personnel have even discovered calendars at the office and residences of cybercriminals in Russia with all federal holidays carefully marked and noted.[91]

On Friday, December 27, 2013—two days after Christmas and four days before New Year's Eve—cybercriminals began injecting malware-ridden advertisements into Yahoo's ad network. While Yahoo had security personnel working through the holidays, the cybercriminals in question were nevertheless successful in their attack. The malware-infected advertisements continued to run until January 3, 2014, when Yahoo discovered the problem, took the ads off their network, and initiated tighter security protocols to prevent future attacks.[92] Though Yahoo initially reported that the advertisements were delivered only to Internet users in Europe,[93] later reports suggest that machines outside of the European Union were also compromised.[94]

---

[90] Id.

[91] Interview with Craig Spiezle, Executive Director and President, Online Trust Alliance, in Wash., D.C. (Mar. 19, 2014).

[92] Yahoo provided the Subcommittee with a detailed briefing concerning the causes of the breach and company's response. The Subcommittee relied on public information when summarizing the event in order to protect Yahoo's confidential security practices.

[93] Faith Karimi and Joe Sutton, *Malware attack hits thousands of Yahoo users per hour*, CNN (Jan. 6, 2014), http://www.cnn.com/2014/01/05/tech/yahoo-malware-attack.

[94] Chris Smith, *Yahoo ad malware attack far greater than anticipated*, YAHOO NEWS (Jan. 13, 2014), http://news.yahoo.com/yahoo-ad-malware-attack-far-greater-anticipated-114523608.html.

34

The malware in question spread without the need for user interaction. Users did not need to click on suspicious-looking ads.[95] Indeed, the advertisement in question was not even visible to the victims who visited ordinary websites. Instead, when a user visited a website with Yahoo ads delivered, the user's browser, at Yahoo's direction, contacted the advertiser's server, which delivered malware to the user's browser instead of the image of an advertisement. The malware then seized control of the user's computer and used it to generate Bitcoins, a digital currency that requires a tremendous amount of computer power to actually create.[96]

In this case, the advertisement made it past Yahoo's security protocols because a hacker had gained access to a Yahoo employee's account and approved the malicious advertisement in question.[97] The attack utilized Yahoo's ad network as a delivery system, but gained access to that system through the sort of hacking that has been going on for years.

Independent security firms estimate that around 27,000 computers were infected through this one malware-laden advertisement.[98] Around 300,000 visitors were exposed to the advertisement, yielding an infection rate of around 9 percent.[99] The virus in question would not trigger on any random computer, but only ones with particular operating systems and programs,[100] making the virus even more difficult to detect through the ordinary scanning implemented by ad networks and security firms and discussed in detail in the next section.[101]

That vulnerability within the network emerged simply because a single Yahoo employee's account was compromised. The Subcommittee's investigation indicates that other ad networks may also be vulnerable to that method of attack. Yahoo, it appears, meets industry standard practice for security in its advertisements. However, the industry standard appears to fall short of the level required to comprehensively protect consumers who visit popular websites from malvertising.

---

[95] Interview with Yahoo, in Wash., D.C. (Jan. 16, 2014).

[96] Chris Smith, *Yahoo ad malware hijacked computers for Bitcoin mining*, BGR (Jan. 9, 2014), http://bgr.com/2014/01/09/yahoo-malware-bitcoin-mining.

[97] Interview with Yahoo, in Wash., D.C. (Jan. 16, 2014).

[98] Karimi and Sutton, *supra* note 93.

[99] *Id.*

[100] The attack targeted Windows users with non-updated version of Java.

[101] *Id.*

4. *Ad Networks Do Not Directly Deliver the*
   Advertisements They Place, Limiting the Effectiveness
   of Their Security Measures: "JS:Prontexi" Malware
   Attack on Multiple Ad Networks, 2010

As discussed in the Background section, ad networks do not deliver the actual image or substantive advertisement (referred to in the online advertising industry as the "creative") that appears on a consumer's browser. Because the ad network must engage in millions of these information exchanges each second, it needs a tremendous amount of bandwidth even to simply retrieve small cookie text files. If the ad network were to host the images for each advertisement itself, its bandwidth needs could be thousands of times greater because image files are so much larger than simple text files. To save on bandwidth and decrease the amount of time it takes to load webpages, the images for the advertisements are kept on another server, which is many times owned by an entity separate from the advertiser.

Because ad networks do not deliver the advertisements they place, they need to perform quality control on the advertisements through two basic processes: human oversight and automated scanning. Ad networks regularly deliver millions of ads per minute, a computationally intensive process requiring powerful networked servers. Ads must be selected and delivered in well-under a second, and consequently there is pressure to deliver ads quickly and not tie up server resources and time doing quality control.

Scanning is the automated process in place for quality-control purposes and is actually a reasonably simple concept. The scanning process replicates a situation in which machines located at a few locations around the world load webpages where advertisements run and monitor what they actually do when running on a user browser. When the advertisements are run through scanning processes, they are tested against multiple browser types, decomposed into component parts, and tested for known viruses or calls to known malicious URLs.[102]

Cybercriminals routinely attempt to circumvent scanning with several inventive tactics. First, just like ordinary advertisers, cybercriminals can target their malware to execute on only certain devices in specific geographic locations.[103] In the most basic sense, if the cybercriminals know that the scanners are located in, for example, Palo Alto and New York City, they might direct their malware-laden advertisements to run only in Ames, Iowa. Second, cybercriminals are

---

[102] Interview with Alex Stamos, Yahoo, in Wash., D.C. (May 12, 2014).
[103] Interview with Craig Spiezle, Executive Director and President, Online Trust Alliance, in Wash., D.C. (Mar. 19, 2014).

becoming increasingly adept targeting the types of machines and operating systems their ads run on. With a plethora of machines and operating systems to choose from, it is almost impossible for scanners to test every device and every configuration.

Those deficiencies help explain how one particular malware attack, the "JS:Prontexi" virus, avoided detection by many major online advertising companies in 2010.[104] The spread of that malware was one of the first published accounts where an advertising malware threat occurred with no user interaction or clicks. JS:Prontexi targeted only Windows operating system users and specialized further by focusing on vulnerabilities in Adobe Reader, Adobe Acrobat, Flash, Java, and QuickTime.[105] Over the course of four months, the JS:Prontexi virus spread to 2.6 million computers.[106] 16,300 of those instances of the virus were delivered through Google's subsidiary DoubleClick, and another 530,000 were from a Yahoo-controlled ad network.[107] The JS:Prontexi virus spread for over four months before its existence was disclosed to the public by a security company.[108]

Both Yahoo and Google claimed at the time to have detected the malicious advertisement, but apparently only after many users' computers were infected with the JS:Prontexi virus.[109] The difficulty that even the most sophisticated ad networks face in providing comprehensive security suggests that the countless other entities that comprise the online advertising industry may also struggle to maintain security at their companies.

5. Epic Marketplace and the Limitations of Self-Regulatory Bodies, 2010-2011

The online advertising industry's self-regulatory groups are tasked with maintaining industry standards for privacy and security. The theory of self-regulation is that membership in such a regulatory body is an indication to consumers of quality and trustworthiness. Many online advertisers hold up their membership in such organizations as evidence of the propriety of their operations.[110] The Subcommittee's investigation has found few instances of companies being expelled or

---

[104] Elinor Mills, *Malware delivered by Yahoo, Fox, Google ads*, CNET (Mar. 22, 2010), http://www.cnet.com/news/malware-delivered-by-yahoo-fox-google-ads.
[105] *Id.*
[106] *Id.*
[107] *Id.*
[108] *Id.*
[109] *Id.*
[110] *See, e.g.*, Turn, Inc. "Social Responsibility", ("As an industry leader, Turn participates actively in industry groups—IAB, DAA, and NAI—that are establishing safety mechanisms, implementing best practices, and enforcing guidelines to safeguard consumer privacy."), http://www.turn.com/company/social-responsibility.

suspended from one of these organizations for non-compliance with the organization's code. Even after wrongdoing is discovered by entities other than the regulators, offending companies are sometimes not suspended or excluded from membership in any of those organizations.

For example, in March 2010, Epic Marketplace, an online advertising company, began to engage in "history sniffing," a method by which a company can determine whether a consumer has previously visited a webpage by examining how the user's browser displays hyperlinks (purple indicating visited hyperlinks, blue indicating non-visited hyperlinks.)[111] History sniffing can be an even more powerful tool for data collection than cookies—it enables companies to record user visits to websites outside of its cookie network.

Through this practice, Epic Marketplace could see that users had visited pages relating to, among other things, fertility issues, impotence, menopause, incontinence, disability insurance, credit repair, debt relief, and personal bankruptcy.[112] Based on that knowledge, Epic Marketplace could identify user interest segments in those areas and use the information for targeted advertisements.[113]

The practice was discovered by Stanford Security Lab in July 2011. Epic Marketplace's privacy policy had stated that "[w]eb surfers may elect not to provide non-personally identifiable information by following the cookie opt-out procedures set forth [on its website]."[114] Because Epic Marketplace's history sniffing contradicted its privacy policy, the FTC brought an enforcement action against Epic Marketplace. The FTC approved a final order settling charges against Epic Marketplace in March 2013.[115]

Epic Marketplace was a member of NAI at the time the practice came to light. Despite that fact, NAI's audits did not discover Epic Marketplace's history sniffing practice. Once Epic Marketplace's misbehavior came to light, NAI said that it would launch its own

---

[111] Complaint, *In the Matter of Epic Marketplace, Inc. et al.*, No. C-4389 (Mar. 13, 2013), http://www.ftc.gov/sites/default/files/documents/cases/2013/03/130315epicmarketplacecmpt.pdf.
[112] *Id.* at 2.
[113] *Id.*
[114] Jonathan Mayer, *Tracking the Trackers: To Catch a History Thief*, THE CENTER FOR INTERNET AND SOCIETY, STANFORD LAW SCHOOL (July 19, 2011), http://cyberlaw.stanford.edu/node/6695.
[115] Press Release, Fed. Trade Comm'n, FTC Approves Final Order Settling Charges Against Epic Marketplace, Inc. (Mar. 19, 2013), http://www.ftc.gov/news-events/press-releases/2013/03/ftc-approves-final-order-settling-charges-against-epic. The terms of the settlement barred further violations and imposed a $16,000 penalty for any violations of the consent decree.

investigation.[116] During that time, Epic Marketplace remained an NAI member, subjected merely to additional auditing requirements.[117] Subsequently, Epic Marketplace went out of business, removing it from NAI's membership lists.

To the extent that the self-regulatory codes are binding, actual detection and punishment of noncompliance is remarkably rare. NAI recently completed its 2013 Compliance Report and, after reviewing 88 members, "NAI still did not find any material noncompliance with [its] Code."[118]

6. Direct Sales of Advertisements are Subject to Compromise: New York Times Malware Attack, 2009

Some major websites sell their advertising through direct sales to advertisers, bypassing most of the technology companies who have traditionally dominated the online advertising industry. Direct sales can, in some ways, be beneficial for security: with fewer parties involved, there are fewer ways in which criminals can slip in malware. As one security researcher noted: "I think there is a problem with ad networks, in general. . . . The problem really is with Web sites handing over control of some of their content to third parties."[119]

By avoiding the major technology companies, however, websites using direct sales have to come up with their own quality control processes, which can be subverted in some cases.[120] One example is the *New York Times* website's front-page malware attack of 2009.

In September 2009, the *New York Times* sold advertising space on its website using both third-party ad networks and direct sales. An advertiser claiming to represent the Internet telephony company Vonage contacted the *New York Times* offering to purchase advertising space on NYTimes.com.[121] Vonage had previously run advertisements through the *New York Times*, so the newspaper allowed a third-party vendor it was unfamiliar with to actually deliver the ad. For several weeks, the advertiser submitted wholly legitimate-looking advertisements, which

---

[116] NAI Compliance, *An Update on NAI Compliance*, NETWORK ADVERTISING INITIATIVE COMPLIANCE BLOG (Oct. 20, 2011), https://www.networkadvertising.org/blog/update-nai-compliance.

[117] *Id.*

[118] Network Advertising Initiative, 2013 ANNUAL COMPLIANCE REPORT (2013), http://www.networkadvertising.org/2013_NAI_Compliance_Report.pdf.

[119] Elinor Mills, *Ads—the new malware delivery format*, CNET (Sept. 15, 2009), http://www.cnet.com/news/ads-the-new-malware-delivery-format.

[120] The incidents in this section are all drawn from publicly available reports, not interviews with the parties involved.

[121] Ashlee Vance, *Times Web Ads Show Security Breach*, N.Y. TIMES (Sept. 14, 2009), http://www.nytimes.com/2009/09/15/technology/internet/15adco.html?_r=2&.

the *New York Times* ran without incident.[122] Then, at the beginning of a weekend, the advertiser replaced the Vonage advertisements with an ad proclaiming that the user's computer was not safe, and that the user should purchase fake antivirus software to protect her computer.[123] That fake antivirus software, once placed on a user's computer, could steal personal data and extort money from consumers hoping to make the virus go away.[124]

The *New York Times* is not the only company victimized by fraudulent advertisers. It is not even the only newspaper that has experienced this type of incident. The website of the *San Francisco Chronicle* (SFGate.com) suffered a similar attack on the same weekend in 2009 as the *New York Times*. One common attack method is to generate an email address that is close or identical to the name of a well-known company and then contact a website claiming to represent that company. Cybercriminals routinely inject malware in that manner, posing as legitimate companies such as Lexus.[125] The online music service Spotify was hit with a malicious advertisement within its desktop program in 2011.[126] User's computers were affected without having to click on any advertisements, and the event led Spotify to shut off all advertising for third parties until it could identify the source of the problem.[127]

These examples illustrate how the infrastructure of online advertising can be subverted for malicious purposes even when the ad networks are not involved. Additional oversight is required in order to validate the identities of would-be advertisers. In many cases, unfortunately, that sort of examination is either not performed, or it is performed in only the most perfunctory manner.

> 7. *First-Party Websites' Cookie Usage Depends Heavily on Extent to Which Online Traffic is the Website's Sole Source of Profit*

Companies that primarily provide free content on the Internet logically must find alternative ways of generating revenue. Selling advertising space is the obvious solution, and the more targeted those

---

[122] *Id.*

[123] *Id.*

[124] *Id.*

[125] Mills, *supra* note 119.

[126] Patrik Runald, *Spotify application serves malicious ads*, WEBSENSE (March 25, 2011), http://community.websense.com/blogs/securitylabs/archive/2011/03/25/spotify-application-serves-malicious-ads.aspx.

[127] Spotify, "We've turned off all 3rd party display ads that could have caused it until we find the exact one." (Mar. 25, 2011, 4:44 AM), Tweet, https://twitter.com/Spotify/status/51248179039059968.

advertisements are, the more advertisers will pay.[128] The placement of cookies and other tracking mechanisms thus becomes more important for websites dependent on advertising. The online advertising industry is teeming with data brokers willing to pay for the right to retrieve information from cookies.[129]

Using Disconnect, an application which detects when a user's browser is directed to a third-party server (the necessary step to placing or retrieving a third-party cookie), the Subcommittee examined a number of websites to determine the number of third-party servers involved when a consumer visits a particular website. The number of calls to third-party servers varied significantly from site to site. It also varied significantly within the same website, depending on the particular page visited or time of day.[130] However, based on Subcommittee analysis, broad trends emerged. The Subcommittee has observed that websites offering free content tended to have a great number of third-party server calls than websites offering goods or services. These relationships with third parties are potentially a large source of revenue for high traffic websites.

---

[128] Julia Angwin, *The Web's New Gold Mine: Your Secrets*, THE WALL STREET JOURNAL (July 30, 2010), http://online.wsj.com/news/articles/SB10001424052748703940904575395073512989404; see also Bryce Cullinane, *Cookies For Sale? How Websites Obtain Permission to Track and Sell Online User Data*, MIRSKY & COMPANY, PLLC BLOG (Feb. 19, 2013), http://mirskylegal.com/2013/02/how-websites-obtain-permission-to-track-and-sell-online-user-data.

[129] Sen. Commerce Committee Data Broker Report, *supra* note 75.

[130] For example, of the websites tested, none that had more than 100 third-party server calls ever had fewer than 100. Some websites would go as low as 120 third-party server calls on one visit and as high as 1500 at other times. The figures listed in this report are all from specific test visits and are representative of the sites in question. All of the websites listed were checked at the same time of the day and week to correct for any increases in advertising activity to correspond with high or low-traffic times.

For example, a visit to the website of TDBank, a consumer bank, led to only 11 calls to third-party servers:

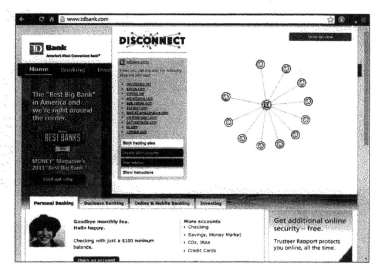

Figure 9. A screenshot of TDBank.com with the Disconnect display identifying third-party server calls.

By contrast, a visit to TMZ.com, whose business model is heavily dependent on Internet traffic, yielded *352* calls to third-party servers.[131]

Figure 10. A screenshot of TMZ.com with the Disconnect display identifying third-party server calls.

In between those two extremes, ESPN—a dynamic company with a suite of business, including activities based on offering free Internet

---

[131] TMZ.com. Third-party server activity measured on Apr. 26, 2014.

42

content as well as other cable broadcasting services—had 83 calls to third-party servers.[132]

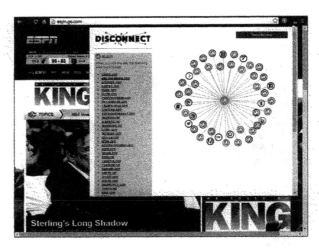

Figure 11. *A screenshot of ESPN.com with the Disconnect display identifying third-party server calls.*

The Subcommittee observed a similar trend with other websites—the extent to which a company's business model depended on online traffic was a strong predictor of the number of calls to third-party servers. Ford, whose profits derive primarily from its automobile sales, not primarily high Internet traffic, also had 18 calls to third-party servers from its website.[133] The Drudge Report, a solely Internet-based news site, had 326 calls to third-party servers.[134] Bank of America had 11 third-party server calls. AT&T had 32 calls to third-party servers.[135] Senate.gov, the website of the U.S. Senate, had no third-party server calls.[136] Wikipedia, wholly dependent on donations from visitors instead of advertising, also had no third-party server calls. Amazon.com, which takes in revenue from sales of goods, had only a single third-party server call.[137]

The results of the Subcommittee's survey suggest a basic problem: data is valuable, and the more a website depends on traffic rather than non-Internet-based revenue, the more it seems to be willing to forge relationships with third parties that may pay to collect that data. As Internet-based companies become a greater portion of the economy, one could reasonably expect that sales of data to third parties will only increase further.

---

[132] Espn.go.com. Third-party server activity measured on Apr. 26, 2014.

[133] Ford.com. Third-party server activity measured from a test visit on Apr. 26, 2014.

[134] DrudgeReport.com. Third-party server activity measured from a test visit on Apr. 26, 2014.

[135] BankofAmerica.com. Third-party server activity measured from a test visit on Apr. 26, 2014.

[136] Senate.gov. Third-party server activity measured from a test visit on Apr. 26, 2014.

[137] Amazon.com. Third-party server activity measured from a test visit on Apr. 28, 2014.

b. Current Online Advertising Regulatory Authorities Do Not Adequately Address Security Concerns in Advertising

Congress has not enacted comprehensive data-security legislation to guide industry standards and establish enforcement benchmarks for federal enforcement agencies to follow. Instead, the Federal Trade Commission (FTC) has regulated the online advertising industry primarily under its authority found in Section 5 of the Federal Trade Commission Act ("FTC Act").[138] Under Section 5 of the FTC Act, the FTC is empowered to begin enforcement actions, levy fines, and seek injunctions against companies that engage in "unfair" or "deceptive" practices.[139]

Following an investigation, the FTC has the authority to initiate an enforcement action against a company if it has "reason to believe" that the law has been violated.[140] The legislative history indicates that Congress intentionally used the general terms of "unfair" and "deceptive" because it believed that providing a list of unfair or deceptive practices would have inevitably left loopholes susceptible to easy evasion.[141] Thus, the FTC was given the task of determining and identifying unfair or deceptive practices through notice and comment rulemaking, on-the-record adjudication, and policy statements.

1. Deceptive Practices Enforcement

To date, the FTC has brought several deceptive practices cases against companies involved in online advertising. However, that enforcement authority essentially requires that a company publicly state a policy that is contradicted by its actions. Thus, FTC deceptive practices enforcement in the online advertising industry has stopped a few clear violations, but has not meaningfully changed what practices are generally considered acceptable.

An act or practice is deceptive when there is (1) representation, omission, or practice, which misleads or is likely to mislead the consumer; (2) a consumer's interpretation of the representation, omission, or practice is considered reasonable under the circumstances;

---

[138] 15 U.S.C. § 45.

[139] *Id.*

[140] Fed. Trade Comm'n, *A Brief Overview of the Federal Trade Commission's Investigative and Law Enforcement Authority* (July 2008), http://www.ftc.gov/ogc/brfovrvw.shtm.

[141] See H.R.REP. NO. 63-1142, at 19 (1914) (Conf. Rep.) (observing if Congress "were to adopt the method of definition, it would undertake an endless task").

44

and (3) the misleading representation, omission, or practice is material.[142]

The most prominent FTC deceptive practices enforcement action to date involving the online advertising industry was against Google. In August 2012, Google agreed to pay a record $22.5 million civil penalty to settle FTC charges that it misrepresented its cookie and targeted-advertising practices to users of Apple Inc.'s Safari Internet browser.[143]

The FTC alleged that Google placed tracking cookies on Safari users who visited websites within Google's DoubleClick ad network. Google had previously told these users that they were automatically opted out from a Google tracking cookie because the default settings on the Safari browser blocked third party cookies. Google further represented that as a member of the self-regulatory organization, the Network Advertising Initiative, it was required to disclose its data collection and use practices. The FTC alleged that despite these promises, Google exploited a loophole in Safari's default setting to place a temporary DoubleClick cookie on user's computers. The initial tracking cookie, in turn, allowed additional tracking cookies from DoubleClick—including advertising tracking cookies that Google represented would be blocked from Safari browsers—to track user's Internet activities.[144] The FTC referred the matter to the Department of Justice on August 8, 2012 which then filed the complaint in the United States District Court for the District of Northern California in San Francisco.[145] District Judge Susan Illston approved the $22.5 million settlement agreement between the two parties on November 17, 2012.[146]

That settlement came after an October 2011 deceptive practices settlement that resolved charges that Google failed to follow its privacy promises when it launched its social network, Google Buzz. The settlement forced Google to implement a privacy program for Google Buzz, submit to FTC audits and reporting for 20 years and face $16,000 fines for any future privacy misrepresentations.[147]

---

[142] Interview with Lisa Harrison, General Counsel, Mark Acorn, Privacy, Molly Crawford, Bureau of Consumer Protection, Maneesha Mithal, Associate Director, Privacy and Identity Protection Division, Chris Olsen, Associate Director, Privacy and Identity Protection Division and Kim Vandecar, Congressional Liaison, Fed. Trade Comm'n. in Wash., D.C. (Mar. 21, 2014).
[143] Press Release, Fed. Trade Comm'n, Google Will Pay $22.5 Million to Settle FTC Charges It Misrepresented Privacy Assurances to Users of Apple's Safari Internet Browser (Aug. 9, 2013), http://www.ftc.gov/news-events/press-releases/2012/08/google-will-pay-225-million-settle-ftc-charges-it-misrepresented.
[144] Id.
[145] United States v. Google Inc., 3:12-cv-04177, U.S. District Court, Northern District of California (San Francisco).
[146] Sara Forden and Karen Gullo, Google Judge Accepts $22.5 Million FTC Privacy Settlement, BLOOMBERG (Nov. 17, 2012), http://www.bloomberg.com/news/2012-11-17/google-judge-accepts-22-5-million-ftc-privacy-settlement.html.
[147] Agreement Containing Consent Order, In re Google, Inc. File No. 102 3136 (Mar. 30, 2011).

While the FTC's enforcement actions against Google were among its most prominent, other deceptive practices enforcement actions have been levied against smaller companies. In March 2011, the Commission brought a deceptive practice action against the online advertising company, Chitika, Inc., alleging that it placed tracking cookies on consumers' browsers after they opted out of receiving targeted advertisements.

Chitika is an online ad network that engages in behavioral advertising. It uses cookies to track consumers' browsing activities online to serve them targeted advertisements based on that individual's Internet activity. When a consumer visits a website within Chitika's network of publishers, Chitika sets a new cookie or receives information from its tracking cookie that has already been imbedded on the user's browser.[148] The Chitika tracking cookie contains a unique identification number that allows the company to connect an Internet user's activity to a particular computer.[149] Each time a Chitika sets a new tracking cookie or receives information from a previously-placed tracking cookie, the company receives more information on the user to tailor advertisements to that particular user.[150] So long as a consumer visits a website in the Chitika network from the same browser on the same computer at least once a year, the consumer will indefinitely retain the Chitika tracking cookie on her browser.[151] Chitika's network consists of over 350,000 publishers and the information gathered within it helps the service of over 4 billion targeted ads per month.[152]

Internet users have the ability to "opt-out" of having Chitika tracking cookies placed on their browsers. When a user opts out, Chitika sets an "opt-out cookie" in the user's browser and when a user visits a website within Chitika's network, Chitika receives the opt-out cookie and does not place any subsequent tracking cookies on the user's browser. It also does not add any additional information to a previously set Chitika cookie or use the data from the cookie to target advertisements to the consumer. Chitika did not indicate how long the opt-out would last if a user opted out.

The FTC alleged that between May 2008 and February 2010, Chitika delivered opt-out cookies that automatically expired after ten days.[153] After the ten days expired, Chitika placed tracking cookies back on consumers' browsers who had opted out and targeted ads to them

---

[148] Complaint at 2, *In re Chitika, Inc.,* No. C-4324 (June 7, 2011).
[149] *Id.*
[150] *Id.*
[151] *Id.*
[152] Chitika Inc., *About Chitika,* http://chitika.com/about.
[153] Complaint at 3, *In re Chitika, Inc.* No. C-4324 (June 7, 2011).

again. The Commission alleged that Chitika's claims about its opt-out mechanism were "deceptive" within the meaning of Section 5.

Chitika settled its case with the Commission. The settlement agreement required Chitika to display a clear notice on their website explaining that it collects consumer data and offers an opt-out function.[154] It also prohibited Chitika from selling or transferring consumer data obtained prior to March 1, 2010 and ordered the company to permanently delete all information stored in Chitika user's cookies and all IP addresses collected while it employed a defective opt-out system.[155] Moreover, the agreement required that every targeted ad include a hyperlink that takes the consumer to a clear opt-out mechanism that allows the user to opt out for at least five years.[156] The order subjected Chitika to five years of FTC monitoring to ensure Chitika's compliance with the consent decree.[157]

One other example of the FTC's deceptive practice enforcement against the online advertising industry came in November 2011, when the FTC settled with the online advertiser, ScanScout. ScanScout is a video ad network that acts as an intermediary between publishers and advertisers. It engages in behavioral advertising, collecting information about consumers' online activities and to serve targeted ads based on the user's interest. The FTC alleged that from April 2007 to September 2009, ScanScout used Flash cookies to collect and store user data in its efforts to facilitate the behavioral targeting of video advertisements.[158] Flash cookies are not controlled through a computer's browser, so if a user tries to change her browsers' privacy settings to delete or block cookies, Flash cookies remain unaffected.[159] Since browsers could not block Flash cookies, users could not prevent ScanScout from collecting data on their Internet activities or from serving them targeted video advertisements.

From April 2007 until September 2009, ScanScout's privacy policy on its website stated in pertinent part, "[Users] can opt out of receiving a cookie by changing your browser settings to prevent the receipt of cookies."[160] The FTC alleged that this false statement constituted a deceptive act or practice in or affecting commerce in violation of Section 5.[161]

---

[154] Decision and Order at 3, *In re Chitika, Inc.*, No. C-4324 (June 7, 2011).
[155] *Id.* at 4.
[156] *Id.*
[157] *Id.* at 5.
[158] Complaint at 2, *In re ScanScout Inc.*, No. C-4344 (Dec. 14, 2011).
[159] *Id.*
[160] *Id.*
[161] *Id.* at 3.

The FTC and ScanScout entered into a settlement agreement on November 8, 2011, which was finalized on December 21, 2011. The settlement required ScanScout to host a notice on its website that read, "We collect information about your activities on certain websites to send you targeted ads. To opt out of our targeted advertisements click here."[162] When selected, the hyperlink takes consumers directly to an opt-out mechanism that allows them to prevent ScanScout from collecting information that can identify them or their computer; redirecting the user's browser to third parties that collect data without their approval; and associating any previously collected data with the user.[163] As part of the settlement, ScanScout submitted to five years of FTC monitoring for compliance with the order.

2. Unfair Practices Enforcement

To date, the FTC has not brought unfair practices enforcement actions against companies in the online advertising industry. That absence of enforcement largely reflects the lack of clear standards of conduct within the industry itself. FTC standards for unfair practice depend heavily on industry common practice and the standards set by self-regulatory bodies.

FTC officials informed the Subcommittee that an act or practice is unfair when it: (1) causes or is likely to cause substantial injury to consumers; (2) cannot be reasonably avoided by consumers; and (3) is not outweighed by countervailing benefits to consumers or to competition.[164] Industry standards and self-regulatory guidelines weigh heavily in the assessment of what constitutes reasonable actions for companies in a given industry.

3. FTC Enforcement Actions Against Online Advertisers Under Other Statutes

The FTC's authority to regulate online advertising under other statutes tends to be for very specific types of data. The most prominent examples include:

- the Children's Online Privacy Protection Act (COPPA),[165]
- the Fair Credit Reporting Act,[166]

---

[162] Decision and Order at 3-4, *In re ScanScout Inc.*, No C-4344 (Dec. 14, 2011).

[163] *Id.* at 4.

[164] Interview with Lisa Harrison, General Counsel, Mark Acorn, Privacy, Molly Crawford, Bureau of Consumer Protection, Maneesha Mithal, Associate Director, Privacy and Identity Protection Division, Chris Olsen, Associate Director, Privacy and Identity Protection Division and Kim Vandecar, Congressional Liaison, Fed. Trade Comm'n. in Wash., D.C. (Mar. 21, 2014).

[165] Pub. L. No. 105-277, 112 Stat. 2581-728, codified at 15 U.S.C. § 6501 (requiring covered website operators to establish and maintain procedures to protect the confidentiality and security of data gathered from children).

- the Gramm-Leach-Bliley Act,[167]
- the Health Insurance Portability and Accountability Act of 1996,[168]
- the Cable Television Consumer Protection and Competition Act,[169] and
- the Health Information Technology for Economic and Clinical Health Act.[170]

One specific enforcement action in the online advertising arena was brought under COPPA. That law was enacted in 1998 to protect the safety and privacy of children using the Internet. The legislation prohibits the unauthorized or unnecessary collection of children's personal information online by operators of Internet websites or online services. The Commission promulgated regulations that applied to any "operator" of a website directed at children that has knowledge that it is collecting or maintaining children's personal information.[171] The FTC's rule under COPPA requires that website operators notify parents and obtain their consent before they collect, use, or disclose personal information from children under 13. The rule also requires that website operators post a privacy policy that is clear, understandable, and complete for users to read.

On March 26, 2012, the FTC filed an action in the United States District Court for the Northern District against RockYou, Inc., alleging that RockYou violated the FTC's COPPA rule. RockYou is a social game website where users could play games and use the site to upload photos from their computers or web, add captions, and choose music to create a slideshow.[172] Users were required to register with RockYou, using an email address and password, if they wanted to save or edit their slideshows. Registrants were also required to enter a birth year, gender, zip code and country with their registration.[173] RockYou stored the email addresses and passwords in their internal database.

---

[166] Pub. L. No. 108-159, 117 Stat. 1953, codified at 15 U.S.C. § 1681 (requiring the FTC and other agencies to develop rules for financial institutions aimed at reducing identity theft against consumers).

[167] Pub. L. No. 106-102, 113 Stat. 1338, codified at 15 U.S.C. § 6801 (instructing the FTC and federal banking agencies to promulgate data-security standards for financial institutions to protect against "unauthorized access to or use of" consumer financial records or information).

[168] Pub. L. No. 104-91, codified at 45 U.S.C. § 1320d (requiring health care providers to maintain security standards for electronically stored health care information).

[169] Pub. L. No. 102-385, 106 Stat. 1460, codified at 42 U.S.C. § 551 (forcing cable companies to enact policies aimed at preventing unauthorized access to certain subscriber information).

[170] Pub. L. No. 111-5, 123 Stat 115, codified at 42 U.S.C. § 17921 (requiring regulated entities to provide notice of unsecured breaches of health care information in particular instances).

[171] 16 C.F.R. Part 312.

[172] Complaint at 4, *United States v. RockYou, Inc.*, (N.D. Cal. filed Mar. 26, 2012), Civil Action No. 12-CV-1487, http://www.ftc.gov/sites/default/files/documents/cases/2012/03/120327rockyoucmpt.pdf.

[173] *Id.* at 5.

The Commission alleged that from December 2008 through January 2010, RockYou accepted approximately 179,000 registrations from children under the age of 13 without parent consent.[174] Since the website asked for registrant's date of birth and other personal information, RockYou fell within the FTC's definition of operator under the rule and it put children's personal information at risk because the slideshows that the children created could be shared online. Specifically, the FTC charged that RockYou violated the COPPA rule by: (1) failing to spell out its collection, use and disclosure policy for children's information; (2) failing to obtain verifiable parental consent before collecting children's personal information; and (3) failing to maintain reasonable procedures to protect the confidentiality, security, and integrity of personal information collected from children.[175]

RockYou and the FTC entered into a consent agreement and settlement order on March 27, 2012.[176] The consent decree enjoined RockYou from future collection of information from children online and forced the company to delete the information it had already collected in violation of the COPPA rule.[177] Moreover, the FTC fined RockYou $250,000 and ordered the company to post a link to the Commission's consumer education website on its own website for five years.[178] Finally, the settlement required RockYou to implement a data security program, submit compliance reports to the Commission allow security audits by independent third-party auditors every other year for 20 years.[179]

4. The FTC's 2010 Proposed Regulatory Framework

The FTC proposed a regulatory framework in December 2010 that noted several of the most pressing consumer hazards in the online advertising industry. That report cast strong doubt on the FTC's "notice-and-choice model," under which companies can avoid enforcement action so long as their privacy policies gave notice to consumers, who could then make an informed choice about whether to use a particular Internet service.[180] The FTC noted that "the notice-and-

---

[174] *Id.* at 7.

[175] Press Release, Fed. Trade Comm'n, FTC Charges That Security Flaws in RockYou Game Site Exposed 32 Million Email Addresses and Passwords (Mar. 27, 2012), http://www.ftc.gov/news-events/press-releases/2012/03/ftc-charges-security-flaws-rockyou-game-site-exposed-32-million.

[176] Consent Decree and Order for Civil Penalties, Injunction and Other Relief, *United States v. RockYou, Inc.*, No. 12-CV-1487, (N.D. Cal. 2012), http://www.ftc.gov/sites/default/files/documents/cases/2012/03/120327rockyouorder.pdf.

[177] *Id.* at 5-6.

[178] *Id.* at 7.

[179] *Id.* at 9.

[180] Fed. Trade. Comm'n., PROTECTING CONSUMER PRIVACY IN AN ERA OF RAPID CHANGE: A PROPOSED FRAMEWORK FOR BUSINESSES AND POLICYMAKERS, at iii (Dec. 2010),

choice model, as implemented, has led to long, incomprehensible privacy policies that consumers typically do not read, let alone understand."[181] Given the FTC's criticism of the model it had hitherto used in its enforcement actions, the need for some protection beyond formal notice seemed evident. The framework went on to suggest some basic principles for regulation, and tasked the businesses within the online advertising industry to come up with policies that matched those principles.

c. Incentives to Limit Responsibility for the Harmful Effects of Online Advertising

Many consumers have developed an expectation that web content delivered by reputable sources will be free of dangerous malware. The Subcommittee's investigation has determined that even the most sophisticated advertisers have difficulty guaranteeing consumer security due in part to numerous structural vulnerabilities in the online advertising model. The current state of law and regulation addressing online advertising is sparse, focusing mainly on criminal actors rather than the responsibilities of intermediaries. While still pursuing criminal actors, the responsibility of industry and private stakeholders to implement precautionary measures should be clarified. The current structure leaves consumers with no recourse when they are victim of a malware attack.

1. Ad-Hosting Websites Often Do Not Know What Advertisements Will be Run on Their Website

Websites that run advertisements delivered by ad networks almost never know all of the advertisers that will operate on their website on any given day. While the host websites can request that certain categories of advertisements be excluded (for example, violent or pornographic advertisements), they are often completely unaware of what advertisers end up operating on their websites until after the fact. Consequently, when a malicious advertisement is delivered to a visitor, the host website can plausibly claim that it had no idea of the danger.

2. Ad Networks do not Control the Advertisement Creative Directly

As discussed above, ad networks—among the most sophisticated technology companies in the world—generally do not have direct control over the advertisements they deliver. Because such control

---

http://www.ftc.gov/sites/default/files/documents/reports/federal-trade-commission-bureau-consumer-protection-preliminary-ftc-staff-report-protecting-consumer/101201privacyreport.pdf.
[181] *Id.*

would incur bandwidth costs and slow delivery, there is a clear disincentive to retain control over the advertisement's content. While there are reputational costs associated with malware attacks through ad networks, such costs are only realized if the attack is (a) detected and (b) linked to an advertisement delivered by that ad network. It is difficult for an ordinary consumer to even identify why, or even if, her computer has been compromised. Learning how and from what entity she acquired the malware in question is a near impossibility for the average consumer.

3. Self-Regulatory Groups do not Provide Sufficient Oversight on Security and Privacy issues

The online advertising industry self-regulatory groups are not currently stand-ins for comprehensive regulators. While they do generate codes and provide enforcement for privacy standards, they could improve their practices by expelling or publicly identifying members who are not in compliance with their codes. Industry participants should also expand their self-regulatory efforts into the security realm. While self-regulatory bodies have, in the privacy context, promulgated standards and rules, there have not been any similarly enforced standards regarding the threat from online advertising malware attacks. One industry effort to address security foundered reportedly due to members of the industry "desiring to refocus their resources on aggressively defending industry practices to policy groups and regulatory bodies."[182] New efforts, such as the recently launched Trust in Ads initiative, should strive to issue meaningful security standards to protect consumers.

\# \# \#

---

[182] Written Testimony of Craig D. Spiezle before the Senate Committee on Homeland Security & Government Affairs Permanent Subcommittee on Investigations, May 15, 2014; *see also* Caitlin Condon, *StopBadware steps down as leader of the Ads Integrity Alliance*, STOP BADWARE BLOG (Jan. 20, 2014), https://www.stopbadware.org/blog/2014/01/20/stopbadware-steps-down-as-leader-of-the-ads-integrity-alliance.

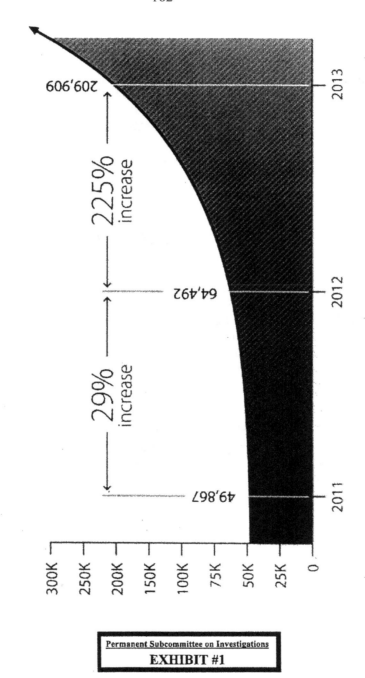

Increase Display Malvertising

209,909

225% increase

64,492

29% increase

49,867

300K
250K
200K
150K
100K
75K
50K
25K
0

2011   2012   2013

Source: RiskIQ

163

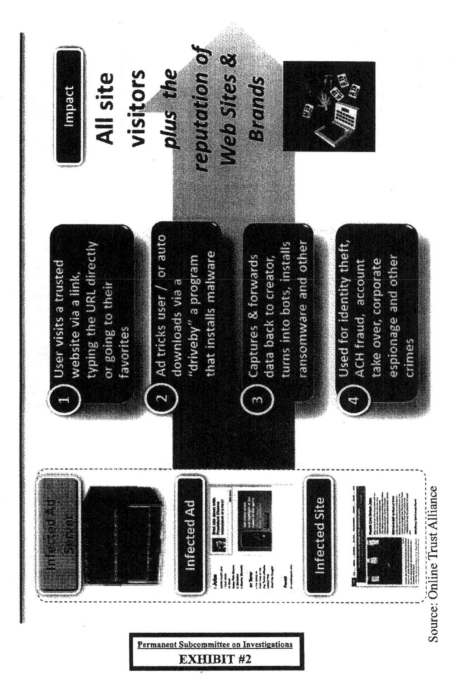

Proliferation & Impact

Impact

All site visitors _plus the reputation of Web Sites & Brands_

1. User visits a trusted website via a link, typing the URL directly or going to their favorites

2. Ad tricks user / or auto downloads via a "driveby" a program that installs malware

3. Captures & forwards data back to creator, turns into bots, installs ransomware and other

4. Used for identity theft, ACH fraud, account take over, corporate espionage and other crimes

Infected Ad Network

Infected Ad

Infected Site

Source: Online Trust Alliance

Third-Party Website Calls on TDBank.com

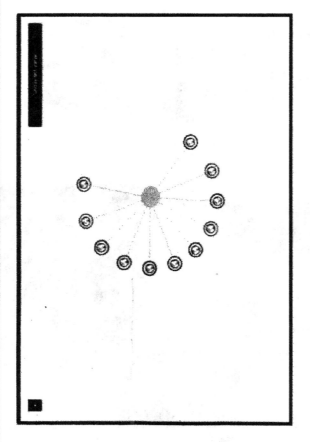

TD Bank

11 calls to third-party websites

Prepared by Permanent Subcommittee on Investigations, May 2014
Sources: TDBank.com, Disconnect Private Browsing

165

Third-Party Website Calls on TMZ.com

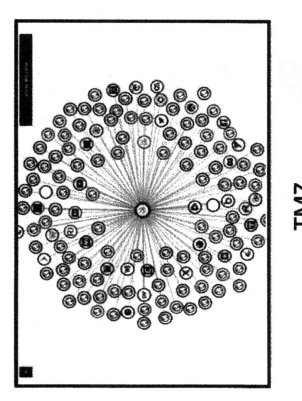

TMZ

Over 500 calls to third-party websites

Prepared by Permanent Subcommittee on Investigations, May 2014
Sources: TMZ.com, Disconnect Private Browsing

Permanent Subcommittee on Investigations
EXHIBIT #4

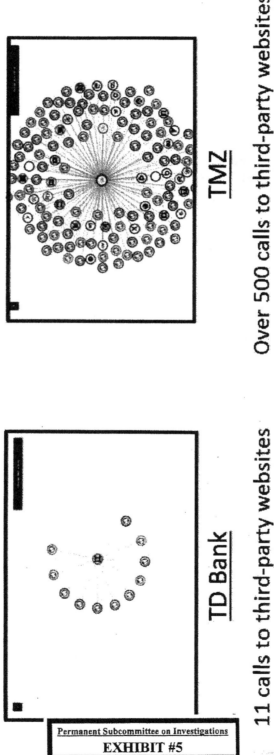

Comparison of Third-Party Website Calls

TD Bank

11 calls to third-party websites

TMZ

Over 500 calls to third-party websites

Prepared by Permanent Subcommittee on Investigations, May 2014
Sources: TDBank.com, TMZ.com, Disconnect Private Browsing

GOOD MONEY GONE BAD

Digital Thieves and the Hijacking of the Online Ad Business

A Report on the Profitability of
Ad-Supported Content Theft

February 2014

www.digitalcitizensalliance.org/followtheprofit

CONTENTS

TABLE OF REFERENCES

Figures

Tables

ABOUT THIS REPORT

In the early days of the Internet, content theft – also known as online piracy – was often shrugged off. While it significantly impacted the creative community – musicians, artists, movie studios and record producers who lost income for their creative works – it was typically viewed as the isolated activity of high school or college students who wanted to listen to music or watch movies for free. But as the Internet has become an increasingly pervasive force in the economy, the harm caused by content theft now extends well beyond the music and movie industries. It robs designers who rely on the Internet to sell their creations, hurts brands that find themselves associated with illegal and inappropriate sexual and violent content, funds online criminals and provides seed money for other illegal activities.

The future of the Internet depends on all users being able to trust that it will serve their interests.

When well-known premium brands, as well as other legitimate secondary brands, appear on content theft sites due to the "blind" sales channels through which most Internet advertising is sold, they involuntarily lend those sites an appearance of legitimacy that potentially deceives consumers. When those brands see their ads placed next to illegal content and bottom-feeder ads for sex trafficking or illegal drugs it makes these brands think twice about the Internet as a vehicle to reach their target audience. That, in turn, hurts consumers who benefit from an abundance of free-to-the-user – and legitimate – ad-supported content on the Internet. When designers and creators have their works stolen by unscrupulous operators, it makes them think twice about the Internet as a platform to launch or expand their business. And that hurts consumers who want online commerce to be robust, pervasive and trustworthy.

In short, ad-supported content theft has become a big business that harms a wide range of players in the digital economy and threatens the future of a free and open Internet. It cannot be dismissed as a benign act or victimless crime. It undermines our basic trust in the integrity of the platforms that make up the Internet.

As a society we need to protect the Internet from those who want to bleed it for their own profit while making it less attractive for generations to come. It is for this reason that Digital Citizens Alliance set out to understand how content thieves operate and profit from the works of others. To understand the problem fully, we have to follow the profits. In commissioning this study we seek to understand how bad actors make money through advertising, and how much they make.

It is important to note that the advertising *profits* garnered by content thieves do not equate with the *losses* incurred by the owners of the content. These losses are unquestionably greater by many orders of magnitude, because content thieves are responsible for illicitly distributing millions of copies of highly valuable works that cost billions to create, depriving their owners and creators of billions of dollars in rightful income. There is no question that the victims in this equation include a wide range of workers in the creative industries, from ordinary craft guild members, who rely on the revenues from creative productions to fund their health and retirement benefits, to independent creators.

But that economic harm is *not* the focus of this study, which instead seeks to estimate the advertising profits that content thieves reap for themselves from illicit distribution.

To determine how much money these bad actors are making through advertising, Digital Citizens commissioned MediaLink LLC – an advisory firm that provides critical counsel and strategic direction to the media, advertising, entertainment and technology industries and to companies and institutional investors that interact with those sectors – to undertake a research project focused on the ecosystem's revenues and profitability. By gaining insight into the ad-supported content theft ecosystem, we can as a society strive to find answers to protect the long-term future of the Internet.

Through this research, we have a snapshot of how much money content thieves make through advertising. We hope that this insight encourages the Internet and advertising industries, consumers, public-interest groups and responsible government officials to strive to make the Internet a stronger, more reliable and open platform for everyone.

EXECUTIVE SUMMARY

Ad-supported content theft is a real and growing threat not only to the content creators whose business it undermines, but also to the credibility of the digital advertising ecosystem that has developed over the last two decades. This research project analyzed advertising-supported web sites that dealt primarily in pirated content, and found that advertising yielded enormous profits.

The web sites MediaLink examined accounted for an estimated **$227 million in annual ad revenue, which is a huge figure, but nowhere close to the harm done to the creative economy and creative workers.** The 30 largest sites studied that are supported only by ads average $4.4 million annually, with the largest BitTorrent portal sites topping $6 million. Even small sites can make more than $100,000 a year from advertising.

Because their business model relies entirely on illicitly distributing millions of stolen copies of highly valuable works that cost others billions to create, their profit margins range from 80% to 94%, underscoring that crime can pay when you steal other people's content.

MediaLink's analysis of the profitability of ad-supported pirate sites provides additional insights into other aspects of the content theft ecosystem, including the prevalence of premium and secondary brand ads, and connections among sites. Below are other highlights of this study:

- **Premium, Secondary Brand Advertisers at Risk:** Weaknesses in the digital advertising ecosystem threaten the value of legitimate brands by allowing ads to be served on offending sites, often alongside offensive ads and links to malware.

  - **Nearly 30 percent of large sites in the sample carried ads for blue-chip premium brands –** highly recognizable household names.

  - In addition, ads for secondary brands - **legitimate gaming, gambling and content aggregation sites - appeared on up to 40 percent** of all the sites studied.

- **Low barriers to entry:** Stealing rights-protected content and setting up a site can be achieved with minimal technical expertise or cost and then can be iterated to avoid detection and policing, especially among the largest segments of sites.

- **Traffic generation:** Attracting a user base requires little effort or investment, as millions of users seek free content for download or streaming and as the Internet population grows.

The profitability and ease of execution, complemented by consumers' desire for free movie, TV, and other content, are the primary drivers of ad-supported content theft. Efforts to deter or degrade these activities through legal, technical, or industry initiatives continue to face a challenge. Nonetheless, the urgency to do so has never been greater in light of advertising trends, technology advances, and a growing intent among individual and organized global bad actors to capitalize on these profitable opportunities.

THREE KEY RELEVANT GROWTH TRENDS

Absent action by stakeholders, ad-supported content theft is likely to continue, supported by three key trends: increased programmatic digital advertising; growth of the global Internet population; and a swelling demand for video content by users who are willing to steal it rather than pay for it.

US Display Ad Spending Share, by Type, 2011–2017
% of total

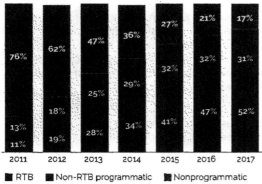

■ RTB ■ Non-RTB programmatic ■ Nonprogrammatic

Note: read as 28% of display-related spending was through RTB in 2013; numbers may not add up to 100% due to rounding.
Source: MAGNA GLOBAL as cited in press release, Oct. 14, 2013

Figure 1: Growth in Programmatic

Trend #1: Programmatic buying and selling of digital advertising: The digital advertising supply chain has many points of vulnerability. As more ad placement is done through automated systems, it becomes easier for bad actors to funnel ads to their sites, and to generate fraudulent clicks via bots and human operations.

An estimated 53% of US online display ad placement was automated in 2013, according to Magna Global, which projects that volume to increase to 83% by 2017. As buying and selling ads programmatically continues to grow, the opportunity to manipulate technology for further advertising gain only increases.

Trend #2: More Infringing Users and Bandwidth: The universe of consumers who view stolen content, and the bandwidth that they use in doing so, are on the rise, according to NetNames' September 2013 report, *Digital Piracy: Sizing the Piracy Universe.* NetNames reported that the number of infringing users in North America, Europe and the Asia-Pacific region rose nearly 10% from 297.6 million in November 2011 to 327 million in January 2013. Meanwhile, bandwidth used to access infringing content jumped dramatically, by nearly 160%, from 2010 to 2012 in the same regions.

Taken together, the two sets of data point to consumers' desire to access content, especially video content, enabled by the ability to discover and access the pirated content through peer-to-peer networks and search.

Trend #3: Global Internet Population Growth: Given the increase in infringing users, the anticipated global explosion in Internet use generally suggests that ever more consumers are likely to want movie, TV, and other digital content, especially as delivery systems increase in speed and decline in cost.

Today's 2.7 billion global Internet users represent only about 40% of the world's population, according to the International Telecommunications Union, and new users are coming online steadily. Just 31% of the population is online in the developing world, compared with 77% in the developed world, according to ITU, so there is ample potential for continued rapid growth.

Implications: The convergence of these growth trends suggests that the market size for ad-supported content theft is on the rise and will continue unless concerted diligence by all stakeholders in the digital media value chain is intensified and coordinated. Only through these kinds of efforts can the highly attractive profitability of ad-supported content theft be slowed and degraded.

METHODOLOGY

Sites Studied

In selecting sites for this research, MediaLink focused on the third quarter of 2013 to provide a recent point in time on which to base calculations. As the basis for finding sites engaged in content theft, it started with Digital Millennium Copyright Act (DMCA) removal request data from the Google Transparency Report.

There are thousands of sites around the world that offer infringing material and are supported by advertising. To allow a deeper dive we focused on a subset, including the largest and most successful. As a result the findings, while significant, reflect only a part of the aggregate profitability of such sites.

The baseline was sites with 25 or more DMCA takedown requests in Q3, that Veri-Site determined were live in the quarter, and for which unique visitor and page view data were available from comScore. The comScore data were used to calculate advertising revenue and to segment the sample by size, as described below. MediaLink validated the sample further using Integral Ad Science ratings on sites determined to be at high risk for content infringement, and its analysts visited and reported on hundreds of sites to further qualify them, and removing from consideration:

- Porn and hate sites;
- Sites where most content appeared to be user-generated, personal in nature or highly localized, e.g., Tamil-language programs or movies unlikely to be interesting to a broader pirating audience; or
- Sites where available content was not primarily movies and TV shows.

Thus, the only sites kept in the sample were those at least partially ad-supported sites where infringing content appeared to be a significant portion of the site.

Because content infringement sites can appear and disappear quickly, a small number of the sites had shut down while subsequent research was conducted in Q4 of 2013, in some cases as a result of civil or police action. Those sites were kept in the sample, as they represented ad-supported content theft within the time frame for this study.

The result was a sample of 596 sites.

Sample Segmentation

The sample sites were categorized into four functional segments, based on technology and business model, before being further segmented by size.

Functional Segments

Figure 2: Example BitTorrent Portal (piratereverse.info)

BitTorrent and Other P2P Portals

BitTorrent is the most popular peer-to-peer (P2P) file distribution system worldwide, and sites based on it have become synonymous with content theft. It is the largest method of content infringement, according to NetNames, which reported that 96.2% of unique visitors to such sites accessed infringing content at least once in January 2013. MediaLink also found BitTorrent sites to be predominant in ad-supported content theft.

These portals let users browse or search for files available on peer-to-peer distribution systems. Users following the links can access media files stored on multiple computers across the P2P network and download the content to their own computers for use at no charge. There were 144 sites in this segment, 24.2% of the sample. Figure 2 shows a typical BitTorrent site.

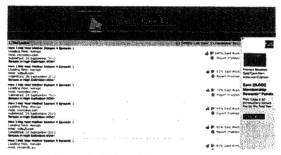

Figure 3: Example Linking Site (free-tv-video-online-me)

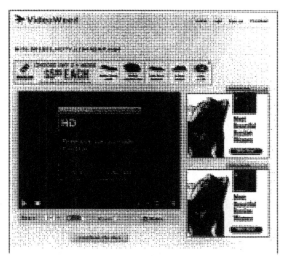

Figure 4: Example Video Streaming Host (videoweed.es)

Figure 5: Example DDL Host (albafile.com)

Linking Sites

These portals aggregate and index links to media content hosted on Direct Download (DDL) Hosts (described below) or other sites. Some allow search within the Linking Site itself to facilitate access to content. They do not host content themselves. Users browse or search for the content they want, all the while exposed to ads. The users then click a link and download the content from the site where it is hosted, at no charge. Many Linking Sites have business affiliations with specific DDLs, promoting their hosted content. There were 283 Linking Sites in the sample or 47.5% of the base. Figure 3 shows a typical Linking site.

Video Streaming Host Sites

This segment includes both the ad-supported portal and a subscription-based storage model. One-third of large, two-thirds of medium and all of the small sites are strictly ad-supported portals with embedded players that allow users to stream videos hosted elsewhere. The remaining sites both stream and host content, offering subscriptions to users who want to store video content and then allow users to stream videos. The sample included 75 Video Streaming Host Sites or 12.6% of the base. Figure 4 shows a typical Video Streaming Host Site.

Direct Download (DDL) Host Sites

Direct Download (DDL) Host Sites allow users to upload media files to cloud-based storage. Users can generate links to be used by themselves or others to download the content for free. DDLs have dual revenue streams: a free, advertising-supported model, and a premium version that lets users pay subscription fees to avoid ads and for faster downloads, and that accounts for the bulk of their total revenue. Ads are typically shown on download pages. DDL Hosts are fundamental to the content theft ecosystem, providing the content to which Linking Sites point. Many of the DDLs offer their users bounty payments for downloads of the users' popular uploaded files, encouraging users to post links widely across the Internet. There are 94 DDL Host Sites in the sample, comprising 15.8% of the 596 total sites. Only DDLs that displayed advertising were included in the sample. Figure 5 shows a typical DDL site.

Size Segments

To account for differences in scale across the sample, the functional segments were further divided by size into small, medium and large sub-segments, based on 3-month average unique visitors. The segments were:

- **Small:** Fewer than 1 million monthly unique visitors
- **Medium:** 1 million to 5 million monthly unique visitors
- **Large:** Greater than 5 million monthly unique visitors

This segmentation allowed for analysis of the traffic and economic realities of the industry leaders separately from myriad small sites. The result was 12 functional/size segments: three sizes for each of the four functional segments. The number of sites per functional and size segment is shown in Figure 6.

	Large	Medium	Small
BitTorrent and Other P2P Portals	15	36	93
Direct Download (DDL) Host Sites	8	35	51
Linking Sites	7	41	235
Video Streaming Host Sites	15	26	34

Figure 6: Sites by Functional and Size Segments

P&L Model

To create the financial model for the analysis of ad-supported content theft profitability, MediaLink considered numerous possible drivers of revenue and cost. Through its industry experience and by interviewing advertising and web site hosting experts, combing webmaster forums and blogs, reviewing US Justice Department filings, and studying the sample sites, MediaLink chose 20 data points that paint a picture of the profitability.

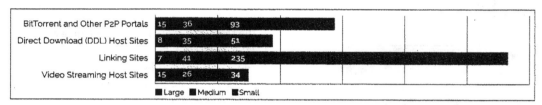

Traffic			Revenue														Direct Costs	Indirect Costs		
Unique Visitors	Page Views		Ads								Ad Metrics						Hosting	Personnel (FTE Cost)		Overhead
UVs/Mo. (mm)	PVs/ Mo. (mm)	% PVs w/ Ads	# of Ad Positions Per Page	Fraud Multiplier %	% of PVs Generating PopUps	Pop-Up Multiplier	% Premium Ads	CTR	CPC	Non-Prem CPM	Prem CPM	% Using CPA	# CPA Links	CTA Rate	CPA	Server Cost/ Month	Head Count	Est. Salary	% of Revenue

Figure 7: Financial Model Data Points

The Key Drivers of Ad Revenue:

- Page views
- Number of ad positions per page
- Amount paid per thousand impressions, per click on a banner or text link, and per completion of an action.

MediaLink based these values on rates for similarly sized legitimate sites, discounted because rates for campaigns on infringement sites would be lower, while still generating significant revenue.

Variables included potential click and impression fraud as well as common click-through and conversion rates.

The Key Drivers of Costs:

- Hosting fees
- Human resources.

With cloud-based hosting becoming a commodity, infrastructure costs are low for all but the DDL segment of the ecosystem, which requires more processing and storage capacity than other segments. Because the focus of this research was on ad-supported content theft, subscription revenue, cost and margins are not reported for sites that were not wholly supported by advertising.

The data points are shown in Figure 7 above. See **Appendix A: P&L Detail** for detailed explanation.

PROFITABILITY ANALYSIS AND KEY FINDINGS

Segment	Ad Revenue	Margin
BitTorrent and Other P2P Portals		
Small	$2,079,334	85.9%
Medium	$3,227,159	84.5%
Large	$23,181,252	94.1%
Linking Sites		
Small	$3,690,915	79.9%
Medium	$8,351,446	89.8%
Large	$4,498,344	87.5%
Video Streaming Hosts		
Small	$529,480	79.9%
Medium	$1,681,477	
Large	$4,661,535	
Direct Download (DDL) Host Sites		
Small	$401,087	
Medium	$1,281,344	
Large	$3,084,123	

Table 1: Q3 Aggregate Ad Revenue, Margin for Ad-Supported Sites

Torrent, Linking Sites Drive Most Ad Revenue

BitTorrent and Linking sites, the segments with the lowest barriers to entry, together accounted for 80% of the aggregate ad revenue, with BitTorrent sites alone generating more than half the total despite making up less than a quarter of the sample. Revenue by segment detail can be seen in Figure 9.

Highly Lucrative, Profitable

The aggregate ad revenue for the sample of 596 sites was an estimated $56.7 million for Q3 of 2013, projecting out to $226.7 million dollars annually, with average profit margins of 83%, ranging from 80% to as high as 94%.

All Sizes Profit

The 45 largest sites, 7.6% of the entire sample, accounted for 62.5% of the total aggregate ad revenue. The average large site makes an estimated $3 million in ad revenue a year – $4.4 million for those that are supported solely by advertising – while even small sites can net $100,000. Small sites comprised 69.3% of the sample but only accounted for 11.8% of aggregate ad revenue. Revenue by size detail can be seen in Figure 8.

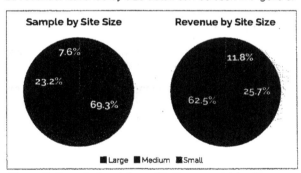

Figure 8: Sample Breakdown (l.), Revenue (r.) by Size

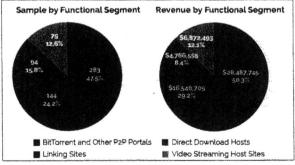

Figure 9: Sample Breakdown (l.), Revenue (r.) by Segment

Problem for Premium and Secondary Brands

Premium brand ads appeared on nearly 30% of large sites, highlighting the ineffectiveness of current approaches to protecting the brands' reputation and value.

Premium brands are those easily recognizable companies familiar to most consumers, and which suffer reputational damage when their ads appear on content theft site, often alongside ads for illicit sites and services.

Premium brands listed in Appendix D are only those whose ads were observed by MediaLink analysts visiting the sites in the sample. MediaLink found that:

- Ads for premium brands appeared on 28.9% of large sites, 17.4% of medium and 13.1% of small sites.

- They appeared on 33.3% of DDL Hosts, 16.4% of Video Streaming Hosts, 11.7% of Linking Sites, and 9.7% of BitTorrent portals.

Advertising is often targeted by geography and by user interests as captured in browser cookies, so MediaLink's US-based analysts would have seen different ads and brands than users in, say, Ukraine.

Many players in the advertising ecosystem profit from placement of ads on content theft sites, whether for premium brands or others. Programmatic placement may involve exchanges, networks, publishers and agencies, and each link in the chain offers weaknesses that can be exploited. While some have taken action in an attempt to prevent premium ads from appearing on infringing sites, clearly more needs to be done, and alternative approaches need to be explored to reduce this contribution by good companies to bad activities.

Secondary Brands and other Advertising

In addition to those blue-chip companies, legitimate "secondary" brands also can find their ads served into content theft sites through the complex and increasingly computer-driven ecosystem of ad networks and exchanges . Categories that MediaLink identified were:

- **Casual Gaming:** These are a range of online single- and multi-player warfare, fantasy and other games that typically require users to create accounts or download software. Game ads appeared on some 40% of the large sites reviewed.
- **Online Gambling:** Ads for online gambling and betting services, many of which may be regulated by consumer protection or other agencies, appeared on 10% of the large sites reviewed.
- **Content Aggregator Sites:** This broad category, which appeared on just over 20% of large sites, included links to non-premium aggregators of news and information, with varying degrees of legitimacy.

The remaining ads studied came from illicit sites and services, often placed next to premium or secondary brands. Categories that MediaLink identified were:

- **Software/Malware Downloads:** These are often hidden behind download buttons, or are presented via links or popups promoting a plug-in the user supposedly needs to view content, or as an update to legitimate software. The actual downloads often contain malware. These ads were extremely common, appearing on 60% of the large sites.
- **Adult Content:** This category includes ads for escort and other sexual services, porn and body part and sexual performance enhancements. Banners frequently display scantily clad or naked women. Adult content ads appeared on just over 20% of the large sites.
- **Easy Money:** This category includes business opportunities and get-rich-quick offers that encourage users to pay to receive the secrets to financial success or to participate in the advertiser's scheme for wealth generation. These ads appeared on roughly 15% of the large sites reviewed.

Note that the categories add up to more than 100% of the sites because these sites typically display more than one of the identified ad types.

Site Affiliations and Bad Actors

Cross-ownership and affiliations between sites help some operators evade enforcement and maximize profits, establishing networks of sites distributing the same stolen content. If one site is shut down by authorities, others may keep running. In addition, some site operators are linked to nefarious activities beyond content theft.

MediaLink asked Veri-Site, a web site risk assessment firm, to analyze the 596 sites in the sample. Veri-Site found *linkages* from 32 of the primary domains. Veri-Site defines these linkages as connections among individuals, businesses and other web sites. It found 976 linkages to other web sites both within

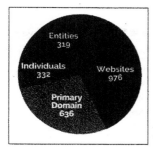

and outside the sample, as well as ownership or business affiliations among those 32 sample sites and 319 individuals and 332 entities, typically companies. This data suggests that while individuals may be operating many of the sites, some individuals and enterprises are operating multiple sites for additional revenue and to hedge their bets against enforcement.

The sites with the three largest networks were **thepiratebay.se** and **bitsnoop.com**, both large BitTorrent portals, and **ufox.com**, a small DDL Host Site. Altogether they had 223 connections: 137 for thepiratebay.se, 52 for **ufox.com** and 34 for **bitsnoop.com**. These networks of sites highlight a strategy to conceal relationships with the parent, according to Veri-Site. With so many layers to the sites' functioning, the risk is distributed, and their ability to evade various laws is enhanced. The sites also operate from various geographies, making it easier to evade legal action. For example, a

Figure 10: Site Linkage Types (Veri-Site)

total of 122 legal actions have been taken against these sites, yet they remained active during Q3 2013.

ThePirateBay.se: This is the most notorious BitTorrent portal currently operating. Veri-Site found 16 entities and 31 individuals with connections to this site. The individuals were identified as domain registrants, co-founders, lawyers and associates. Several of the co-founders have been convicted of copyright infringement and fined millions of dollars. In addition, Veri-Site identified 90 web sites linked to thepiratebay.se, many of them simply with different country-specific domains but also other BitTorrent portals and mirrors. Between April and December 2013, The Pirate Bay switched to domains of six different countries to evade authorities. Several of its co-founders have been convicted of hacking, fraud and copyright infringement.

Ultramegabit.com: Less well known, perhaps, is this medium-sized DDL that has linkages to 16 sites, entities and individuals. Its owner was convicted of consumer fraud and fined $400,000. His associates through a web of other sites include two companies that violated consumer protection laws while marketing PC registry-cleaning software. The owner of one was fined $400,000 and the other's president was fined $75,000.

Bitsnoop.com: Two registrants are connected to bitsnoop.com through 32 sites that include torrentcrazy. com, a medium BitTorrent portal, and torrentreactor.net, a large BitTorrent portal, both of which are in the MediaLink sample. There also are linkages to zooqle.com, a BitTorrent site outside the sample, and to a number of mirror sites that contain copies of the content found on bitsnoop.com and other BitTorrent portals. Eight of the linked web sites are mirrors of thepiratebay.se.

Ufox.com: Two entities connect 50 web sites to ufox.com. Unlike the other two top sites, however, none of the linked sites in this example are content theft sites; almost all are either porn or unsavory content.

Other examples include:

- **Torrentzap.com**, a small BitTorrent portal, is linked by a common postal address to fileindexer.com, a small Linking site also in the sample, and to fulldls.com, a small BitTorrent portal outside the sample.
- **Desitorrents.com**, a small BitTorrent portal, is linked by address and registrant to rutor.org, a large BitTorrent portal, and to argentinawarez.com, a medium Linking site. All three are in the MediaLink sample.

Veri-Site analysts research linkages among sites using open source and public domain information, as well as government agencies, news sources, domain registrations and payment registries. The company also includes in its research information from intellectual property holders attesting to infringement, governing bodies and law enforcement bulletins. Its analysts also visit and report on sites to capture data.

Segment Analysis

BitTorrent and Other P2P Portals

BitTorrent portals generate more ad revenue than any of the other segments, and the largest sites have the highest average operating margins, about 94%.

	Ad Revenue	Cost	Margin
Average Quarterly Results			
Small	$22,358	$3,147	85.9%
Medium	$89,643	$13,877	84.5%
Large	$1,545,417	$91,724	94.1%
Aggregate Quarterly Results			
Small	$2,079,334	$292,691	
Medium	$3,227,159	$499,556	
Large	$23,181,252	$1,375,863	

Table 2: Torrent Portal Average/Aggregate Results

The portals represented 23.5% of the sample sites but accounted for 50.3% of advertising revenue, accounting for $28.5 million in the quarter, or $114 million annually. Large BitTorrent portals represented just 10.4% of the 144 sites in the segment but accounted for 81.3% of the aggregate segment ad revenue and 40.9% of the aggregate ad revenue across the entire sample.

Average monthly page views for the segment (52.5 million) are significantly more those of any other, most of them displaying ads, along with the second highest average monthly number of unique visitors (2.7 million) account for the sites' significant revenue. While small BitTorrent sites have the lowest top-line revenue, the average small site can still make nearly $100,000 annually with very little overhead or infrastructure.

Despite BitTorrent portals' notoriety as sources of stolen content, premium brand ads appeared on 13.3% of large, 13.9% of medium and 7.5% of small BitTorrent portals.

Linking Sites

	Ad Revenue	Cost	Margin
Average Quarterly Results			
Small	$15,706	$3,149	79.9%
Medium	$203,694	$20,868	89.8%
Large	$642,621	$80,462	87.5%
Aggregate Quarterly Results			
Small	$3,690,915	$740,069	
Medium	$8,351,446	$855,597	
Large	$4,498,344	$563,233	

Table 3: Linking Sites Average, Aggregate Results

Linking Sites represented 47.5% of the representative sample, reflecting the extremely low barriers to entry in this segment. In fact, the 235 small Linking sites alone represent 39.4% of the entire representative sample; however, they only accounted for 6.5% of overall aggregate ad revenue.

Nonetheless, even small Linking sites, like small BitTorrent sites, can net $100,000 in ad revenue a year, with margins of 80% or more. Large portals, on the other hand, make up just 2.5% of the 283 sites in the segment but account for 27.2% of the aggregate quarterly ad revenue of $16.5 million.

Large Linking sites made up just 1.2% of the entire sample, while accounting for 7.9% of the aggregate quarterly ad revenue.

Overall, Linking Sites had the lowest average number of unique visitors compared with other segments, at less than 1 million, reflecting the large percentage of small sites in the segment. The large sites averaged 8.7 million unique visitors, reflecting the value of scale. Overall, Linking Sites averaged 13.0 million page views, the lowest segment. Note that the average is reduced by the extremely large number of small sites.

Premium brands appeared on nearly a third (28.6%) of large, 17.1% of medium and 10.2% of small Linking sites.

Video Streaming Host Sites

Ad Revenue	
Average Quarterly Results	
Small	$15,573
Medium	$64,672
Large	$310,769
Aggregate Quarterly Results	
Small	$529,480
Medium	$1,681,477
Large	$4,661,535

Table 4: Video Streaming Host Average, Aggregate Ad Revenue

Video Streaming Host Sites represented 12.6% of the sample, and accounted for 12.1%, or $6.9 million, of the aggregate quarterly advertising revenue, or $27.6 million per year. Large sites represented 20% of the 75 sites in the segment and accounted for 67.8% of the aggregate segment ad revenue. Margins are not reported here because a number of the sites in this segment offer subscription access, requiring infrastructure for account management, e-commerce and storage that is not directly related to advertising revenue.

Video Streaming Hosts attracted an average monthly 2.3 million unique visitors and averaged 33.4 million page views for the quarter.

Premium brands appeared on 33.3% of large, 15.4% of medium and 8.8% of small Video Streaming Hosts.

Ad Revenue	
Average Quarterly Results	
Small	$7,864
Medium	$36,610
Large	$385,515
Aggregate Quarterly Results	
Small	$401,087
Medium	$1,281,344
Large	$3,084,123

Table 5: DDL Host Sites Average, Aggregate Ad Revenue

Direct Download (DDL) Host Sites

DDLs generate some ad revenue but are primarily subscription-based. Ads are displayed on upload and download pages, and the sites offer premium accounts for a monthly subscription fee that ranges from $5 to $15 to get rid of ads and for increased download speeds.

DDLs have higher barriers to entry and overall costs than other segments. Because DDLs' infrastructure and operations are scaled to support user management, e-commerce and storage and not directly tied to advertising revenue, their margins are not reported here.

DDLs comprised 15.8% of the sample but accounted for 8.4%, or $4.8 million, of the aggregate quarterly advertising revenue – or $19.2 million per year. Large DDLs represented just 8.5V% of the 94 sites in the segment but accounted for 64.7% of the aggregate segment ad revenue.

DDLs attracted the largest average monthly number of visitors at 2.6 million, and ranked third in average total page views at 29.4 million.

Premium brands appeared on 50% of large, 22.9% of medium and 39.2% of small DDLs.

SUMMARY AND RECOMMENDATIONS

Content theft sites are making millions in revenue, at high margins, from advertising. Creating a content theft site is inexpensive and requires little technological expertise, making ad-supported content theft "easy money" for bad actors. Exacerbating the problem for rights-protected content owners and many unwitting premium and secondary brand advertisers are the concurrent trends of a dramatically growing online global universe hungry for cheap, new content, and the explosion of programmatic buying and selling of advertising.

To date, efforts to degrade the viability of ad-supported theft have had only marginal impact and success, as the perpetrators evade detection with considerable ease.

The presence of ads for legitimate brands on content theft sites should be an incentive for those brand marketers to press agencies, ad networks and exchanges to strengthen current blocking methods and to develop new ones.

Advertisers and ad agencies, networks and exchanges can start by enhancing their voluntary best practice standards. The technology and services to identify and filter out content theft sites are available and should be adopted in the online advertising community. Just as brands do not advertise on porn or hate sites, they can take steps to assure they are not on content theft sites.

The online advertising industry knows this is a problem. As an ad industry insider told MediaLink, "Even one premium brand ad on one of these sites is too many." Another said that having one's brand appear on content theft sites alongside the kinds of ads that are common there "is a bad day at the office for a brand marketer."

DCA is not alone in sounding this call to action.

In an August 2013 op-ed, Bob Liodice, the President and CEO of the Association of National Advertisers wrote about the threat of online piracy: *"The volume and availability of traffic on rogue sites may be tempting. But rest assured, it is in everyone's best interest to demonstrate support for brands by protecting them from compromising situations. Our industry must combat and halt the content pirates hijacking our ads."*

Randall Rothenberg, the President and CEO of the Interactive Advertising Bureau, said at IAB's Annual Leadership Meeting in February 2014: *"Advertising, much of it purchased via automated systems, inadvertently supports web sites that deliberately steal and distribute movies, music, and other copyrighted intellectual property, leading to an untold fortune in losses annually to news and entertainment companies."*

A coordinated effort by all stakeholders in the online advertising ecosystem is urgently required to preserve the value of digital media and help make the Internet a safer marketplace for legitimate commerce.

ACKNOWLEDGEMENT

Digital Citizens Alliance greatly appreciates the effort and care that MediaLink and its partners have put into this project. In addition to MediaLink's own researchers, significant contributions of analysis and data were provided by:

- **Veri-Site**, a global leader in assessing and mitigating risk associated with the rapidly changing online environment. Veri-Site provides risk-relevant intelligence regarding rogue websites, intellectual property theft, cybercrime, web-enabled transnational organized crime, and sanctioned entities operating online. Veri-Site uniquely targets these threats with intelligence to manage operational, regulatory, and reputational risk. More information at **veri-site.com**.

- **Integral Ad Science Inc.**, the leading global provider of actionable advertising intelligence data for buyers and sellers of digital media and the industry's standard for rating media quality. Since launching the industry's first preventative brand safety solution in 2009, powered by constant growth and innovation, Integral has evolved into a global media valuation platform that is essential to the buying and selling of quality media. Integral focuses on a comprehensive solution set that enables advertising to appear in quality environments and receive favorable exposure — while the sell side can monitor and control its quality and performance. Integral's technology drives improved visibility, efficiency, and ROI for players across the digital media landscape. More information at **integralads.com.**

- **DoubleVerify**, the market leader in technology and insights that assure brand performance and effectiveness for the world's largest advertisers online. DV solutions create value for media buyers and sellers by bringing transparency and accountability to the market, ensuring ad viewability, brand safety, fraud protection, accurate impression delivery and audience quality across campaigns to drive performance. Learn more at **doubleverify.com**.

- **comScore Inc.**, a global leader in digital measurement and analytics, delivering insights on web, mobile and TV consumer behavior that enable clients to maximize the value of their digital investments. Through its Audience Analytics, Advertising Analytics, and Digital Enterprise Analytics product suites, comScore provides clients with a variety of on-demand software, real-time analytics and custom solutions to succeed in a multi-platform world. The proprietary comScore Census Network™ leverages a world-class technology infrastructure to capture trillions of digital interactions a month and power big data analytics on a global scale for its more than 2,000 clients. More information at **comscore.com**.

APPENDICES

APPENDIX A: P&L DETAIL

As noted above, sites that offered infringing content with no advertising were excluded from the research.

Ad-Supported: BitTorrent and Other P2P Portals, and Linking Sites examined by MediaLink were exclusively ad-supported. The research found impression-, click-, and action-based models in use. The action-based approach applied to what was sometimes identified as affiliate programs, wherein the sites generated revenue by displaying to users opportunities to sign up for a program or a gaming service, or where they could download software, which often turned out to be loaded with malware.

Ad- and Subscription-Supported: Direct Download (DDL) Hosts and about one-third of Video Streaming Hosts were supported by subscription access as well as advertising. These were typically "freemium" services where users could create a free account, but with throttled download speeds and ads displayed. To eliminate ads and to get full-speed downloads, users have to buy a premium package, typically at one-, three-, six- and 12-month terms with discounts as high as 50% off the monthly rate for longer subscriptions. Direct exploration of the sites, including creating both free and premium accounts and uploading and downloading content, verified the sites' fees and download bounties. Some sites offer users bounties for downloads of the users' content and for subscriptions resulting from downloads.

The goal of this research was to understand the profitability of ad-supported content theft, so the discussion focuses on just the ad-supported aspects of the business, and the costs and margins for subscription-supported sites are not reported here. What follows is an explanation of the data points and assumptions underlying ad-supported content theft sites.

Revenue

Advertising revenue, as noted, has three components: CPM- or impression-based, CPC- or click-based, and CPA- or action-based. Impression revenue derives from a fee per thousand views of an ad; click-based advertising, a la Google AdWords, generates revenue only when users click a banner or link; and CPA pays when a user completes some action, such as downloading and installing software or registering on a site.

CPM Revenue

Impression-specific data points are:

- **Page Views (PVs):** The monthly average of page views for July, August and September 2013, from comScore. For the model, this data was used to estimate ad revenue.

- **Percent of Page Views with Ads (% Ads):** These assumptions are part of the ad revenue calculation and are based on MediaLink visits to the sites as well as external research. The percentage assumptions by segment are as follows:

  - **BitTorrent and Other P2P Portals:** These sites generally do not show ads on the home page but do on almost all other pages displayed. Assumption is 80% (a 20% reduction of the comScore average) to be multiplied by CPM (cost per thousand) defined below to arrive at CPM ad revenue.

  - **Linking Sites:** Assumed 95% as virtually all pages on all Linking Sites display ads.

  - **Video Streaming Host Sites:** Assumed 75%. One-third of sites are DDL-model sites, which we assume have ads on 30% of page views; two-thirds are linking-type sites, which we assume have ads on 95% of page views. Average is roughly 75%. Sources are MediaLink site visits and external research.

  - **Direct Download (DDL) Host Sites:** Assumed 50%. Ads only display on upload and download pages, conservatively estimated at half of page views.

- **Number of Ad Positions per Page (# Ads):** This is an average by functional and size segment based on MediaLink researchers' site visits and direct observation.

• **Fraud Multiplier (% Fraud):** Impression fraud is a significant challenge to the advertising ecosystem and is likely to be even more significant in the content theft ecosystem. Fraud includes such benign practices as pop-unders, where ads are launched behind a user's primary browser window, as well as activities such as stacking ads in nested iframes and embedding ad calls in single-pixel images that viewers can never see. The research did not include analysis of log files or data streams, and assumptions for the financial model rely on a combination of third-party sources and direct observation of sites' business models.

  - **BitTorrent and Other P2P Portals:** Assumed 30%, based on industry reports.
  - **Linking Sites:** Assumed 30%, based on business model equivalence to P2P sites.
  - **Video Streaming Host Sites:** Assumed 20%, adjusting the 30% metric for P2P and Linking sites to account for the number of Video Streaming sites with a DDL-like business model.
  - **Direct Download (DDL) Host Sites:** Assumed 10%, adjusting the 30% metric based on site visit observations that DDL sites have by far more functional pages for account management and signup, and don't show ads to premium users, resulting in less apparent opportunity for fraud.

• **Percent of Page Views Generating Pop-ups (% Pop-Ups):** Based on MediaLink site visits, researchers extrapolated that 30% of page views and clicks generated pop-up or pop-under ads.

• **Pop-Up Multiplier (# Pop-Ups):** While visiting sites, MediaLink researchers counted the number of pop-ups and pop-unders displayed. This data point is an average by functional and size segment.

• **Percent of Premium Brand Ads (% Prem):** MediaLink researchers visited each site and counted the number of premium ads displayed. This data point is an average by functional and size segment.

• **Non-Premium CPM ($ Non-Prem):** Based on MediaLink expertise and research with advertising industry members, ads on content theft sites are likely delivered at low CPMs. This reflects the overwhelmingly low quality of most advertisers, including adult dating and gambling sites, games, get-rich-quick schemes, etc. The assumption was a CPM of $0.50 (50 cents) per thousand ads displayed.

• **Premium CPM ($ Prem):** Based on MediaLink expertise and research with advertising industry members, the assumption is that where premium ads appear they are delivered programmatically by exchanges to fulfill the dregs of campaigns. As such, rates are assumed to be the same for premium and non-premium ads.

Average CPM revenue per site was calculated by functional and size segment, and derived as shown here:

Base Impressions = (PVs x % Ads x # Ads)
Fraudulent Impressions = Base Impressions x % Fraud
Pop-Up Impressions = Base Impressions x % Pop-Ups x # Pop-Ups
Total Ad Impressions = Base Impressions + Fraud Impressions + Pop-Up Impressions
Premium CPM Revenue = $ Prem x (Total Ad Impressions x % Prem)
Non-Premium CPM Revenue = $ Non-Prem x (Total Ad Impressions - % Prem)
Total CPM Revenue = Premium CPM Revenue + Non-Premium CPM Revenue

Cost-Per-Click (CPC) Revenue

The second advertising model involves payment for each user click on a banner or text link. For click-based (CPC) advertising, these additional data fields and calculations apply:

• **Click-Through Rate (CTR):** Based on MediaLink expertise and research with advertising industry members, assumed a click-through rate of 0.08% (eight one-hundredths of one percent).

- **Cost Per Click (CPC):** Based on MediaLink expertise and research with advertising industry members, assumed a cost-per-click rate of $0.21 (21 cents) per click.

CPC Revenue = Total Ad Impressions x CTR x CPC

Cost-Per-Action (CPA) Revenue

The final ad model involves paying for users' completion of an action, generally as part of lead generation activities. Based on MediaLink site visits, the participants in this model in the content theft ecosystem are overwhelmingly software (and malware) distributors, as well as gaming and gambling sites.

For action-based (CPA) advertising, these additional data fields and calculations apply:

- **Percent of Sites with Affiliates (% Affils):** Based on MediaLink site visits, this is an average percentage by functional and size segment of those with ads linking off-site to pages where actions were to be completed.
- **Number of Affiliate Links (# Affils):** Based on MediaLink site visits, this is an average number by functional and size segment of CTA links in sites.
- **CTA Action Rate (CTA):** Based on MediaLink expertise and research with advertising industry members, assumed conversion rate of 0.01% (one one-hundredth of one percent).
- **Cost-Per-Action Fee (CPA):** Based on MediaLink expertise and research with advertising industry members, assumed revenue per completed action of $0.75 (75 cents).

CPA/Affiliate Revenue = (PVs x % Affils x # Affils) x CTA x CPA

Operating Costs

Sites in the content theft ecosystem do not report revenues or operating costs, so assumptions were based on generally accepted practices for similar types of ad- and subscription-supported sites, and used some third-party data. The research considered direct costs for hosting and indirect costs for staff and other overhead.

General Costs

Regardless of business model, web sites have hosting costs and some cost for human resources, whether those are employees or freelancers. The following additional data points and calculations were used for these costs applicable to all sites.

- **Monthly Hosting Costs:** MediaLink used the site MuStat (**www.mustat.com**) for hosting costs. The site compiles data from a number of sources and appears to base its calculations on a combination of unique visitors, page views, bandwidth utilization estimates and location. While more detail about its observations is not available, Mustat provides a consistent and conservative number for the sites.
- **Head Count:** Estimated number of people involved in operating the sites, based on research and general expertise in web site operations. This varies significantly based on the size and type of site. For example, small BitTorrent and Linking sites are likely run by one person, probably with no additional full-time employees. The need for staff likely increases with size as more effort is required to manage additional servers and to deal with affiliate and advertising relationships and compliance with DMCA takedown requests. DDLs and DDL-like Video Streaming sites, on the other hand, are more complicated. They involve e-commerce, subscription and account management, significant content storage infrastructure, and integration with content distribution networks (CDNs), to name a few key functions.

- **BitTorrent and Other P2P Portals:** Assumed 0.25 FTE for small, 1.0 FTE for medium and 5 FTE for large sites. Torrent software is increasingly common and not difficult to operate, and once sites are built ongoing operation would mainly focus on monitoring, indexing and dealing with advertising.
- **Linking Sites:** Assumed 0.25 FTE for small, 1.5 FTE for medium and 5 FTE for large sites.
- **Video Streaming Host Sites:** Assumed 0.25 FTE for small sites, which operate the same as small BitTorrent and Linking sites. The DDL model only exists in the medium and large segments, where the average FTE count was adjusted downward slightly to accommodate the blend of DDL-type and portal-type sites. For medium sites, assumed 2.0 FTEs and 4.0 for large sites.
- **Direct Download (DDL) Host Sites:** Assumed 0.5 FTE for small, 2.5 FTE for medium and 6 FTE for large sites. As noted above, these are more complicated to maintain and there's need for customer service and marketing resource that doesn't apply to torrent and Linking sites.

- **Average Monthly Salary:** Based on published salaries for web and system administrators and developers, assumed an average monthly salary per person of $4,000.
- **Overhead:** Most sites in the content theft ecosystem are presumed to operate without offices and that the only significant infrastructure beyond hosting and network. That likely changes as the sites grow and especially in regard to DDLs, which as noted have more complex needs. To account for overhead despite the opacity of the business, researchers assumed overhead of 0%-1% of revenue for BitTorrent, Linking and Video Streaming sites and 1% across the board for DDLs.

APPENDIX B: COST & REVENUE DETAIL

Q3 2013 Average Site Performance by Segment

Segment	CPM Rev	CPC Rev	CPA Revenue	Total Ad Revenue	Total Cost	Margin %
BitTorrent and Other P2P Portals						
Small	$ 14,144	$ 7,920	$ 294	$ 22,358	$ 3,147	85.9%
Medium	$ 56,173	$ 31,457	$ 2,014	$ 89,643	$ 13,877	84.5%
Large	$ 969,597	$ 542,974	$ 32,845	$ 1,545,417	$ 91,724	94.1%
Linking Sites						
Small	$ 9,793	$ 5,484	$ 429	$ 15,706	$ 3,149	79.9%
Medium	$ 129,790	$ 72,683	$ 1,221	$ 203,694	$ 20,868	89.8%
Large	$ 405,959	$ 227,337	$ 9,325	$ 642,621	$ 80,462	87.5%
Video Streaming Host Sites						
Small	$ 9,517	$ 5,330	$ 726	$ 15,573	$ 3,127	79.9%
Medium	$ 39,870	$ 22,327	$ 2,475	$ 64,672		
Large	$ 188,511	$ 105,566	$ 16,691	$ 310,769		
Direct Download (DDL) Host Sites						
Small	$ 4,736	$ 2,652	$ 477	$ 7,864		
Medium	$ 19,417	$ 10,873	$ 6,319	$ 36,610		
Large	$ 205,998	$ 115,359	$ 64,158	$ 385,515		

Q3 2013 Aggregate Site Performance by Segment

Segment	CPM Rev	CPC Rev	CPA Revenue	Total Ad Revenue	Total Cost	Margin %
BitTorrent and Other P2P Portals						
Small	$ 1,315,359	$ 736,601	$ 27,374	$ 2,079,334	$ 292,691	85.9%
Medium	$ 2,022,214	$ 1,132,440	$ 72,505	$ 3,227,159	$ 499,556	84.5%
Large	$ 14,543,956	$ 8,144,615	$ 492,681	$ 23,181,252	$ 1,375,863	94.1%
Linking Sites						
Small	$ 2,301,393	$ 1,288,780	$ 100,742	$ 3,690,915	$ 740,069	79.9%
Medium	$ 5,321,407	$ 2,979,988	$ 50,050	$ 8,351,446	$ 855,597	89.8%
Large	$ 2,841,712	$ 1,591,359	$ 65,274	$ 4,498,344	$ 563,233	87.5%
Video Streaming Host Sites						
Small	$ 323,594	$ 181,213	$ 24,674	$ 529,480	$ 106,305	79.9%
Medium	$ 1,036,612	$ 580,503	$ 64,362	$ 1,681,477	$ 1,117,063	
Large	$ 2,827,670	$ 1,583,495	$ 250,370	$ 4,661,535	$ 1,575,050	
Direct Download (DDL) Host Sites						
Small	$ 241,524	$ 135,253	$ 24,310	$ 401,087		
Medium	$ 679,593	$ 380,572	$ 221,180	$ 1,281,344		
Large	$ 1,647,986	$ 922,872	$ 513,266	$ 3,084,123		

APPENDIX C: SITES STUDIED

Note: Sites marked with an asterisk were no longer active as of January 2014, but were active during Q3 2013.

BitTorrent and Other P2P Portals

Large
bitsnoop.com
extratorrent.com
fast-torrent.ru
isohunt.com*
rutor.org
rutracker.org
t411.me
tfile.me
thepiratebay.sx
torrentdownloads.me
torrenthound.com
torrentino.com
torrentreactor.net
torrentz.eu

Medium
bigtracker.org
bitlordsearch.com
cpasbien.me
gamestorrents.com
ilcorsaronero.info
jptorrent.org*
katmirror.com
katushka.net
kinozal.tv
limetorrents.com
megashara.com
monova.org
nowfilms.ru
pirateproxy.net
rarbg.com
seedpeer.me
smartorrent.com
tfile.org
tnttorrent.info
torlock.com
torrent.cd
torrentcrazy.com
torrentfunk.com
torrent-games.net
torrentino.ru
torrentline.net
torrentor.net
torrentportal.com
torrentroom.com
torrents.net
torrentszona.com
vertor.com

vitorrent.org
yify-torrents.com
yourbittorrent.com
yyets.com

Small
10torrent.net
5gg.biz
absolutorrent.com
ahashare.com
ba3a.org.ua
bayproxy.org
bigtorrent.org
bit2bit.org
bitcoca.com
bitnova.info
bitreactor.to
bit-torrent.bz
bt-chat.com
btmon.com
byte.to
chhola.com
crazy-torrent.com
cztorrent.net
desitorrents.com
dht-tracker.org
emuleday.com
filesstoreroom.com
firebit.org
freestorrent.com
free-torrents.org
friends-torrent.com
fulldls.com
goldenshara.com
hdreactor.org
helltorrents.com
jarochos.net
kickassunblock.info
kinokubik.com
kino-zal.tv
kinsburg.ru
lanunbay.org
limetorrents.net
megatorrents.kg
megatorrents.org
netz.ru
newtorrents.info
nowtorrents.com
online-freebee.ru

opensharing.org
ourrelease.org
piratebayalternative.me*
pirateby.info
pirateproxy.nl
piratereverse.info
polskie-torrenty.pl
pslan.com
psychocydd.co.uk
publichd.se
rapidzona.com
realtorrentz.com
rustorka.com
rustorrents.org
rus-torrents.ru
silvertorrent.org
sparkmovies.com
streamzone.org
tamiltorrents.net
tapochek.net
titanshare.to
torentilo.com
torrentazos.com*
torrentbar.com
torrentbee.com*
torrentbutler.eu
torrent-cinema.net
torrentdownloadz.com
torrentfilms.net
torrent-films.net
torrent-finder.info
torrent-francais.com
torrent-free.ru
torrentkereso.hu
torrent-loco.com.ar
torrentman.com
torrento.net
torrentom.com
torrents.to
torrent-shara.net
torrent-shara.org
torrents-load.net
torrentv.org
torrentz.me
torrentzap.com
torrtilla.ru
tvboxnow.com
unionpeer.org
utorrents.org
ziotracker.org

Linking Sites

Large
filestube.com
filmix.net
free-tv-video-online.me
kinox.to
myegy.com
watchfreemovies.ch
zerx.ru

Medium
1channelmovie.com
1kinobig.ru
1tvlive.in
argentinawarez.com
bobfilm.net
castordownloads.net
cinetube.es
couchtuner.eu
cwer.ws
desirulez.net
desitvforum.net
divxonline.info
ekino.tv
eqla3.com
filetram.com
filmlinks4u.net
ganool.com
gratispeliculas.org
identi.li
ikinokz.net
kinobar.net
kinopod.ru
letmewatchthis.ru
m5zn.com
masteetv.com
newalbumreleases.net
nnm-club.ru
peb.pl
peliculasyonkis.com
primewire.ag
seedoff.net
stepashka.com
torrentfrancais.com
uakino.net
urgrove.com
video.az
vn-zoom.com
watchseries.lt
watchseries-online.eu
worldfree4u.com
zone-telechargement.com

Small
1movie.ru
300mblinks.com
3dl.tv
5fantastic.pl

720pmkv.com
720pmovies.net
990.ro
actorpedia.net
ajo.pl
albumhunt.com
alive-ua.com
allcandl.org
allyoulike.com
astatalk.com
atomload.at
baixardegraca.com.br
baixeturbo.org
bajui.com
bartzmovie.com
bergfiles.com
berglib.com
bochinchewarez.com
btarena.org
burning-seri.es
byhero.com
cinemaaz.com
cinevip.org
cokeandpopcorn.ch
collb9.org
come.in
coolmoviezone.com
copywarez.com
dacho.co.il
dangbuon.com
darkmachine.pl
ddl-search.biz
ddlvalley.eu
derinport.in
descargamela.com
descargarpelicula2.com
desicorner.net
directoriow.com
divxadresi.com
divxatope.com
divxm.com
divxm.net
dl4all.com
dl4v.com
downloadarquivo.com
downloadbox.me
downtr.co
downtwarez.com
dupemonkey.com
egybest.com
enlacewarez.com*
epidemz.net
ergor.org
esdvx.com
estrenosgo.com
estrenosonline.org

exclusivitees.eu
excluzive.net
exsite.pl
fastdown.info
fdmovie.com
filebeta.com
filebox8.com
fileindexer.com
filemirrors.info
filenewz.com
filerapid.pl
files4you.org
fileshut.com
fileslinx.com
filesocean.net
filesresidence.com
filessearcher.com
fileszona.com
film-stream.tv
forum-maximus.net
forumtv.pl
free-filmy.ru
freerutor.com
french-movies.net
freshupnow.com
ftdworld.net*
fullepisode.info
fullmovie-kolkata.com
fullpelis.com
fullseries.net
fzmovies.net
general-search.net
getmediafire.com
golden-ddl.com
gram24.pl
hatemtai.com
hdkinoklub.ru
hd-world.org
hinditvlinks4u.ch
hnmovies.com
hotfilesearch.com
hotshare.pl
identi.info
ineedfile2.com
itvmovie.eu
iwannawatch.ch
iwatchonline.to
kinodoma.net
kinoxa-x.ru
kinoylei.ru
klipzona.net
kohit.net
leecher.to
letitbit-files.net
libertyland.tv
linexdown.net

Linking Sites (continued)

linxdown.me
majaa.net
mamega.com
mayonez.net
mechoddl.com
mechodownload.com
mediafire.li
mediafire.vc
mediafiredownloads.net
mediafirehbo.com
mediafiremoviez.com
mediafiretrends.com
megaparadiz.com*
megauploaders.com
megawarez.eu
mesddl.net
moloto4ka.net
mov1.ru
movie2k.tv
movie2kproxy.com
moviedetector.com
moviesberg.com
moviesdatacenter.com
moviesnhacks.com
movieswamp.com
moviezet.tv
moviz.net
mp4yukle.com
nabolister.com
neomaks.ru
netzor.org
newdivx.net
newpct.com
nizaika.ru
norapidsearch.com
novycinema.ru
onlinemix.ru
onlinemoviesplayer.com
ourphorum.com
peliculaswarez.com

pirat.ca
planetakino.com
plus-soft.ru
pordescargadirecta.com
posteando.com
powerddl.com
precyl.com
proc.com.ua
programaswarez.com
prostokino.net
ps3iso.com
qiq.ru
qkshare.com
raidrush.ws
rapidbizz.com
rapide-ddl.com
rapidfiledownload.com
rapidmoviez.com
rapidog.com
rlsbb.com
rlslog.net
rl-team.net
roomyshare.com
rpds-download.net
rslinks.org
ru-admin.net
saugking.net
scteam.net
sharepirate.com
sharethefiles.com
skatay.com
soft-6.com
soft-best.ws
soft-catalog.net
softvnn.com
speedlounge.in
streaming-ddl.net*
streamxd.com
super-warez.net
takeavailable.com

tehparadox.com
telechargementz.org
telecharger-tout.com
teluga.com
thalathalapathy.com
thedarewall.com
timeparty.com
tinydl.com
tkshare.com
tnt24.info
todotaringa.com
top-hitz.com
tumejortv.com
tvcric.com
tvmuze.com
twilight.ws
ultra-vid.com
vagoslatino.com
vcdq.com
videoanons.ru
vidics.ch
viz4u.net
vostfr-gb.com
vpsite.ru
war4u.sk
warcenter.cz
warez-home.net
warmacher.com
watch-free-movie-online.net
watchonlineseries.eu
watchtvfree.me
watchtvseries.ch
wawacity.su
waz-warez.org
wewatchmoviesfree.net
xitwarez.ru
xmovies8.com
za-friko.com
zonaplus.net

Video Streaming Host Sites

Large
allmyvideos.net
bigcinema.tv
chomikuj.pl
ex.ua
flashx.tv
kinobanda.net
kinostok.tv
movshare.net
novamov.com
nowvideo.eu
played.to
sockshare.com
veoh.com
videoweed.es
vodly.to

Medium
allserials.tv
baskino.com
bestkino.su
faststream.in
films-online.su
kinohome.net
kinomaniak.tv
kinomoov.net
kinoprosmotr.net

minizal.net
moiserialy.net
movierulz.com
movpod.in
movreel.com
movzap.com
nosvideo.com
online-life.ru
playtube.pl
purevid.com
the-cinema.ru
tushkan.net
uploadc.com
vidbull.com
vidbux.com
videobam.com
ziddu.com

Small
2gb-hosting.com
300mbfilms.com
arm-tube.am
delishows.com
dom-filmov.ru
dpstream.tv
esoft.me
fifostream.tv

film4ik.ru
filmodrom.net
glowgaze.com
hddiziizle.com
kino-az.net
kinoclips.net
kinolot.com
kinolubim.ru
kinomatrix.com
kinovam.com
levtor.org
linecinema.org
mytv.kz
mytvline.com
nzbmovieseeker.com
series-cravings.tv
smotri-filmu.ru
smusla.net
tubemotion.com
videobb.com
videonette.com
videoxalyava.ru
vipzal.tv
vreer.com
vzale.tv
zalaa.com

Direct Download (DDL) Host Sites

Large
4shared.com
bitshare.com
depositfiles.com
freakshare.net
rapidgator.net
sendspace.com
turbobit.net
uptobox.com

Medium
180upload.com
1fichier.com
akafile.com
billionuploads.com
cloudzer.net
crocko.com
divxstage.eu
eyny.com
filecloud.io
filepost.com
fshare.vn
ge.tt
hipfile.com
hugefiles.net
junocloud.me
lumfile.com
megafiles.se
megashares.com
novafile.com
queenshare.com
rghost.net
sharebeast.com

share-online.biz
solidfiles.com
tusfiles.net
uloz.to
ulozto.net
ultramegabit.com
uploadbaz.com
uploading.com
vidhog.com
vidup.me
vip-file.com
xvidstage.com
yunfile.com

Small
4upfiles.com
albafile.com
arabloads.com
batshare.com
bayfiles.com
cramit.in
creafile.net
data.hu
dataport.cz
davvas.com
easybytez.com
easyfiles.pl
epicshare.net
euroshare.eu
exoshare.com
expressleech.com
fastshare.cz
fileflyer.com

fileparadox.in
fileplaneta.com
files2upload.net
filesflash.com
filevice.com
gigasize.com
hellupload.com
henchfile.com
hitfile.net
hostingbulk.com
hulkfile.eu
hulkload.com
jheberg.net
jumbofiles.org
load.to
muchshare.net
multiup.org
myuplbox.com
myupload.dk
prefiles.com
project-free-upload.com
rapidfileshare.net
rodfile.com
sanshare.com
sendmyway.com
sendspace.pl
sharefiles.co
sinhro.net
speedshare.eu
swankshare.com
ufox.com
upfile.biz
uploadboy.com

APPENDIX D: PREMIUM BRANDS APPEARING ON SAMPLE SITES

The following premium brands were observed by MediaLink analysts during visits to the sites in the sample.

Aereo
Air Wick
Airborne
Allstate
Ally Bank
Amazon
Amazon (Audible)
American Express
American Girl
Ancestry.com
Angry Birds
Ann Taylor
AT&T
Autonomy
Banana Republic
Benjamin Franklin Paint
Birchbox
Bose
BP
Broadway Theatre
Cablevision
Chevrolet
Chromecast
Citrix
Clarks
Clinton Foundation
Crate & Barrel
Crest
Deli
Delsun

Delsym
Delta
Dish Network
Dominos
Durex
Extended Stay America
Facebook
Fiat
Ford
GE
GEICO
GloboTech
Google
Google Nexus
Grainger
H&M
Hulu Plus
Iceland
istockphoto.com
Jcrew
Keller Graduate School of
Management
Keurig
L.L. Bean
Lego
LG
Lime-a-way
McDonalds
Merck & Co.
Microsoft

Microsoft (Bing)
Monster.com
Motorola
NYU Langone
Opel Auto
Petsmart
Progressive
Puffs
Rackspace
RAM
REI
Sapphire
Seattle's Best
Sensodyne
Target
TD Bank
Time Warner Cable
Toyota
Ugg
UNICEF
Verizon
Wall Street Journal
Walmart
Western Union
Whole Foods
Xfinity
Zales
Zappos
zipcar

APPENDIX E: REFERENCES

Research

BAE Systems Detica (2012), *The six business models for copyright infringement: A data-driven study of websites considered to be infringing copyright*, at **http://bit.ly/H7R9GM**.

DoubleVerify (2013), *DV Fraud Lab Report*, at **http://bit.ly/1edET3u**.

Envisional, (2011), *Technology Report: An Estimate of Infringing Use of the Internet*, retrieved from **http://bit.ly/H6yMm1**.

Felten, E., (2010), Census of Files Available Via BitTorrent, from Princeton Center for Information Technology Policy, referenced at **http://bit.ly/HPeQ7i**.

Hochman Consultants, (2012), *The Cost of Pay-Per-Click (PPC) Advertising – Trends and Analysis*, retrieved from **http://bit.ly/1chpDFp**.

International Telecommunications Union (2013), ICT Facts and Figures, retrieved from **http://bit.ly/1haYMt6**.

Mahanti, A., Carlsson, N., Williamson, C. (2010), *Characterizing the File Hosting Ecosystem: A View from the Edge*, retrieved from **http://bit.ly/16VcSye**.

Millward Brown Digital (2013), *Understanding the Role of Search in Online Piracy*, at **http://bit.ly/1fIjItB**.

NetNames, (2013), *Digital Piracy: Sizing the Piracy Universe*, retrieved from **http://bit.ly/1aRR01P**.

Sanju`as-Cuxart, J., Barlet-Ros, C., Sol´e-Pareta, J., (2009), *Measurement Based Analysis of One-Click File Hosting Services*, retrieved from **http://bit.ly/17jTxRl**.

Springborn, K., Barford, P., (2013), *Impression Fraud in Online Advertising via Pay-Per-View Networks*, for m.Labs, retrieved from **http://bit.ly/19E4uRv**.

US Department of Justice, (2012), Indictment of Kim Dotcom et. al. in US District Court, retrieved from **http://bit.ly/17iFJww**.

Watters, P. (2013), *A Systematic Approach to Measuring Advertising Transparency Online*, retrieved from **http://bit.ly/1hHQWFS**.

Published Reports

Get Money: How to Scam Big Brand Ad Budgets, DigiDay, October 2013.

Here Come the Bots: Assessing the Latest Ad Fraud Fear, DigiDay.com, October 2013.

How sites like MegaUpload make millions from pirated video, c|net, February 2012.

How the gambling industry funds copyright theft, The Kernel, December 2013.

Meganomics, The American Assembly, Columbia University, January 2012.

Online Ad Fraudsters are Stealing $6 Billion from Brands, adweek.com, October 2013.

Pirate sites are raking in advertising money from some multinationals, theguardian.com, February 2013.

The Pirate Bay Is Now the World's Largest File-Sharing Site, Gizmodo, April 2013.

Why is Ad Tech Still Funding Piracy?, DigiDay, August 2012.

RESPONSES TO SUPPLEMENTAL QUESTIONS FOR THE RECORD
from
SENATOR CARL LEVIN
for
MANEESHA MITHAL
Associate Director, Division of Privacy & and Identity Protection
Federal Trade Commission

PERMANENT SUBCOMMITTEE ON INVESTIGATIONS
Hearing On
Online Advertising and Hidden Hazards to Consumer Security and Data Privacy

May 15, 2014

1. In your testimony before the Subcommittee you stated, "the Commission continues to reiterate its longstanding bipartisan call for enactment of a strong Federal data security and breach notification law." Please provide recommendations that address these concerns, as well as any recommendation to promote greater privacy and consumer choice in Internet advertising.

   The FTC supports federal legislation that would (1) strengthen its existing tools with regard to data security requirements for companies and (2) require companies, in appropriate circumstances, to provide notification to consumers when there is a security breach. We have recommended that legislation in both areas – data security and breach notification – should give the FTC the ability to seek civil penalties to help deter unlawful conduct, jurisdiction over non-profits, and rulemaking authority under the Administrative Procedure Act.

   Under current laws, the FTC only has the authority to seek civil penalties for data security violations with regard to children's online information under the Children's Online Privacy Protection Act (COPPA) or credit report information under the Fair Credit Reporting Act (FCRA).[1] To help ensure effective deterrence, we urge Congress to allow the FTC to seek civil penalties for all data security and breach notice violations in appropriate circumstances. Likewise, enabling the FTC to bring cases against non-profits would help ensure that whenever personal information is collected from consumers, entities that maintain such data adequately protect it.[2]

---

[1] The FTC can also seek civil penalties for violations of administrative orders. 15 U.S.C. § 45(*l*).

[2] A substantial number of reported breaches have involved non-profit universities and health systems. *See* Privacy Rights Clearinghouse Chronology of Data Breaches (listing breaches including breaches at non-profits, educational institutions, and health facilities), *available at* http://www.privacyrights.org/data-breach/new.

Finally, rulemaking authority under the Administrative Procedure Act would enable the FTC in implementing the legislation to respond to changes in technology. For example, whereas a decade ago it would be very difficult and expensive for a company to track an individual's precise geolocation, the explosion of mobile devices has made such information readily available. Rulemaking authority would allow the Commission to ensure that as technology changes and the risks from the use of certain types of information evolve, companies would be required to adequately protect such data.

With respect to your question regarding privacy in Internet advertising, the Commission has recently recommended legislation that would improve the transparency of data broker practices, including the practice of delivering online advertising to consumers based on their offline purchases.

RESPONSES TO SUPPLEMENTAL QUESTIONS FOR THE RECORD
from
SENATOR JOHN McCAIN
for
MANEESHA MITHAL
Associate Director, Division of Privacy & and Identity Protection
Federal Trade Commission

PERMANENT SUBCOMMITTEE ON INVESTIGATIONS
Hearing On
Online Advertising and Hidden Hazards to Consumer Security and Data Privacy

May 15, 2014

1. Do you believe that additional legislative authority is required for the FTC to adequately protect consumers' security and privacy online?

   Yes. Although the FTC makes effective use of its existing tools to protect security and privacy of consumer data, the FTC has urged Congress to pass data security and breach notice legislation; legislation providing greater transparency of data broker practices; and baseline privacy legislation.

   With regard to data security, a unanimous Commission has reiterated its longstanding call for federal legislation that would (1) strengthen its existing tools with regard to data security requirements for companies and (2) require companies, in appropriate circumstances, to provide notification to consumers when there is a security breach. As described in detail above, such legislation should give the FTC the ability to seek civil penalties to help deter unlawful conduct, jurisdiction over non-profits, and rulemaking authority under the Administrative Procedure Act.

   To help rectify a lack of transparency about data broker practices, as explained in a recent Commission report, the Commission has encouraged Congress to consider enacting legislation that would enable consumers to learn of the existence and activities of data brokers and provide consumers with reasonable access to information about them held by these entities. More specifically, the Commission urged Congress to consider enacting legislation to require data brokers to, among other things, create a centralized mechanism, such as an Internet portal, where data brokers can identify themselves and provide links to access tools and opt-outs; give consumers access to their data at a reasonable level of detail; and disclose the names and/or categories of data sources. In addition, the Commission advocated that such legislation require consumer-facing entities – such as retailers – to provide prominent notice to consumers when they share information with data brokers, along with the ability to opt-out of such sharing, and to obtain affirmative express

consent from consumers before sharing sensitive data (such as health information) with data brokers.[1]

In addition, as set forth in the March 2012 report *Protecting Privacy in Era of Rapid Change: Recommendations for Policymakers and Businesses* ("Privacy Report"), the Commission has urged Congress to consider enacting baseline privacy legislation that is technologically neutral, sufficiently flexible to allow companies to continue to innovate, and that authorizes the Commission to seek civil penalties to deter statutory violations.[2] Such legislation, which could be informed by the Commission's Privacy Report, would provide businesses with the certainty they need to understand their obligations as well as the incentive to meet those obligations, while also assuring consumers that companies will respect their privacy.

2. What recommendations can the FTC offer regarding changes or additions to the 2011 Kerry-McCain privacy bill (official title: *Commercial Privacy Bill of Rights Act of 2011*) in order to protect consumers' privacy and security online?

The Commission supports the goals of protecting consumer privacy, and we appreciate your leadership on this important topic. As discussed above, the Commission, as set forth in its 2012 Privacy Report, called for baseline privacy legislation. There are some provisions of the 2011 Kerry-McCain privacy bill that FTC staff believes could be revised in order to ensure that the Commission has the tools it needs to best protect consumer privacy in the marketplace. For example, the bill contained a broad exception to its notice and choice requirements, if a company engages in first-party marketing. This might result in, for example, an ISP, browser, or operating system being able to track consumers' every click online for marketing purposes simply because they have a first-party relationship with the consumer in order to serve as a gateway to the Internet. Such a relationship does not imply consent to be tracked across the Internet. The Commission stated in its 2012 Privacy Report that it has strong concerns about such comprehensive tracking for purposes inconsistent with a company's interaction with a consumer, without express affirmative consent or more robust protection.[3]

Additionally, although the bill authorized the Commission to conduct rulemaking in some areas, it did not give the FTC general APA rulemaking authority or otherwise allow it to modify definitions, such as the definition of personal information, in the Act. General rulemaking authority would allow the Commission to ensure that, as technology changes and the risks from the use of certain types of information evolve,

---

[1] *See* Fed. Trade Comm., *Data Brokers: A Call For Transparency and Accountability: A Report of the Federal Trade Commission* 49-54 (May 2014), *available at* http://www.ftc.gov/system/files/documents/reports/data-brokers-call-transparency-accountability-report-federal-trade-commission-may-2014/140527databrokerreport.pdf.
[2] *See* Fed. Trade Comm., *Protecting Privacy in an Era of Rapid Change: Recommendations for Policymakers and Businesses* 13 (2012), *available at* http://www.ftc.gov/sites/default/files/documents/reports/federal-trade-commission-report-protecting-consumer-privacy-era-rapid-change-recommendations/120326privacyreport.pdf.
[3] *Id.* at 56.

companies would be required to give adequate protection to such data. We would be happy to work with your staff on this legislation.

RESPONSES TO SUPPLEMENTAL QUESTIONS FOR THE RECORD
from
SENATOR RON JOHNSON
for
MANEESHA MITHAL
Associate Director, Division of Privacy & and Identity Protection
Federal Trade Commission

PERMANENT SUBCOMMITTEE ON INVESTIGATIONS
Hearing On
Online Advertising and Hidden Hazards to Consumer Security and Data Privacy

May 15, 2014

1. How many employees does the FTC currently have dedicated to cybersecurity? What about online advertising?

   The Commission has three divisions responsible for examining a variety of data security, advertising, and malware issues. The Division of Privacy and Identity Protection consists of approximately 40 staff with expertise in privacy, data security, and identity theft. The Division of Advertising Practices, which protects consumers from unfair or deceptive advertising practices, employs approximately 40 individuals. The Division of Marketing Practices consists of approximately 40 employees charged with responding to ever-evolving problems of consumer fraud – including malware – in the marketplace. In addition, the agency also has regional office employees who work on privacy and security matters on an occasional basis.

2. According to the Interactive Advertising Bureau, companies spent $42.3 billion on online advertising in 2013. How would civil penalties from the FTC serve as a greater incentive for protecting consumers from malvertising than this enormous loss in revenue?

   Malvertising affects individual consumers or businesses whose computers are infected by malware disseminated through the ad system. In most cases, victims have no way to know that the malware ended up on the computer because of a malicious advertisement, and no way to know which of the many companies in the advertising chain -- many operating behind the scenes -- might have been responsible for inserting the malicious ad into the system. Victims of identity theft often would not know that the harm done to them was even related to malware in the first place. For these reasons, individual players in the advertising ecosystem may not be held to account if they do not have reasonable procedures to prevent malware. In such cases, allowing the Commission to seek civil penalties would serve as an important deterrent.

RESPONSES TO SUPPLEMENTAL QUESTIONS FOR THE RECORD
from
SENATOR KELLY AYOTTE
for
MANEESHA MITHAL
Associate Director, Division of Privacy & and Identity Protection
Federal Trade Commission

PERMANENT SUBCOMMITTEE ON INVESTIGATIONS
Hearing On
Online Advertising and Hidden Hazards to Consumer Security and Data Privacy

May 15, 2014

1. As a former Attorney General, I am always concerned about coordination between law enforcement agencies. Can you discuss how you coordinate with other agencies? What is your relationship like with state and local authorities when it comes to combating malware and online identity theft?

Cooperating with other state and federal agencies helps the FTC to effectively leverage its resources for the benefit of consumers. With that goal in mind, the FTC works closely with law enforcement agencies and coordinates with them on a regular basis. This is true throughout the FTC's work to protect consumers, including the data security and identity theft arena. For example, the FTC coordinated its data security investigation of the TJX Companies, Inc. with 39 state attorneys general. This cooperative effort contributed to an FTC action alleging that TJX's failure to use reasonable and appropriate security measures resulted in a hacker obtaining tens of millions of consumers' payment card data, and a settlement of those charges. The 39 states, which settled separately with TJX, made similar allegations in their subsequent action. At the federal level, criminal law enforcement authorities investigated and prosecuted some of the hackers involved in the TJX and other data breaches. As the TJX matter illustrates well, in the data security context, the goals of FTC and federal criminal agencies are complementary: FTC actions send a message that businesses need to protect their customers' data on the front end while actions by criminal agencies send a message to identity thieves that their efforts to victimize consumers will be punished.

More generally, the FTC's Criminal Liaison Unit (CLU) partners with prosecutors to bring criminal consumer fraud cases. Since CLU's launch in 2003, prosecutors have indicted more than 550 FTC defendants and their associates. In fiscal year 2013 alone, prosecutors initiated 76 indictments or complaints against FTC defendants and their associates and obtained 65 convictions or guilty pleas with an average sentence of more than 40 months.

2. In 2012, Senator Pryor and I introduced and passed legislation that reauthorized the SAFEWEB Act, which renewed the FTC's authority to combat cross-border spam, spyware and fraud for an additional 7 years, through 2020. This is a very important tool for law enforcement. Can you talk about how it has been used to work with your international counterparts to combat malicious actors in online advertising who seek to steal identities and compromise security?

Thank you, Senator Ayotte, for your leadership in passing legislation to reauthorize the SAFE WEB Act, a critical tool to enhance FTC enforcement against cross-border fraud threatening American consumers in the global marketplace. The Act arms the FTC with key enforcement tools to combat Internet scams, fraudulent telemarketing, spam, spyware, and other cross-border misconduct that harms our consumers.

We have used the SAFE WEB Act for information sharing in cases involving scareware, spyware, and other types of malware. For example, in our case against Innovative Marketing, the FTC used the SAFE WEB Act to work with the Canadian Competition Bureau to target a company promoting fake security scans. The FTC alleged that the defendants used elaborate and technologically sophisticated Internet advertisements that they placed with advertising networks and many popular commercial websites. These ads displayed to consumers a "system scan" that falsely claimed to detect viruses, spyware, and illegal pornography on consumers' computers and would then urge consumers to buy the defendants' software for $40 to $60 to clean off the malware. As part of the settlement, the defendants are prohibited from making further deceptive claims and paid $8 million.

3. This report claims that malvertising has increased over 200% last year and there were 209,000 incidents generating over 12.4 billion malicious ad impressions. Has the FTC been able to keep up with this growing problem? How has your approach to this problem evolved over the past few years as this problem has gotten worse?

The Commission shares this Committee's concerns about the use of online ads to deliver malware onto consumers' computers. This practice implicates the FTC's considerable enforcement and education efforts in three areas: privacy, malware, and data security. First, with respect to privacy, we have brought many enforcement cases against online advertising networks, such as our cases against Chitika and Google. Second, the Commission has brought several cases under Section 5 of the FTC Act against entities that unfairly downloaded malware onto consumers' computers without their knowledge (for example, the FTC's cases against Seismic Entertainment Inc., Enternet Media, Inc., and CyberSpy Software LLC), and also has made consumer education on malware issues a priority. Finally, while going after the malware purveyors is important, it is also critical that ad networks and other companies take reasonable steps to ensure that they are not inadvertently enabling third parties to place malware on consumers' computers. To

this end, online ad networks should maintain reasonable safeguards to ensure that they are not showing ads containing malware.

We will continue to actively monitor this problem. We also encourage several additional steps to protect consumers in this area, including enactment of a strong federal data security and breach notification law that would give the Commission the authority to seek civil penalties for violations; more widespread consumer education; and meaningful industry self-regulation.

4. The FTC should be focusing on enforcement and consumer education in regards to identity theft. For the past 14 years, identity theft has been the number one complaint to the FTC, including nearly 300,000 complaints this year. What is the FTC doing to focus on identity theft?

The Commission has used its existing authority and resources to implement a comprehensive program to combat identity theft, on three fronts: law enforcement, data collection, and consumer and business education. The Commission has brought 53 law enforcement actions challenging businesses that failed to reasonably protect sensitive consumer information that they maintained, including matters that resulted in identity theft. For example, in one of the best-known FTC data security cases – the 2006 action against ChoicePoint, Inc. – a data broker allegedly sold sensitive information (including Social Security numbers in some instances) concerning more than 160,000 consumers to data thieves posing as ChoicePoint clients. In many instances, the thieves used that information to steal the consumers' identities. In settling the case, ChoicePoint agreed to pay $10 million in civil penalties for violations of the FCRA and $5 million in consumer redress for identity theft victims, and agreed to undertake comprehensive data security measures.

Also a primary focus for the Commission has been child identity theft. In 2011, the Commission hosted a public forum to discuss the growing problem of child identity theft, which brought to light that a child's Social Security number alone can be combined with another person's information, such as name or date of birth, in order to commit identity theft.

In addition to law enforcement, the Commission collects and analyzes identity theft complaint data in order to target its education efforts and assist criminal law enforcement authorities. Identity theft victims can provide information to Consumer Sentinel, the FTC's consumer complaint database, via an online complaint form or by calling a toll-free hotline and speaking with a trained counselor. The Commission makes this and other data available to thousands of international, federal, state, and local law enforcement agencies who have signed confidentiality and data security agreements.

Finally, the FTC makes available a wide variety of consumer educational materials, including many in Spanish, to help consumers deter, detect, and defend against identity theft. For example, the FTC has long published a victim recovery guide –

Take Charge: Fighting Back Against Identity Theft – that explains the immediate steps identity theft victims should take to address the crime; how to obtain a credit report and correct fraudulent information in credit reports; how to file a police report; and how to protect personal information. And, the Commission recently held a number of events as part of Tax Identity Theft Awareness Week to raise awareness about tax identity theft and provide consumers with tips on how to protect themselves, and what to do if they become victims.

5. Does law enforcement have sufficient resources to investigate and enforce against distributing malicious software? What agencies have primary authority?

On the civil side, the FTC has authority to combat spyware and other malware using Section 5 of the FTC Act, which prohibits unfair or deceptive acts or practices, as do the state attorneys general. Intentionally distributing spyware and other malware may also violate criminal laws enforced by the Department of Justice and state attorneys general.

The FTC's Section 5 cases to combat the installation of spyware and other malware reaffirm three key principles. First, a consumer's computer belongs to him or her, not to the software distributor, and it must be the consumer's choice whether or not to install software. Second, burying material information in a disclosure, such as an End User License Agreement, will not shield a malware purveyor from Section 5 liability. Third, if a distributor puts a program on a computer that the consumer does not want, the consumer should be able to uninstall or disable it. And, we will continue to challenge harmful practices involving spyware and other malware. Finally, to provide further deterrence, the Commission has also recommended that Congress enact legislation giving it the authority to seek civil penalties against purveyors of malware.

6. This report states that the FTC's authority under Section 5 to address deceptive practices has not been effective in going after malware criminals. However, Commissioner Ohlhausen said this week "FTC has brought over 100 spam and spyware cases and over 40 data security cases under Section 5."

Question: Does this suggest to you that the FTC has ample authority it needs to be an effective law enforcement presence? Given this, how do you justify the need for more regulations at the FTC to address the problem of consumers being attacked by malware?

The Commission has effectively used its existing authority under Section 5 of the FTC Act, which prohibits deceptive and unfair commercial practices, to combat malware, unreasonable data security practices, and email and text message spam. While these cases have helped to protect consumers, the Commission believes that additional legislation is needed to (1) strengthen its existing tools with respect to data security requirements on companies and (2) require companies, in appropriate circumstances, to provide notification to consumers when there is a security breach. Currently, the FTC lacks authority in most data security cases to obtain civil

penalties, an important remedy for deterring violations. Also, the FTC currently lacks authority over non-profits, which have been the source of many breaches.

207

June 12, 2014

Response of George Salem, Senior Product Manager, Google Inc.
Senate Permanent Subcommittee on Investigations
Hearing on "Online Advertising and Hidden Hazards to Consumer Security and Data Privacy,"
May 15, 2014

Questions for the Record from Senator Ron Johnson

1. What can the government do in terms of enforcement to target cybercriminals responsible for malvertising? What about cybercriminals generally?

Google believes that enforcement is a strong deterrent to the continued growth in the number of cybercriminals who target innocent consumers. Google supports the training of and resources for US law enforcement units and agencies to prosecute these cybercriminals, many of whom reside outside the United States.

The cybercrime of malware exists because it is profitable. The government should increase its collaboration with law enforcement agencies globally in order to detect and prosecute cybercriminals. In particular, the Federal Trade Commission (FTC) should prioritize pursuing additional memorandums of understanding to promote increased cooperation and information sharing with enforcement agencies in countries that serve as havens for cybercriminals. Targeted and effective enforcement will avoid collateral damage to the advertising industry and protect American consumers.

At the same time, enforcement alone is not enough to combat the cybercrime of malware. The Federal Government can be very effective in assisting industry with consumer education on how to prevent malware infections — for example, by helping consumers become better informed on how to execute free and quick virus scans of their computers. We believe the FTC could greatly help by prioritizing more resources for outreach to teach Americans how to protect themselves from malware and the crime of identity theft.

2. How many employees does Google currently have dedicated to cybersecurity? What about online advertising security?

Google has 569 full time employees dedicated to cybersecurity. Separately, Google has 466 full time employees dedicated to ads security. There are numerous other full and part time employees, as well as vendors and contractors, that directly or indirectly support these teams.

June 13, 2014

Mary D. Robertson
Chief Clerk
Permanent Subcommittee on Investigations
199 Russell Senate Office Building
Washington, DC 20510

SUPPLEMENTAL QUESTIONS FOR THE RECORD
from
SENATOR RON JOHNSON
for
ALEX STAMOS
Yahoo! Inc.

PERMANENT SUBCOMMITTEE ON INVESTIGATIONS
Hearing On
Online Advertising and Hidden Hazards to Consumer Security and Data Privacy

1. You suggested that perhaps the most important thing the government can do to combat cybercriminals is remove financial incentives associated with cybercrime. Can you provide specific examples of what the government can do to make it more difficult for cybercriminals to realize profits from their cybercrimes?

   First and foremost, I would suggest that better prioritization of law enforcement resources could go a long way in helping to disrupt the financial networks that allow spammers and malware actors to profit off of their deeds. Additionally, law enforcement could work with financial institutions to shut down accounts being used for this kind of illegal activity.

2. What can the government do in terms of enforcement to target cybercriminals responsible for malvertising? What about cybercriminals generally?

   I would suggest that government could focus on development of and support for foreign law enforcement officials and cybercrime response teams across the globe. And, as mentioned previously, better prioritization of law enforcement resources could help with combating these cybercriminals, especially those with financial networks in the United States.

Permanent Subcommittee on Investigations
EXHIBIT #9

1

3. How many employees does Yahoo currently have dedicated to cybersecurity?
   What about online advertising security?

   **Yahoo has a core security team of 42 employees. Online advertising
   security is done by a cross-functional team of 18 dedicated personnel
   and 62 support, analytical, and technical support staff. We also have a
   growing cybercrime team that I am working on building up.**

210

Online Trust Alliance

Via email to mary_robertson@hsgac.senate.gov

June 18, 2014

Ms. Mary Robertson
Chief Clerk
U.S. Senate Homeland Security and Governmental Affairs Committee
Permanent Subcommittees on Investigations
223 Hart Senate Office Building
Washington, D.C. 20510-6250

Re: Supplement Questions from Senator Johnson

Dear Ms. Robertson,

Thank you for your request to provide additional insights responding to the May 15th Hearing "Online Advertising and Hidden Hazards to Consumer Security and Data Privacy". Since the Hearing the impact of malvertising continues to grow. Ransomware and related threats deployed by malvertising is on the rise, with high profile sites such as the Disney, Facebook and the FIFA World Cup sites impacting innocent site visitors.[1, 2, 3]

The Online Trust Alliance (OTA) agrees with the industry that ad networks are under attack. Cybercriminals and fraudulent businesses have recognized the advertising ecosystem provides a highly scalable infrastructure to target and exploit consumers, businesses and government services simultaneously. The lack of security controls and low adoption of best practices makes ad networks soft targets and ripe for abuse. Yet when faced with the facts, industry trade groups continue to defend their practices and attempt to shift accountability to others.[4, 5]

Consumer's expectation of safety offline should be not different when online. A consumer visiting a shopping mall, has an expectation that systems are in place to help deter, detect and mitigate threats. While such incidents may be infrequent, mall owners and merchants have recognized the need to collaborate, invest in security staff, surveillance systems and training of first responders. Retailers work with law enforcement, share data with other merchants and report incidents. Although there is no guarantee of physical security against determined criminals, similar safeguards are needed online to help protect online consumers from malvertising.

---

[1] Malicious website ads lead to ransomware
http://www.computerworld.com/s/article/9248886/Malicious_major_website_ads_lead_to_ransomware?source=CTWNLE_nlt_security_2014-06-06
[2] Malvertising scheme uses Flash exploit to profit from World Cup buzz
http://www.scmagazine.com/malvertising-scheme-uses-flash-exploit-to-profit-from-world-cup-buzz/article/351289/
[3] http://www.fifa.com/worldcup/index.html
[4] http://netchoice.org/catch-criminals-dont-pass-buck/
[5] http://trustinads.org/about.html

Online Trus| **Permanent Subcommittee on Investigations** |455-7400
EXHIBIT #10

In response to Senator Johnson's questions;

1. Given the enormous free market incentive to make sure malvertising does not drive consumers away, why is regulation from other organizations or government entities necessary?

In the absence of meaningful self-regulation and an enforceable code of conduct governing the integrity of online advertising, the need for regulatory oversight is fast becoming warranted. In a perfect world, industry would recognize the long-term impact and be willing to address the vulnerabilities of their business models. Yet due to the inability of consumers and publishers to correlate an incident to a specific ad, the advertising industry is not realizing reputational harm. Unfortunately consumers have little if any visibility to know how, where and when they have been compromised by a malicious ad.

In the near decade since the threat of malvertising was identified, the general response from industry has been one of dismissing the threat and attempting to discredit those who have raised the alarm.

Society and our economy are increasingly reliant on web services funded by advertising. The knowledge of this dependency by cybercriminals is placing the Nation's critical infrastructure at risk. Inaction suggests the need for regulatory oversight, not unlike what is being demanded of network providers. Recently the Federal Communications Commission Chairman Tom Wheeler called on industry to step up cybersecurity measures or face new regulations. He called on ISPs and carriers to take the lead in ensuring their networks are secure against cyber-attacks.[6]

As outlined in my testimony, we must work towards a framework addressing five key areas: Prevention, Detection, Notification, Data Sharing and Remediation. It is important that remediation be addressed. One such idea is industry establish a "super fund" offering remediation to impacted consumers. A victims' fund could cover financial losses, provide technical support along with reimbursement from ransomware. Such a program would instill consumer trust and serve as an incentive for networks and their trade groups to invest in prevention and detection technologies and operational procedures.

2. What can governments do to combat cybercriminals responsible for malvertising? What about cybercriminals generally?

Malvertising is not unique to other forms of cybercrime plaguing critical infrastructure. It is being driven by sophisticated organized criminals operating outside of our borders with a great deal of anonymity and immunity from many of the countries they operate from. Without formal data sharing mechanisms, law enforcement efforts are limited. With only partial and unstructured data sharing, law enforcement lacks a 360 degree view of the threat landscape.

In the aftermath of the Target breach, the advertising and banking industries formed an Information Sharing and Analysis Center (ISAC) to foster data sharing and adoption of best practices. Other mechanisms such as: InfraGard, a partnership with the FBI and the private sector; the Homeland Security Information Network; and the adoption of STIX (Structured Threat Information Expression) should be considered as part of required incident reporting.[7][8][9]

---

[6] http://online.wsj.com/articles/fcc-urges-an-industry-led-approach-on-cybersecurity-to-protect-u-s-communications-networks-1402594627?mod=WSJ_TechWSJD_NeedToKnow&cb=logged0.681783548510998

[7] http://stix.mitre.org/

[8] https://www.infragard.org/

[9] http://www.dhs.gov/homeland-security-information-network

Combined they would facilitate threat intelligence sharing with both other industry sectors and law enforcement, providing an early warning system and aid in shutting down criminal networks. The biggest factor impacting law enforcement today is that malvertising incidents remain largely unreported and what data that is being shared is typically unstructured and incomplete.

Recently U.S. Security and Exchange Commissioner Aguilar made a plea to public companies for mandatory incident reporting. He stated, "It is possible that a cyber-attack may not have a direct material adverse impact on the company itself, but that a loss of customers' personal and financial data could have devastating effects on the lives of the company's customers and many Americans."[10] The same obligation should apply to the interactive advertising industry. In the absence of such reporting, law enforcement's and stakeholder's efforts to fight malvertising will remain stymied.

Such data sharing should protect reporting parties from oversight and include controls to prevent personal identifiable information and competitive data from being shared outside of law enforcement. The National Cyber-Forensics & Training Alliance (NCFTA) is a public-private partnership where threat intelligence data is shared with law enforcement and back to partipating stakeholders with such privacy and confidential provisions.[11]

In summary, as our society and economy are increasingly reliant upon the internet and advertising-supported services, we have a shared responsibility to harden our systems. The OTA favors the adoption of an enforceable code of conduct and mandatory reporting over regulation.

As cybercriminals remain determined and in the absence of meaningful security controls, we can only expect the impact to consumers and our economy to grow. OTA looks forward to working with the Committee and industry to help fight these abuses and threats.

Respectfully,

Craig Spiezle
Executive Director & President
Online Trust Alliance

Cc: Jack Thorlin, Daniel Goshorn

---

[10] http://www.reuters.com/article/2014/06/10/sec-cybersecurity-aguilar-idUSL2N0OR13U20140610
[11] http://www.ncfta.net/